THE STRATHSPEY MUTINEERS

Published by

Librario Publishing Ltd

ISBN: 1-904440-23-1

Copies can be ordered via the Internet
www.librario.com

or from:

Brough House, Milton Brodie, Kinloss
Moray IV36 2UA
Tel /Fax No 01343 850 617

THE STRATHSPEY MUTINEERS

A history of the First Highland Fencible Regiment
1793-1799

G. M. Fraser

Librario

Dedication

To my wife Sue for listening with great patience to the exploits of Sir James, the Lt Colonel, Watson and Rippachie and the other officers and men of the First Fencible Regiment.

Contents

Acknowledgements   **9**

Foreword   **11**

List of Illustrations   **12**

Chapter 1. Recruitment   **15**

Sir James Grant of Grant of Castle Grant, Bart is invited to raise a Fencible regiment for the defence of Scotland – the Royal Warrant – the officers of the regiment – Sir James Grant is Colonel – Lt Colonel A. P. Cumming of Altyre in command – attestation forms – some not signed by the surgeon – recruitment – methods employed by recruiting parties – the quality of the recruits – some aged nearly eighty years – the cost of raising the regiment – regimental head quarters at Forres – training the recruits – desertions – inspection by Lt General A. Leslie – composition of the individual companies – trouble with the civil authorities – meal riots – first floggings – court martials and the frequent use of corporal punishment – contemporary views on the neccesity and severity of corporal punishment in the army – views of private soldiers – officers mess dinners – alcohol consumption and drunkeness in the army – family tragedies of Sir James Grant and Lt Colonel Cumming.

Chapter 2. Glasgow   **55**

The march to Glasgow – the sick and the families travel by boat – bigamy – one wife 'with her belly to her chin' – more desertions – civilians assaulted – syphilis and sibbens – maltreatment alleged – nothing 'to cover his nakedness only an old petticoat of his wifes' – drunkeness among the non commissioned officers – the quartermaster making money on the side – criticism of the quality of the uniforms provided by the clothier, Mr Gloag – Mr Gloag's mother lying a corpse – Captain Alasdair Ranaldson Macdonell of Glengarry causing trouble – the major takes a mistress – two sergeants court martialled for getting drunk and fighting – the sergeant major gets himself 'so drunk & so beat that he is not fit to be seen' – the raising of the 97th Regiment of Foot – recruiting irregularities – the Lt Colonel's young son dies of whooping cough – Captain-Lieutenant John Grant of Rippachie 'balqued :and mortified' at being past over for the second majority.

Chapter 3. Linlithgow   **82**

Fears of a French invasion of England – the regiment marches to Linlithgow – the army Purchase System and the Riding System – the regiment is asked to march to England – No volunteers step forward – The regiment breaks ranks and takes possession of Linlithgow Palace – accounts of the mutiny sent to the factor of Strathspey by his son assistant surgeon John Grant, Adjutant James Watson, the chaplain and Lt John Grant junior – 'the mutinous fellows huzza'd and flew to the storehouse and took possesion of the ammuniton' – the adjutant goes among them – support for the mutineers from the people of Linlithgow – order is restored – the Lt Colonel disposes of vast quantities of ammunition – the men fire their muskets through the hedges 'to the great risk of the lives of the country people' – further attempts to get the men to go to England but they refuse because it is contrary to their terms of engagement – Captain Macdonell resigns his commission and takes command of the first Catholic regiment – augmentation of the regiment to one thousand rank and file – the major gets his mistress pregnant.

Chapter 4. Paisley and Dumfries   123
The march to Paisley – the regiment is widely scattered – The Lt Colonel is taken ill which threatens to 'number me with my fathers' – recruiting for the augmentation – more recruiting irregularities – army barracks and their inadequacies – army wives – further proposals to widen the terms of engagement are dropped – mutiny of the Breadalbane Fencibles in Glasgow – the First Fencibles are involved in a riot – the regiment marches to Dumfries in dreadful weather – the Lt Colonel inherits a fortune and changes his name to Cumming-Gordon – unsatisfactory state of recruits for the augmentation – a 'deformed idiot' and a 'Kings-eviled drunken change keeper' – the Lt Colonel asks for pistols for the officers in case of another mutiny – dispute amongst the Captains regarding seniority – the Major, the Adjutant and Sir James's son go recruiting to Stranraer, Wigton and Kirkcudbright through six foot deep snow drifts – the regiment is scattered and is without a doctor – bad weather prevents the men from getting any leave – the Lt Colonel disobeys the Commander in Chief's orders – further trouble with Mr Gloag's uniforms – the regiment is re-united at Dumfries – the sergeant major defrauds the new recruits – a detachment is sent to arrest some tinkers – three of the soldiers are wounded and one later dies of his wounds – Sir James's efforts on behalf of the wounded soldiers.

Chapter 5. A second Mutiny   157
A Grenadier is impertinent on parade and is arrested – is released from the guard room by his comrades – the regiment in open defiance of authority – the mutiny is quelled by the Lt Colonel and his officers – five mutineers are arrested and marched under close guard to Edinburgh Castle – the court martial – the adjutant's evidence – the evidence of other commissioned and non commissioned officers – the Lt Colonel's evidence – his reason for carrying a pistol is not allowed as evidence – evidence on behalf of the prisoners – the verdict of guilty – four are sentenced to death and one to receive a thousand lashes – Sir James begs the Commander in Chief to show mercy – two of the prisoners are 'shot to death' on Gullane Links and three are reprieved – one is freed but the other two are sentenced to be deported – Sir James's efforts on behalf of the prisoners are successful and they are allowed to enlist in the 78th Regiment – the freed prisoner is caught poaching salmon on the River Spey.

Chapter 6. Dundee and Ayr **181**
Inducements to transfer from the Fencibles to Regiments of the Line are thwarted
– the regiment is posted to Dundee and is reduced to five hundred rank and file –
food riots in Dundee – the London Lottery pays out huge prizes – Sir James is
deeply in debt to Mr Gloag – the regiment tries to enlist a Black soldier – private
soldiers and their families in Strathspey – Captain Cumming 'near kills himself by
eating up large bowlfuls of thick cream' – the regiment marches to Ayr – money is
docked from their pay to pay for bread but is refunded – a further dispute
amongst the captains regarding seniority – French landing in Bantry Bay in
Southern Ireland – the regiment holds itself ready to march 'on the shortest
notice' – an 'infamous anonymous letter' – the Lt Colonel has a bad fall and 'his
testicles is so swelled that he is in continuous agony' – the regiment camps on the
links at Ayr – is involved in a riot and is ordered to Edinburgh Castle.

Chapter 7. Edinburgh Castle, Irvine and Disbandment **216**
The march to Edinburgh Castle – cow gut used to prevent foot sores – 118
women and 214 children as camp followers – escape of Dutch prisoners from
Fountainbridge – the major is arrested – the adjutant falls in love – The Earl of
Home molests the adjutant's fiancee – the regiment camps on the shores of the
Forth – the regiment is posted to 'that shocking hole Irvine' – the French land at
Killala Bay – the Lt Colonel threatens to shoot the Inn Keeper – Lady Grant 'slips
her foot' and breaks her leg – the regiment is asked to serve abroad – but refuses
and is disbanded.

Chapter 8. Epilogue **245**
Why did the regiment mutiny? – the behaviour of the officers – Sir James Grant,
Lt Colonel Cumming-Gordon and adjutant Watson – the conduct of the non
commissioned officers – The views of the private soldiers on flogging – passionate
impetuosity and pride of the Highlander – the regiment's role as a police force.

Chapter Notes **251**

Index **263**

Acknowledgements

I am greatly indebted to the staff of the National Archives of Scotland (The Scottish Record Office), where most of the research for this book was done, for their unfailing help and courtesy. My thanks are also due to the staff of the National Library of Scotland, the Scottish National Portrait Gallery, the National Gallery of Scotland, the Glasgow Art gallery, the British Library and the Library of the Royal College of Physicians of Edinburgh. I am grateful to Dr Stephen Lloyd the Assistant Keeper of the Scottish National Portrait Gallery for his expert opinion, to Molly Duckett the Manager of the Grantown Museum and Heritage Trust who was the inspiration behind this book, to the Earl of Seafield for permission to publish material from the Seafield Muniments and I am indebted to Mr George Dixon for drawing my attention to the existence of this huge wealth of historical material.

I am also greatly indebted to Mr Allan Carswell, the Curator of the National War Museum of Scotland at Edinburgh Castle, for his encouragement and for writing the foreword to this book, and to Mark Lawson and Stephen Young at Librario Publishing for their speed and expertise.

Foreword

By Allan L Carswell, Curator, National War Museum of Scotland

In the popular view, the history of the British army is often seen as being nothing much beyond the glorious stories of familiar sounding regiments battling in the establishment and defence of Britain's overseas empire or struggling against the perennial enemy, the French. Scotland, of course, figures large in this view of history – few regiments can match the Highlanders for sheer reputation and distinct identity.

Yet this is an incomplete version of events and what follows is not the story of a familiar or well-known regiment. This Highland Regiment did not go abroad and it never even saw a Frenchman, nor did it hear the sound of battle. Instead, it stayed in Scotland to try to keep the peace in an age of revolutions and defend the country against the dire threat of invasion.

Undoubtedly, active service abroad was dangerous and difficult, but it was also clear in its purpose. The duty of the 'Fencible' regiments of the late Eighteenth Century was less straightforward and it is the pressures of this service which define the experience brought so vividly to life in this book. Sedition and riots, recruitment and desertion, crime and punishment, appalling barracks and disease, absent officers and drunken NCOs, even open mutiny itself are all covered in the contemporary letters and papers that provide the source material for this regimental history.

What emerges, apart from a vivid portrait of the officers and men of the Strathspey Fencibles, is a striking impression of Scotland in the late Eighteenth Century – Highland and Lowland, urban and rural, rich and poor and civil and military. This is a country at war and in the midst of massive social upheaval and it is a view of Scotland that will be strange to any with comfortable notions of this period of our history. The work also illuminates an aspect of Britain and Scotland's military history that is all too often overshadowed by the familiar exploits of the regiments of Britain's overseas army.

List of Illustrations

COVER

Sir James Grant addressing soldiers of the First Fencible Regiment National Library of Scotland. From 'The Grant, Strathspey or First Highland Fencible Regiment' by H.B. Mackintosh. Colour copy of John Kays Original Portraits volume 1.

PORTRAITS and PAINTINGS

Sir James Grant of Grant of Castle Grant, Bart. by William Stavely, Scottish National Portrait Gallery. PG 1956.

Lady Jane Grant, wife of Sir James Grant by William Stavely. Grantown Museum and Heritage Trust

Major John Grant of Glenmoriston. By kind permission of Mrs Sally Grant of Glenmoriston.

Captain Alexander (Alasdair Ranaldson) Macdonell of Glengarry by Sir Henry Raeburn. National Gallery of Scotland. NG 420.

Captain John Rose of Holme. From John Kays Original Portraits volume 2.

Dr John Grant

Lord Adam Gordon, by Henri-Pierre Danloux. Scottish National Portrait Gallery. PG 192

Henry Dundas, by Sir Thomas Lawrence. National Portrait Gallery, London

The Duke of York, by Sir David Wilkie. National Portrait Gallery, London

Sir James Grant addressing soldiers of the First Fencible Regiment, from John Kays Original Portraits. Volume 1.

Recruits on the way to Join. A romantic view of recruitment. From 'The Life of a Regiment: The History of the Gordon Highlanders'. Gardyne, C. G.: NF 1206.G.14. National Library of Scotland

Linlithgow Palace and Loch where the first mutiny took place, by L. David. Glasgow Museums: Art Gallery & Museum, Kelvingrove, 1970.3.p 8

Dumfries from the Dock where the regiment was dismissed immediately before the second mutiny, by John Clerk of Eldin. The National Gallery of Scotland. L91

MAPS (by Graham Neish)
Postings of the First Highland Fencible Regiment
Route by land and sea from Aberdeen to Glasgow
In May 1794 the regiment was widely dispersed

LETTERS
Attestation form of John Grant dated 1st April 1793 [GD248/464/4/1]
Private John Fraser to Sir James Grant 21st June 1793 [GD248/684/1/3]
Lt Colonel Cumming's letter of 8th September, 1793, to his brother in law, Sir James Grant [GD248/684/4/1]
Dr John Grant to Sir James Grant, 7th October, 1793 [GD248/684/5/1]
James Grant, the factor to Sir James Grant, 20th January, 1794 [GD248/685/3/1]
Adjutant James Watson to James Grant, the factor, 4th April, 1794 [GD248/469/9]
John Grant, junior, to factor James Grant, 10th April, 1794 [GD248/464/9]
Resignation letter of Captain Alexander (Alasdair Ranaldson) Macdonell, dated 2nd May, 1794 [GD248/465/9]
Lord Adam Gordon to Sir James Grant, 6th April, 1795 [GD248/690/3/1]
Sir James Grant's draft petition to the King purporting to come from the condemned mutineers [GD248/2028]
Private Malcolm Grant to the factor regarding his cow 8th August, 1796 [GD248/456/5]
Sergeant Donald McIntosh to Adjutant James Watson 1st December, 1798 [GD248/467/3]

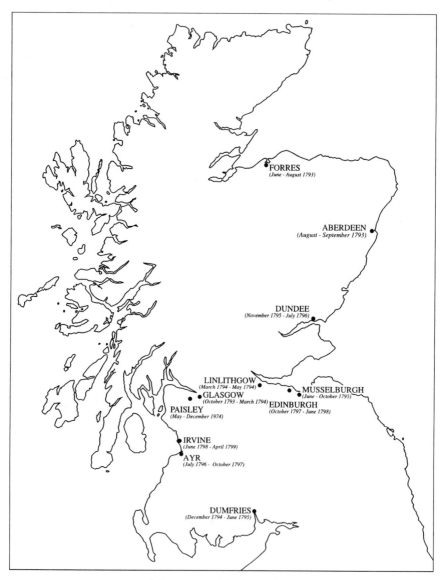

FORRES
(June - August 1793)

ABERDEEN
(August - September 1793)

DUNDEE
(November 1795 - July 1796)

LINLITHGOW
(March 1794 - May 1794)

GLASGOW
(October 1793 - March 1794)

MUSSELBURGH
(June - October 1795)

PAISLEY
(May - December 1974)

EDINBURGH
(October 1797 - June 1798)

IRVINE
(June 1798 - April 1799)

AYR
(July 1796 - October 1797)

DUMFRIES
(December 1794 - June 1795)

Postings of the First Highland Fencible Regiment.

Chapter One

Recruitment

'The Duke and Sir James understand each other perfectly'

In 1778 at the outbreak of the American war of Independence four Scottish Fencible regiments were raised. These were the Argyll or Western, the Southern, the Northern or Gordon and the Sutherland Fencibles, the name 'Fencible' being an abbreviation of the word 'Defensible'. The distinctive conditions of service of the these regiments were that the men were voluntarily enlisted – a bounty of £3. 3s* being given to each – and in all respects of pay, clothing, arms and equipment they were on the same footing as soldiers of the regular army. They were to serve in any part of Scotland but not out of it, except in the case of an invasion of England, and in no event were they to serve outside Great Britain.[1]

In the autumn of 1779 the Argyll Fencibles mutinied. Like many other regiments they were in arrears of pay and bounty money but that was not their main grievance. They had been issued with cartridge pouches and sporrans, the cost of which had been deducted from their pay and this became a running sore with them. In early October whilst on parade at Edinburgh Castle they threw their sporrans to the ground declaring that they would not wear them any longer. They were perfectly willing to obey all other commands and on October 7th they were marched to Leith Links where they were to exercise but on arrival there they were confronted by the 10th Dragoons who overpowered them. Six of the ring leaders were tried at once by Regimental Field Court Martial, two being acquitted but four were found guilty and sentenced to be flogged. The sentence was carried out there and then on the links.[2] These four Fencible regiments were disbanded at the end of the American War of Independence in 1783.

Ten years later, in January 1793 King Louis XVI was executed by the French Revolutionary government. On February 1st France, already at war with Austria and Prussia, annexed the Austrian Netherlands and declared war on Holland and Great Britain. Thus began a war that was to engulf not only all Europe but also the United States of America which

Footnote:
*12 pence [d] equalled one shilling [s]. 20 shillings equalled one pound [£].

was now to be our enemy. It was to end twenty two years later with the final overthrow of Napoleon on the battlefield of Waterloo.

At the outbreak of war the British government under William Pitt put together a small expeditionary force of some 5,000 men to help their Dutch allies protect their frontiers from invasion.[3] The regular troops in Scotland were required to form part of this force and to fill the gap the government again decided to raise Fencible regiments. Feelers were put out to the great landed gentry by Henry Dundas*, Secretary of State at the Home Department, to find out if they would be willing to raise these regiments. Two men in the North East of Scotland who were specifically approached were the Duke of Gordon** and Sir James Grant of Grant of Castle Grant, Bart.*** Dundas was concerned that the Duke and Sir James might start recruiting each others' tenants and thus cause bad blood between them. He need not have worried for Sir James immediately despatched the following note dated February 16th to the Duke:

> As your Grace and I have both offered for Fencible Regiments Mr Dundas wishes us to understand one another so that there may be no inconvenient Interference – Supposing us to have so large a district as from Aberdeen to the west Sea besides any aid we may get otherwise I do not see there can be any difficulty for us to make out the Twelve Hundred men that is Six Hundred for each Regiment neither interfering by themselves or their parties with the others property.

Footnotes:

* The Right Hon. Henry Dundas (1741-1811). A Scot and personal friend of William Pitt, the Prime Minister. Secretary of State for the Home Department 1793. Secretary of State for the War Department 1794-1801. Created Viscount Melville in 1802. Impeached in the House of Lords in 1806 on ten counts of investing government money for his own profit. Was found Not Guilty on all ten counts.

** Alexander, 4th Duke of Gordon KT (1743-1827). Succeeded to the Dukedom on the death of his father in 1752. Raised the Gordon Fencibles in 1793 and the Gordon Highlanders in 1794. Lord Lieutenant of Aberdeenshire 1794-1808. Rebuilt Gordon Castle.

*** Sir James Grant of Grant of Castle Grant, 8th Baronet. (1738-1811) Only son of Sir Ludovick Grant. Educated at Westminster and Cambridge. Married Jane Duff, only daughter of Alexander Duff of Hatton, 1763. Founded the town of Grantown on Spey in 1766 on a barren heath moor. Succeeded to the baronetcy on the death of his father in 1773. Inherited debts which, with interest, amounted to £71,800. M.P. for Moray 1761-1768 and for Banffshire 1790-1795. Raised the First Fencible regiment 1793 (Disbanded 1799) and the 97th Regiment of Foot 1794 (Disbanded 1795). Lord Lieutenant of Invernesshire 1794-1809. General Cashier of the Excise in Scotland 1791-1811. Father of seven sons and seven daughters. Known widely as 'The Good Sir James'.

On receiving a favourable response from the Duke, Sir James replied to Henry Dundas:

Sir James Grant presents his most respectful Compliments to Mr Dundas begs leave to acquaint him that he has just now had a Communing with the Duke of Gordon.

The Duke and Sir James understand each other perfectly, and Sir James is willing to undertake to raise the Fencible Regiment.[4]

Having given this undertaking Sir James, who was in London attending the House of Commons as M.P. for Banff, immediately sent off a flurry of letters. To his brother in law, Alexander Penrose Cumming of Altyre* he wrote: 'I have named you as Lieut. Col. and Major Grant of Achernick as Major and request that you will pick up all the clever fellows you can in your Estate and Neighbourhood before other parties interfere wt you.' To his factor and namesake, James Grant of Heathfield,** he wrote desiring him 'to lose no time in acquainting the Gentlemen upon Sir James's Estate of Strathspey that he hoped that they would not engage to assist others untill they heard further from him'. The factor faithfully carried out his instructions and reported back to Sir James that he had 'made out, and which was read today, at the different Kirks, an intimation acquainting them all...that you depended upon all married, bachelors & young men upon your Estate within Strathspey that could be spared or be absent from their Families friends & occupations, to enter voluntarily in to your Regiment...That the great probability was that your Regiment would be constantly stationed along the Coast from Inverness to Aberdeen and in a year or two at most would be dispensed with'.[5] In the event the regiment was stationed mainly in the south west of Scotland and served not for 'a year or two' but for six

---

Footnotes:
* Alexander Penrose Cumming of Altyre (1749-1806) Ensign in 13th Regiment of Foot 1768. Captain in the Northern Fencibles 1778. Married 1773, Helen (Nelly) daughter of Sir Ludovick Grant. Succeeded to the Gordonstoun Estates on the death of Sir William Gordon in 1795. Changed his name to Cumming-Gordon (The family surname was changed again by his son William, to Gordon-Cumming). M.P. for Inverness 1802. Created a Baronet in 1804. He was even more virile than his brother in law fathering no less than seven sons and nine daughters.
** James Grant of Heathfield. (1733-1821) Parochial schoolmaster of Duthil 1761. Clerk to [Sir] James Grant of Grant 1765-1790. Factor to Sir James 1790-1809. Justice of the Peace1792. Deputy Lieutenant of Invernesshire 1794. Father of Dr John Grant, surgeon to the First Fencibles and great great grandfather of the author.

years. To John Grant, son to Patrick Grant, clan chief of the Grants of Glenmoriston, Sir James offered command of a company adding: 'I trust that the spirit of our clan will enable us soon to embody the Regiment.' When Achernick declined the Majority it was then offered to Glenmoriston who accepted it.[6]

Other officers whom Sir James appointed were Captain John Grant of Achindown as Captain and Paymaster. 'I hope he will do well in both,' Sir James wrote to the newly appointed Lt Colonel adding: 'He is very active & intelligent and has worked like a Horse for me.' Another important appointment, as far as Sir James personally was concerned, was the appointment of the second Lieutenant in his own company and he wrote to the Lt Colonel: 'I have settled John Grant Commy as my second Lieut. as I shall have constant occasion for his writing about the Regimental business.' The newly appointed Lt John Grant was Commissary of Moray. His name frequently appears in this account as he was a prodigious letter writer. John Prebble[7] refers to him as 'Delcroy' after his father's farm and Mackintosh[8] calls him simply 'Lieutenant John Grant'. The factor annotates his letters 'Commissary' and although Sir James occasionally refers to him as 'Commy' he more frequently calls him 'Lt. John Grant junior' so that is how he will be referred to in this account. It is clear from his distinctive legible handwriting that Lt John Grant 'commy', 'Delcroy' and 'junior' are one and the same person. As well as being a good writer of letters he had a sense of humour for when he came to know him better he addressed one letter to Sir James,[9] which arrived safely at its destination:

> Colonel Sir James Grant
>
> etc etc etc
>
> at his House
>
> Edin.

With respect to the staff officers, Sir James wrote to the Lt Colonel: 'I have got an excellent Quartermaster (one Sutherland) recommended from the Artillery who knows all Scotland and every part of service.' Sutherland had been recommended to Sir James by no less a person than the Duke of Richmond, but this was an appointment that Sir James was soon to come to regret. The quartermaster was responsible for supplying the regiment with all its requisites including ammunition, accommodation and food.[10] A much shrewder appointment was that of James Watson as adjutant. Watson was a sergeant in the Artillery and his mother who was known to

Sir James as 'an excellent mother' lived in Strathspey, as did his aunt. Of Watson, Sir James wrote to the Lt Colonel: 'I prefer'd James Watson Serjeant in the Royal Artillery to any other Competitor for the Adjutancy as he is highly recommended by all his officers, is a perfect Master of his profession, has the warmest Attachment and Zeal for the Honor of the Corps.' The adjutant had a particular responsibility for drill and discipline, and was often commissioned from the ranks.[11] Initially, the Lt Colonel was dubious regarding Watson's suitability for the post, replying to Sir James that he 'saw Watson your Intended adjutant here two years ago, & much fear he has not education for it – he ought at least besides being a good <u>drill</u> to be an excellent pen & ink man – if he is not entirely up to his office, the Regt. will be crippled indeed'.[12] Fortunately, the Lt Colonel's fears proved to be groundless and he soon came to recognise Watson's excellent qualities. Sir James appointed Dr Peter Grant*, son of the Rev. John Grant minister of Abernethy, as regimental surgeon and Dr John Grant, his factor's son, as surgeon's mate. Lt John Grant junior wrote of Dr John Grant: 'Among the number of Candidates for that appointment is Mr John Grant Surgeon, Son of Sir James Grants factor, who is an exceeding clever young man and thoroughly recommended by a number of the officers of the Regt.' It is of interest to note that James [later Sir James] McGrigor** who was an exact contemporary of John Grant at the Medical School in Aberdeen was able to purchase a surgeoncy rather than an assistant surgeoncy in the 88th or Connaught Rangers because his father was able to pay for it.[13] The Rev. James Grant, minister of Urquhart, was appointed regimental chaplain.[14]

* * *

On 1st of March 1793 Sir James received the Royal Warrant to raise a Regiment of Fencible men.

Footnotes:
*Prebble[15] states that surgeon Peter Grant was the son of the factor which he was not, but this is an understandable error with so many Grants in the regiment.
**James McGrigor (1771-1858). Founded the Aberdeen Medical Society together with John Grant, Alexander Mitchell and nine other medical students. Surgeon to the Connaught Rangers 1793-1804. Chief of the Medical Staff in the Peninsular Campaign under the Duke of Wellington 1812-1813. Knighted 1813. Appointed Director General of the Army Medical Department 1813. Created Baronet 1831.

George R.

Whereas we have thought it fit to order a Regiment of Fencible men to be forthwith raised under your command which is to consist of 8 companies of 3 sergeants 3 corporals 2 Drummers & 60 private men in each, with 2 pypers to the Grenadier company beside a Serjeant Major, & Quarter Master Serjeant, together with the usual Commissioned Officers which men are not to be sent out of Great Britain.

These are to authorize you by beat of Drum or otherwise, to raise so many men in any county or part of our Kingdom of Great Britain as shall be wanted to complete the said Regiment to the above mentioned numbers, and all Magistrates, Justices of the Peace, Constables & other our Civil Officers, whom it may concern are hereby required to be assisting unto you in providing Quarters, impressing Carriages & otherwise as there shall be occasion – Given at our court at St. James this 1st day of March 1793 in the 33 year of our Reign.

By His Majestys Command

(signed) Geo. Yonge

To our T. & lvd Sir James Grant Bart

Colonel of a Regiment of Fencible men to be forthwith raised or to the Officer appointed by him to raise Men for our said Regiment.[16]

Sir George Yonge, who signed the warrant, was the Secretary of State at War. The following year he was replaced in this office by William Windham. Also in 1794 a new post was created, that of Secretary of State for War. William Pitt transferred Henry Dundas from the Home Department to this post. In 1795 William Huskisson was appointed Under Secretary of State for War, so in practise there were three ministers involved in the administration of the army instead of one. It can be readily understood therefore, that the administration of the army was, at this stage, somewhat haphazard.[17]

Seven Scottish Fencible regiments were raised in 1793. The regiment Sir James raised and commanded was initially called the 'Grant Fencibles' but this was then changed to the 'First or Strathspey Regiment of Fencible Highlanders'. For the sake of brevity the regiment soon became known simply as 'The First Fencibles'. The other six Fencible regiments were the

Second or Sutherland, the Third West Lowland or Montgomerie, the Fourth or Breadalbane, the Fifth or Argyll, the Sixth or Gordon and the Seventh Southern or Hopetoun Fencible regiment.[18]

Sir James, who was now aged 55 years was Colonel of the regiment and drew up a list of gentlemen whom he recommended to His Majesty for commissions in the Grant Fencibles. Alongside the names of the recommended officers Sir James appended his own comments with regard to their military experience. To these have been added the ages of the officers where these are known. The full list of officers as given in the returns from regimental headquarters in Forres on 30th April 1793 was:

Lieutenant Colonel
> A. P. Cumming of Altyre – aged 43 years, Captain late North Fencibles, 6 years a subaltern in the 13th Regiment of Foot.

Major
> John Grant of Glenmoristone, aged 34 years, late Captain in the 73rd Regiment. At present on half pay of the 24th Regiment.

Captains
> John Grant of Achindown, aged 54 years. Late Captain of the 42nd Regiment. To be Paymaster.
> Alexander Macdonell, Esq., of Glengarry, aged 19 years.
> Robert Cumming, Esq., of Logie, aged 47 years. Lieutenant in the late North Fencibles.
> Simon Fraser, Esq., of Foyers, aged 32 years. Lieutenant in the late North Fencibles.
> John Rose, of Holme, Esq., aged 47 years. Lieutenant in the late North Fencibles.

Captain–Lieutenant
> John Grant of Rippachie, aged 49 years. Half pay of the 89th Regiment.

Lieutenants
> James Grant of Bellintomb, aged 48 years, from the half pay of Sir James Campbell's late Independent Company.
> John Grant, aged 35 years, senior of Rosefield. Half pay late 80th Regiment.
> William Grant, aged 35 years, of Callendar. Half pay late 90th Regiment.

Allan Grant, aged 53 years, of Mulben. Half pay of the late 108th Regiment.

Francis W. Grant, aged 15 years, Gentleman.

James Macdonell, aged 15 years, Gentleman.

John Urquhart, Gentleman.

John Grant, Junior, Commissary of Moray, Gentleman.

Ronald Macdonell, Gentleman.

Ensigns

James Grant. Half pay of the late Garrison Battalion.

Duncan Grant, senr.

Peter Grant.

John Grant, Kinchirdy.

Duncan Grant, Junr.

Harry Cumming, from The Royal Irish Artillery.

Staff

Chaplain – James Grant, Aged 36 years.

Adjutant – James Watson, aged 33 years.

Quartermaster – Angus Sutherland.

Surgeon – Peter Grant.

Surgeon's Mate – John Grant, aged 21 years.[19]

Lieutenant Colonel Alexander Penrose Cumming of Altyre was a man of considerable personality and presence with a wonderful command of the English language and a caustic wit. He had former military experience which was important for Sir James had none. The Major and the Captains who were to be the company commanders all had some military experience apart from Alexander [or Alasdair Ranaldson as he is better known] Macdonell*, who was still only nineteen years of age. He owed his place in the regiment not only to the fact that he was Sir James Grant's ward but also because as chief of the Macdonell of Glengarry branch of the Clan Macdonald he could bring recruits to the regiment. However, his company of Macdonells were later to be the cause of considerable unrest within the regiment. Alexander

Footnote:

*Alexander [Alistair Ranaldson] Macdonell (1773-1828) 15th chief of the Glengarry branch of clan Macdonald. Educated at Oxford University. Raised the Glengarry Fencible regiment of which he was appointed Colonel 1794.

Macdonell brought with him his younger brother James* and his cousin Ronald, as Lieutenants in his company.

Every officer, in order to purchase his rank, was to raise an allotted number of recruits for the regiment as follows:[20]

Colonel	68
Lt. Col.	65
Major	55
Each Captain	40
Captain Lieutenant	23
Each Lieutenant	10
Each Ensign	8
The Adjutant	16
Quartermaster	16
Chaplain	10
Surgeon	10
Surgeon's mate	6

Recruiting started at once and was undertaken with great urgency. As early as March 2nd, Sir James issued the following instructions to all involved in recruiting:

No man is to be inlisted above 45 years of age, or under five feet four inches; but well made, growing Lads, between 16 and 18 years of age, may be taken at five feet three inches. You are not, however, absolutely restricted to half an inch, when you find stout well made Lads, who are likely soon to be fit for service. Every Recruit, before he is attested, should be examined by an experienced surgeon, who will at the foot of the Attestation certify that he is fit for service.

...Each Serjeant, Corporal, Drummer, and Private, will from that period [the date of Attestation] have an allowance of three

Footnote:
*James Macdonell (1778-1857) Younger Brother of Alexander Macdonell. Educated at Cambridge University. Served under the Duke of Wellington as Lt Colonel of the 1st Battalion Coldstream Guards in the Peninsular campaign. Distinguished himself at the Battle of Waterloo where he succesfully defended the fortified chateau of Hougomont against all attempts by the French to take it. He was knighted after the battle and went on to have a distinguished military career. Promoted full General in 1854.

half pence per day of Bread-money...in aid of the expence of this Levy, you will be allowed Three Guineas *[a guinea was one pound and one shilling]* for each Recruit...but you are requested not to beat up for more than Two Guineas and a Crown for each Man.

At the time of Inspection each Recruit must have the following Articles

Two Shirts

Two pairs of Shoes

Two pair fine Hose

A Bonnet and Feathers

A Black Stock

A Haversack

all of which to be purchased out of his Bounty

The Regiment is to serve in any part of Scotland, but not to march out of it, except in case of Invasion of the more Southern parts of the Kingdom...

When you want an advance of money towards recruiting, you will please to draw upon the paymaster for £50; and when you return him 12 men recruited...he has instructions from me to advance £50 more...

You are to have your quota of Men completed in three Months from the date of your Beating order. Should you fail in completing the number of Men you engage for, you are to pay Three Guineas for each man, necessary to make up your deficiency, or your Commission to be void and null[21]

Attestation forms were printed immediately but curiously the wording and layout of these forms were not all identical. Several different versions were printed and distributed. Some had a grand Royal Crest, others did not. Some had the Articles of War printed on them but others did not. Some forms stated: 'I am a protestant' and in others these words were omitted. The Scottish Emancipation Act was not introduced into the House of Commons until April 3rd 1793[22] but despite this Alexander Macdonell, who was a Catholic, was allowed to raise and command a company. Occasionally, recruiting officers ran out of forms and then they had to be duplicated by hand by a clerk.[23] A typical attestation form is set out below:[24]

I John Grant do make Oath, that I am by Trade a Tayler and to the best of my Knowledge and Belief, was born in the Parish of Abernethy in the county of Inverness that I have no Rupture, nor ever was troubled with Fits, that I am no ways disabled by Lameness or otherwise, but have the perfect Use of my Limbs; and that I have voluntarily enlisted myself to serve his Majesty KING GEORGE the THIRD as a private Soldier in the Regiment of Fencible Men, commanded by Sir JAMES GRANT of GRANT, Baronet, upon condition that I am not to be marched out of Scotland, except in case of an actual Invasion of England; and upon Condition also, that I am not to be draughted out of the said Regiment into any other Corps; and that I am no Apprentice, nor belonging to any Militia, or any other Regiment or to His Majesty's Navy; and that I have received all the enlisting Money which I agreed for. As Witness my Hand this first day of April 1793 years

John Grant

Witness present

To wit

These are to certify, that the aforesaid John Grant Tayler aged 27 Years 5 Feet 8½ Inches high, Brown Complexion, Brown hair, Grey Eyes, Came before me one of His Majesty's Justices of the Peace for the County aforesaid, and acknowledged that he hath voluntarily enlisted himself to serve His Majesty KING GEORGE the THIRD, in the abovesaid Regiment. He also acknowledged that he has heard the Second and Sixth Sections of the Articles of War read to him, against Mutiny and Desertion, and took the Oath of Fidelity mentioned in the Said Articles of War.

I have examined the above-named Man, and find him fit for His Majesty's Service.

Surgeon

Sworn before me at Castle Grant this first day of April 1793

James Grant J.P.

ARTICLES of WAR

[Sect II. Art. 3.] Any Officer or Soldier who shall begin, excite, cause or join, in any Mutiny or Sedition in the Troop, Company, or Regiment, to which he belongs, or in any other Troop or

Company in our Service, or in any other Party, Post, Detachment, or Guard, on any Pretence whatsoever, shall suffer Death, or such other Punishment as by a Court-Martial shall be inflicted.

[Sect.VI. Art.1.] All Officers and Soldiers, who having received Pay, or having been duly enlisted in our Service, shall be convicted of having deserted the same, shall suffer Death, or such other Punishment as by a Court-Martial shall be inflicted.

[Art. 2.] Any non-commissioned Officer or Soldier, who shall, without Leave from his Commanding Officer, absent himself from his Troop or Company, or from any Detachment on which he shall be commanded, shall, upon being convicted thereof, be punished according to the Nature of his Offence, at the Direction of a Court-Martial.

It is interesting to note that in this example, and in many other attestation forms, the recruit's signature was not witnessed nor was he examined by a surgeon.

* * *

There was considerable uncertainty regarding the amount of bounty money that should be paid to each recruit and on March 4th the factor wrote to Sir James: 'We are at a loss as to the size...of the Bounty money.' Without waiting for a reply from Sir James he wrote the same day to the Reverend James Grant of Urquhart, the regimental chaplain: 'By last nights newspaper five guineas is the Bounty money'.[25] Captain–Lieutenant John Grant of Rippachie* was equally confused, writing to Sir James: 'I have never yet learned for certainty what is the money allowed by Government – I have taken it for granted that it is five pounds but I have given a little more.'[26] In fact the bounty paid by the government was only three guineas, so Rippachie may well have been required to pay the difference out of his own pocket.

Recruiting parties were none too scrupulous in their activities. According to Richard Glover[27] the prime incentive for getting men lay in the bounty. This was a sum of money partly to pay for clothing and equipping the recruit and partly to induce him to volunteer by giving him a handsome bonus out

[Footnote:

*In 1806 Strathspey was shocked when Captain and Mrs Grant of Rippachie were found dead in their beds having suffocated after lighting a fire in their bedroom with English coals.[27a]

of the residue. Indeed the bounty worked in two ways as an incentive. The hope of receiving it induced the recruit to enlist and determination to secure the best part of it made the recruiting sergeants very industrious in getting their men. Nor was that all. Many of the recruiting sergeants became very adept in their 'sales talk' with tales of glory, honour and fame and they encouraged the prospective recruit to join by holding out prospects of promotion. If a man showed interest he was plied with ale and given as little time as possible to reflect on the consequences of enlisting. Once he was attested the deed was done and there was no going back on it – except by desertion – and when he joined his regiment the unfortunate recruit was in for a shock for most of his bounty (which had probably already been spent on drink) had to be given back to pay for his uniform and knapsack – so most recruits started their army life in debt.[28] For the recruiting sergeants desertion was a problem. Some men made a practice of 'bounty jumping', taking the money, deserting, and then repeating the process with another regiment. According to Michael Glover[29] a man was hanged in Ipswich in 1787 who had 'made the extraordinary confession that he had enlisted forty nine times and had had three hundred and ninety seven guineas as bounty money thereby'. Haythornthwaite[30] gives an account of a man who in April 1794, in the grassmarket in Edinburgh, put himself up for public auction to the various recruiting parties present, allowing no bid of less than a guinea; he was eventually knocked down for 20 guineas. Another case involved a man selling himself like butchers meat, asking for bids of so much a pound.

Most officers threw themselves into the task of raising their allotted quota of recruits with alacrity and many raised more than they were required to do. Sir James raised at least 180 men. 93 of these came from Strathspey and 11 from Urquhart. In his return of men recruited from Strathspey Sir James wrote 'This is not the right list to be look'd at', so it could be inaccurate but there appears in it the name of an Edward Wheeler, a 17 year old gardener who was born in the parish of Stratford in Warwickshire. It is surprising that such a young man should travel all the way from Warwick to Strathspey to find employment. The remaining 76 of Sir James's recruits came from 'besouth the Forth'. Many of these men had been born as far north as Caithness and Sutherland and as far south and west as Sussex and Cork and had come to Edinburgh to find work.[31]

From the available records it would seem that the Lt Colonel only managed to raise 36 men and Major John Grant of Glenmoriston 30, but

Captain Cumming of Logie raised 56 men. The first 14 on his list were all local men from Moray, Nairn & Inverness but his last five recruits came from Lanark. Unfortunately another five are recorded as having deserted. Captain Alexander Macdonell of Glengarry being the clan chief had no difficulty in bringing 70 volunteers along with him. They were mainly labourers and shepherds. Thirty two of them were Macdonells and all were local men from Invernesshire. One of the Duke of Gordon's recruiting parties headed by a Mr Macpherson strayed into Glengarry country and endeavoured to recruit a man whom Macdonell believed had undertaken to enlist with him. According to Macdonell both Macpherson's and his own recruiting party adjourned with the new recruit 'to a Whiskie house, and as is the invariable practice on such occasions gave him money while in liquor, it is to be observed that my party gave him money in my name & Mr Macpherson in the Duke of Gordons name from the state of intoxication the whole were in I think it is very difficult to say who gave him money first'.[32] Captain John Grant of Achindown managed to raise 44 men, Captain Fraser of Foyers his allotted 40, Captain–Lieutenant John Grant of Rippachie 22 and Captain Rose of Holme 20. Quartermaster Angus Sutherland was two short of his quota, raising 14 men who came from all over the country from York, Sussex, Edinburgh, Inverness and Sutherland. The chaplain, the Reverend James Grant of Urquhart raised 14 men, four more than his quota, most of these coming from Urquhart.[33]

Lieutenant John Urquhart did not do at all well and his recruiting efforts were, to say the least, chequered. In an undated memorandum it is recorded that he initially managed to get 10 recruits but 3 of these promptly deserted and 4 were deemed to have been 'returned too much' whatever that meant. John Heron 'never was known to be inlisted and was deemed discharged' and John Grant 'was allow'd to be a mistake by inserting his name twice'. In a note dated 22nd May 1793 only two recruits, Hugh Rose and Thomas Robb[34] were listed as being raised by Lt Urquhart, but despite this John Urquhart was not a bad officer for when he left in December to join another regiment Sir James wrote of him: 'It is with regret he parts with Lieut. Urquhart for he is a valuable man and deserving officer.'[35] Lt William Grant did not do much better than John Urquhart raising only 5 men.[36]

Dr John Grant, the surgeon's mate, recruited 12 men, six more than he was required to do, between March 1st and April 13th. The first man on his list and allegedly the first volunteer of the Grant Fencible regiment was

Charles McIntosh. In one return he was listed as aged 20 and in another as aged 22. He was 5'1½" in height, had brown hair, black eyes and his complexion was brown. He was a labourer by trade, came from the parish of Inverallan and enlisted on March 2nd 1793.[37] McIntosh must have been known and liked by the factor and his family as there appears in the factor's cash book a page of entries headed 'Charles McIntosh private Dr' with the following entries:[38]

1793		£	S	D
Feb. 27	Gave him inlisting money	–	1	–
	Gave do to acct.		5	
Mar 9	Gave do to acct.		5	
16	Gave do to acct.		15	
	5 [yds] tartan @1/10		2	3½
	4 yds red & green Rib @ 5d		1	10
	1½ bl. do 7d			10½
	Bonnet		1	6
30	Gave do cash		10	

Perhaps McIntosh would not have enlisted so enthusiastically had he known he was to be sentenced to death for mutiny and shot on Gullane links some two years later.

The regimental officers were not the only ones involved in recruiting. Sir James invoked the services of others, in particular James Geddes, a merchant in Perth and Hugh Hutcheon, an advocate in Aberdeen. It is not clear how many men James Geddes recruited. It was at least 39 but this is likely to be a conservative estimate. On March 20th Geddes wrote to Sir James:

> I intend sending a party to Recruit at Dundee as I am informed a great many young men have come there from the North Country seeking Employment at the manufactures.

Geddes wrote again on March 29th:

> It is out of my power to get recruits at less than his Majesty's Bounty as there are so many parties recruiting and the young men are too knowing to take less; and I would recommend if it can be done not to call the recruits from this place till the Regiment is nearly completed, for the reason that every Recruit encourages his companions to Inlist.
>
> I have been very hard on George Ellis for spending so much money at the Markets which however cannot be avoided – He is

a Genteel young Fellow proper to encourage young men to engage with him and is doing the duty of a serjeant upon the pay of a Private. I hope you will allow him serjeants pay while he is recruiting.[39]

George Ellis had certainly been spending a great deal on drink as the following bill run up by him and sergeant William MacDonald at Mrs Cairn's Inn at the Shoegate in Perth on March 16th shows

5 Muckins* whisky @ 8d per mutckin	– 3	4
1 Mutchkin & 1 bottle ale	9^1/$_2$	
^{1}/$_2$ Dozen Beer	9	
1 Mutchkin & Gill whisky	10	
^{1}/$_2$ Muckin Do	4	

	£– 6 0^1/$_2$	

On the same day a bill paid by James Geddes at the Kings Arms in Perth for '5 Recruits Eating and Drinking' came to £1-4-6. Geddes treated his recruiting sergeants well and on March 28th he paid John Norrie, a tailor in Perth ten shillings and two pence for making coats for Mathew Grant and George Ellis. Meanwhile, George Ellis continued his spending spree running up a bill of £1-11-2 at the fairs** on April 10th.[40]

On April 2nd Geddes, when sending four completed attestation forms to Sir James, wrote:

John Fraser has past ware [experience] at the siege of Giberalter and has nineteen years service in his Discharge who is a decent well behaved man....I am hopefull at the reducement of your Honours Regiment that you will recommend him to the benefit of Chelsea Hospital...

Ld Bredalbin Regt is just over 450 strong he is taking men from 70 to 80 years of age the like I never seed in a Regt before.[41]

James Geddes sent recruiting sergeants far and wide reporting to Sir James on April 26th that sergeant Mathew Grant had no success at Kinross. In the same letter he told Sir James that George Ellis, now a sergeant, was on his way

Footnotes:
*A mutchkin was a rather loose measure of volume. Sometimes it would be a pint but more usually three-quarters of a pint. A gill was a quarter of a mutchkin.
**Markets

to Forres with 18 recruits and that he, Geddes, had 'conveyed them six miles out of the town gave them 5/- to drinke to encourage them on the way'.[42]

It was not only Lord Breadalbane who recruited very old men for Geddes concluded his letter with the observation that:

> Willm Farquson a recruit lying here some time ago on my subsistence and Bedfast – Inclosed is the Doctors attestation – he is an old man of no use to the Regt. I believe he is about eighty years of age I thinke his Discharge ought to be sent him and Dismiss him from the service with Directions what Cash to Carrie him to Edinbr. he is doing no good here.

The enclosed doctor's certificate stated only that Farquharson had a bad ulcer on his right leg.[43]

By March 23rd Hugh Hutcheon, the advocate in Aberdeen, had raised 31 men mainly from Aberdeen. Two were aged 45 and three were only 5' 2" tall, but these were recruited before Mr Hutcheon had received orders 'restricting him in point of age and size'. By April 5th Hutcheon had recruited 57 men including 15 year old Samuel Ramsay who was 5' 2½" tall who Hutcheon noted 'not being certain if Samuel Ramsay would pass, no bounty is paid him till he goes North'.[44]

Captain-Lieutenant John Grant of Rippachie was not impressed by Hugh Hutcheon's recruits writing to Sir James: 'The Aberdeen recruits, severals of which I am sory to say I think but indifferent & some very bad indeed tho Mr Hutcheon writes me the Duke's are worse.'[45]

There was a considerable amount of administrative work involved in the recruiting and large bills as well as smaller ones to pay. Alexander Grant, W.S. who was involved with Hugh Hutcheon in raising recruits in Aberdeen had by April 24th paid out on behalf of Sir James the sum of £449. 1. 1.

Hugh Hutcheon was presented with an account by J. Chalmers & Co. Printers in Aberdeen for placards and posters

1793 – March 12th

50 Placards and posting up	£– 12 6
200 Handbills for Recruits	– 10 –
March 22nd	
50 Placards and Posting	12 6
April 1st	
100 do do	1 5 –
Advertising Regiment complete	4 6

Another small account which Hugh Hutcheon sent to Sir James was for cash paid to a William Wright who was:

> a man of 24 years of age 6 ffeet high who was willing to inlist, and is so still, but who has a sore upon one of his legs about which the surgeon has some scruple, for himself and Donald MacDonald who brought him, to drinks £- 2. - .

On March 25th Hugh Hutcheon noted:

> Geo: Pringle deserted by sea to Leith but H.H. has wrote to get him secured & it is expected he will come back as he only went off in a fit of Drunkenness.[46]

Quartermaster Angus Sutherland was one of those recruiting for Sir James 'besouth the Forth' and on March 24th he wrote to Sir James from Edinburgh:

> The Inclosed is the Return of what Recruits has been Inlisted for your Regiment hear besides the 12 men that is Gon North to join, their Remains hear 46 men I think we have been very successful this past week...this morning I am going with a party for Glasgow by the approbation of both messrs Jack & Alex Grant, we are credibly informed that about 500 weavers are out of Imploy.[47]

A small recruiting party, under the command of Sergeant Peter Kilgour, was sent to 'Cromerty' on the Black Isle but although they did 'their best endeavours, yet because the people here prefer the sea to the Land service they have no success'.[48]

A total of 317 recruits came from Edinburgh, Glasgow, Perth and Aberdeen. Various individuals also got involved in obtaining recruits out of enthusiasm for the cause. Provost George Brown from Elgin raised three recruits.[49] Lady Grant received £1 for John Grant, a taylor* and Miss Grant five shillings for enlisting a recruit.[50] On March 16th, Adam Stewart in the Mains of Dalvey wrote to the factor:

> I shall dow my best in getting for the doctor some recruits – as I wrote you before I have one I think – I shall have a chance of two more.[51]

Footnote:
*John Grant's attestation papers are set out on pages 25 and 26

In 1792, the year before the outbreak of war, the pay and conditions of service had been drastically overhauled and a deduction or 'poundage' as it was called was abolished.[52] Private soldiers were now paid 6d per day, Corporals 8d and Sergeants 1/-. Each soldier received a penny halfpenny a day in 'Bread Money' and 6d per day subsistence.[53] Literacy was essential for promotion to sergeant, a sergeant being required to keep the company's clerical records.[54]

Whilst the recruiting was in full swing Sir James was still attending Parliament in London. He set out for the north in the second week of March and wrote to the Lt Colonel from Edinburgh on March 14th: 'We arrived here on saturday evening having left London on Monday evening as soon as we possibly could'. The journey from London to Edinburgh by coach had taken five days but Sir James was impatient to get to his house in Elgin for he wrote again to the Lt Colonel on March 16th from Coupar Angus: 'The Highland road is impracticable, and we are stop'd here for want of Horses in the middle of the day.'[55]

Ostensibly the cost of raising the regiment was borne by the government but in practice much of the burden fell upon Sir James, who was reminded by his brother in law the Lt Colonel that by April 1st the regiment owed him as much as £1,500.[56] On April 12th the Lt Colonel again reminded Sir James of the financial burden the regiment was becoming writing to him 'If you arn't very guarded in your extra allowances, you will find the Regt. a very expensive undertaking & I wou'd therefore propose taking the slop jackets into store & selling them out to raggamuffins'. Beside the address on this letter was written 'wt a salmon' a present for Sir James which no doubt had come from the River Findhorn near the Lt Colonel's home at Altyre.[57] A further expense was soon to fall upon Sir James as he explained to Sir James Abercromby Bart., of Birkenbog, Sheriff of Moray in a letter of April 13th:

> I beg leave to acquaint you that it is highly proper that an investigation be made immediately as to the State of the Country in regard to Meal – When I came to Forres the other day there was an absolute want and very great murmuring, And I really cannot say what might have been the consequence had I not got the immediate Command for the Town of 250 Bolls*...That will not

---

Footnote:
  *A Boll usually weighed 9 stone and cost approximately 16 shillings

last long as our Regt. being ordered to assemble at Forres as soon as possible will add to the demand...every one says there is grain enough in the country, let me intreat your immediate attention & presence that such measures may be adopted as the present circumstances require.[58]

* * *

The regimental headquarters was at Forres and the recruits marched there in separate parties from where they had been enlisted. Detachments were also stationed at Elgin and Nairn and the Macdonell company was initially quartered at Fort Augustus[59] as Alexander Macdonell had specifically asked Lord Adam Gordon* for permission 'for having my Recruits drill'd in Ft. Augustus at the time of forming them – as there is plenty of Barrack room and a sufficiency of arms in the store'.[60] It is likely that the main body of the regiment was encamped in tents outside Forres as this was the normal practice of the time but some may have been billeted in local Inns.[61] On their march north to Forres the new recruits had plenty of time to rue their decision to enlist and many deserted. Some no doubt got well away but others were not so lucky. On April 27th, Wm Binnie the Inner Keeper of the Edinburgh Tolbooth sent a note to 'Captain Cummin' of the Grant Fencibles at Forres, stating that he had 'Received into the Tolbooth Edinr. this day the persons of James Smith and Wm. Turner deserters from Sir James Grant's Regiment of Fencibles.[62]

Training of the recruits began in mid April but got off to a bad start mainly due to the misplaced kind heartedness of Sir James as explained by the Lt Colonel in a letter of April 12th: 'These <u>benevolences</u> or free gifts of 2/6 each which you ordered to your Edin. recruits are the devil & all, for at my first Evening parade of 24 men, the whole Edin. party were as drunk as Dragoons'.[63] Sir James ought to have known better as this was only to be expected. Haythornthwaite[64] describing life in the army at that time writes: 'The consumption of alcohol was prodigious in the extreme.' On April 13th

---

Footnote:
* Lord Adam Gordon (1728-1801) Fourth son of the 2nd Duke of Gordon. M.P. for Aberdeen 1754-1768 and Kincardine 1774-1788. Lt Colonel 66th Regiment of Foot 1762. Lt General and Commander in Chief North Britain (Scotland) 1789-1798. Promoted to full General and appointed Governor of Edinburgh Castle 1796.

the Lt Colonel ordered: 'The whole recruits in the town to parade tomorrow at ¹/₂ past ten oclock clean dressed & powdered to go to church; they will also parade in the same manner at 6 oclock in the evening' and on the following day he ordered the non commissioned officers to 'parade with the adjutant or Drill three times a day viz. at 7 in the morning, 2 in the afternoon & six in the evening – the rest of the recruits...will attend parade at 8 in the morning & 7 in the evening.'[65] The same daily drill routine was to be followed over the next few months.

On April 16th the Lt Colonel gave orders that 'The Serjeants will...make a report of such men who have not had the Small Pox'.[66] The reason for this order is unclear as vaccination against smallpox was not introduced by Dr Jenner until 1796.[67]

On April 20th Lord Adam Gordon informed Sir James that he had directed Mr Ben Bartlet, Store Keeper at Edinburgh Castle to issue 'the Grant Fencible Regiment of Foot Commanded by Sir James Grant Bart – Five Hundred and four Musquets & Bayonets compleat'.[68] These were flintlock muskets nicknamed 'Brown Bess'. They weighed 12 lbs and had an effective range of 200 yards, but the ball could not carry straight for more than 100 yards. Each musket ball weighed just under one ounce.[69]

At the same time the factor wrote to the chaplain:

> upon the whole 36 [recruits] out of Urquhart is not amiss tho I am persuaded it could well offer 20 more...
>
> You will with pleasure have heard before this reaches you that the Grant Fencible Regt. is considerably more than compleat and I may safely say that the Regt. was raised in the short space of three weeks and do now think that if Sir James had got the raising of two battalions they would have been completed within the three months – He has got about 140 in this country & except a very few all fine fellows and we have a number still of good men could be well spared without hurt to the farmers – which as much as possible ought always to be avoided – and what is very agreeable all we have are free volunteers

He then went on to ask the minister to use his influence with the doctor to allow his son, the surgeon's mate, time off to continue with his medical studies:

> Inclosed is a letter to you from my son John whom Sir James has been pleased to appoint Surgeons mate to his Regiment – I trust

you will use your interest on his behalf wt. Dr Peter Grant the surgeon & prevail with him to make matters as easy with John as possible – John served as apprentice during three years wt. Dr French at Aberdeen & at the Infirmary there where he saw and had a good deal of practice – I see very good certificates with him from Dr French and Dr Livingstone but still he is exceedingly anxious to attend the classes at Edinr. – I intended sending him there beginning of last winter but his health not being then confirmd after, the fever he had in harvest last, I put off his going to Edin. till May next – Through your interest I expect he will be allowed to prosecute his interest in the medical line a little further and have as much as can be of his pay as S. mate to enable him to do so & lessen his Expence on me which already has been pretty weighty.[70]

The factor also wrote to Lt John Grant junior:

I am really sorry that the two addl companies askd are not granted – From that I suspect the offer for a second battalion will not be accepted of...

The bearer John Grant Balnaclash goes to be attested at Elgin that, if it can be, his attestation may be antedated as far back as possible...but if you have given in at Forres the general List of the whole I am afraid it can't be done...

I have done nothing in the factory line since about 20th Feby. last...

14 Edin. fine Recruits arrived at Grantown Friday Evening and set out this morning for Forres...

The Perth recruits 15 in number arrived last evening at Grantown and will set out early tomorrow along with the Strathspey Lads for Forres – Hugh Ellis who got two of his Fingers frost bit in Baynack remains at Grantown for some days under Dr Stewarts care.[71]

The 15 Perth recruits were very probably from the party of 18 to whom James Geddes had given '5/- to drinke to encourage them on the way'. The three that did not reach Grantown could have either fallen ill or deserted.

* * *

At this stage there were high hopes for the regiment and a certain well earned satisfaction not only because of the speed with which it had been raised but also with the amount of his own personal money that Sir James had put in to the venture. Alexander Grant WS, Sir James's Edinburgh law agent wrote to him on April 30th:

> I doubt notwithstanding the additional men you are allowed the first year will scarce reimburse you but you have established one object the dignity and influence of the family.[72]

Because so many men had been recruited so quickly Lord Adam Gordon had written to Sir James on April 25th informing him that 'His Majesty has been pleased to order an augmentation of Fifteen men pr Company'.[73] These were the 'additional men you are allowed' which meant that the establishment of each company was now increased from 60 to 75 men.

The 'General Return for all the Strathspey Fencibles' for 1793 showed that 742 men had been recruited. In the 'Remarks' column it was noted that some had been rejected, some were deemed to be 'suspicious' and some were sick[74] so that the effective strength of the regiment on April 30th, apart from the officers, was one sergeant major, one quartermaster sergeant, 24 sergeants, 24 corporals, 16 drummers, two pipers and 624 rank and file.[75]

Lt Colonel Cumming was impressed with the competence of the adjutant and wrote to Sir James at the beginning of June proposing that he be promoted to Lieutenant adding that he 'was more deserving of it than half the Regt put together – for if he does not take the better care of himself & feed & drink wine, which his present pay will not admit of, it's more than probable he goes into a consumption'.[76] Despite this plea it was September 1st before Watson was appointed Ensign[77] and February 1794 before he was promoted to Lieutenant.[78]

* * *

On June 5th the regiment was inspected by Lt General A. Leslie* who was second in command to Lt General Lord Adam Gordon. General Leslie

---

Footnote:
* Lt General the Hon. Alexander Leslie (1731-1794) Younger brother of the 6th Earl of Leven and Melville. Served as Lt Colonel of the 64th Regiment during the American War of Independence 1778-1783. Deputy C. in C. Scotland.

expressed his satisfaction at the regiment's appearance. Not a single man was deemed to be unfit at the inspection and none was discharged which prompted factor James Grant to comment to Sir James 'Poor Charlie McIntosh He of low Stature has had good luck...I would have been sorry had he been cast at the Inspection'.[79] If he had known what the future had in store for him Charles McIntosh would not have been at all sorry had he been discharged there and then. Lord Adam Gordon wrote to Sir James on June 10th: 'I congratulate you on the very flattering report General Leslie makes of yr. Battn.' which is surprising as the recruits had not yet all been provided with uniforms. Lord Adam must have been aware that the regiment was not yet properly clothed and equipped for he wrote to the Lt Colonel at the end of June 'It being of the greatest Importance to His Majesty's Service, that the Fencible Battalions should be clothed, accoutred, & Disciplined as soon as possible; I am to recommend to you, to give your most earnest attention to these objects, and to desire that you will report to me, from Time to Time, the progress made therein'. The contract for clothing the regiment had been won by John Gloag of Edinburgh who had shipped 2,640 yards of cloth from Leith to Findhorn for the regiment and on June 24th Lt John Grant junior reported to Sir James that 'about 30 Taylors are busy in making the Hose & kilts for the men'.[80] MacIntosh[81] states that they had all received their uniforms by the end of July but from subsequent correspondence it is clear that the regiment had not been clothed or equipped to the satisfaction of the officers as late as December 1793. Indeed the first rumblings of dissatisfaction with John Gloag had occurred as early as March 24th when Sir James had written to Mr Isaac Grant, W.S. in Edinburgh:

> Any impropriety to the Cloathing Settlement is owing to Mr Sutherland hanging on so long at London when he shd have been at Edin before I left it – I have desired Lt John Grant to write to him & Mr Gloag this Evening that at least such alterations as to the making the Cloaths may be made as do not prove too late if Mr Gloag has not already ordered the making of them at London so as to be beyond recall, they can settle as to sending the Materials of all kinds And we have Taylers enough to make them But we must not fall between two stools – They must be made in time whatever method is adopted.[82]

The regiment was made up of one company of Grenadiers, one of Light Infantry and six 'Battalion' companies. On parade the Grenadier company was on the right of the line and the Light company on the left with the Battalion companies in the middle. On the march the Grenadier company was in front and the Light company in the rear. The Grenadier company was composed of the tallest and biggest men and the Light company was composed of those who were more intelligent and athletic. On parade each company was drawn up in three ranks, there being 26 men in each rank. The tallest and best looking men were in the front rank to give the best possible overall impression, the shortest in the middle rank and those of medium height were in the rear rank. The tallest men in each rank were at either end of the rank and the shortest men in the middle. The hair was worn long and was powdered for all regimental parades and all the men were clean shaven.[83]

The Grenadier company commanded by Captain Robert Cumming contained five men standing over 6 feet tall and was drawn up thus:[84]

	Front Rank	Centre Rank	Rear Rank
Age	18-39	18-40	18-40
Height	6'0¼"-5'9"	5'5½"-5'9¾"	5'8½"- 5'11¾"

The Light company commanded by Captain Simon Fraser was drawn up

	Front Rank	Centre Rank	Rear Rank
Age	17-30	15-30	16-40
Height	5'6"-5'9½"	5'3½"-5'6"	5'4½"-5'8½"

The Light Company was mainly made up of young men, more than three quarters being aged between 18 and 22 years.

The Muster Roll of a typical Battalion company [Captain John Grant's company] dated Forres, June 5th 1793 was as follows:

	Front Rank	Centre Rank	Rear Rank
Age	20-40	15-39	16-40
Height	5'6"-5'10"	5'3"-5'6½"	5'4"-5'7"

The Captain-Lieutenant, John Grant of Rippachie, was the senior lieutenant and he commanded the first Battalion company or the Colonel's Company. The second Battalion company was commanded by Major John Grant of Glenmoriston and his second in command was Sir James's son Francis [or Frank as he was known to the family] who was only fifteen years old! The third Battalion company was commanded by Captain Alexander

Macdonell, the fourth by Captain John Rose, the fifth by Captain John Grant of Achindown who was also Paymaster and the sixth by Lt Colonel Cumming who had Lt James Grant as second in command of his company.[85]

*　*　*

Even at this early stage in the life of the regiment a note of disharmony was introduced by Alexander Macdonell as an undated draft letter from Sir James to the Secretary at War reveals:

> Capt. Alex. McDonell claims presedence as given him in the Return before Capts. R. Cumming Simon Fraser & John Rose as having compleated his Compy. before either of those Gentn. They on the contrary claim rank of him as having been officers in the late North Fencible Regt. whereas Capn. M.D. never was in the army. This Point is ref'd to His Majestys Secretary at War which he will please decide accordingly.[86]

The final outcome of this dispute is not recorded but it was not so petty as at first sight it might appear for seniority was all important to the officers. Nobody could gain promotion without at the same time selling, thus requiring a chain of purchasers involving everyone at or below the rank that had become vacant.[87] Thus if Macdonell had been successful in his claim to be senior captain, then if the majority had become vacant it should have been his for the asking as long as he could pay for it.

*　*　*

The Lt Colonel had an aversion to gambling in all its forms and issued the following order on June 9th:

> The Commanding Officer is extremely sorry to have observed a shameful spirit of gambling prevail amongst some of the men & Drum Boys – He hereby expressly forbids it and is determined that any person in future caught at pitch & toss or any gambling, shall be punished severely.

Not much notice was taken of this order for on July 6th he had to issue another one:

> The Commanding Officer is sorry to observe that the order relative to gambling has not been complied with – He hereby expressly forbids every species of such a ruinous vice, as he is

determined to try every person by a court martial, who shall be reported to him; & allow the sentence to be inflicted in its fullest extent – all Raffles are expressly prohibited.

In an effort to tighten discipline the Lt Colonel issued a series of orders. The first on June 18th ordered that:

The officer of the day is in future to attend particularly to the awkward Squads and to be answerable that they are keept properly to their exercise & to admit of none lying down or quitting the field.

and ten days later:

a guard is to mount in future consisting of one Subaltern one Serjeant one Corporal one Drum and twenty Private...the Officer of the Guard is to be very particular & exact in posting his Sentries giving them proper instructions how they are to behave on their posts, & what marks of respect they are to pay to the different Officers who passes them – He...is to confine such as get drunk...He is expressly to prohibit any Spirits from being brought in to the Guard room and immediately to confine any person who attempts it – He is to parade his guard regularly at Retreat beating and examine their arms and the same at 7 o clock in the morning; and see that his mens hair are combed, & their shoes brushed.

and again on July 6th:

The Officer of the guard is in future to send Patroles round the town & thro' the closes soon after tattoo beating, who are to apprehend & confine all soldiers who they find out of their quarters after that hour.[88]

A typical guard was the one mounted on August 4th:

Report of the Guard mounted by the 1st or Strathspey Fencible Regt at Forres 4th August 1793.

Parole* Calcutta

John Grant's company

1 subaltern

1 serjeant

1 corporal

1 Drummer

Footnote:
*The 'parole' and the 'countersign' were the passwords. They were listed in general orders and were changed daily.[90]

20 Privates

All orders of the Guard obey'd I visited the Centinells frequently thro' the Night and found them all at there posts

(signed) James Mcdonell

Relieving Officer.[89]

* * *

The regiment remained at Forres for some months and on July 1st it was reported in the regimental returns that Capt Alexander Macdonell had not yet joined 'tho' hourly expected'. In fact Macdonell did not join the regiment until December having obtained leave of absence to continue his studies at Oxford University.[91] Lieut Ronald Macdonell was reported 'absent with leave for his health' and chaplain Mr James Grant had 'not yet joined'. The regimental strength consisted of '662 Rank and File'. There were 7 sick in hospital and 48 sick in quarters.[92]

In July John Hayes, a merchant in Forres brought an action against Lt Colonel Alexander Penrose Cumming, Capt.-Lieut John Grant, Rippachie, Capt Grant Achindown, Lt John Grant, Ballintomb, Sergeant Mackay and Adjutant Watson. The reason for this was that Thomas Duncan, another merchant in Forres, who was indebted to Hayes to the tune of £12. 2. stg. and who was about to be incarcerated in the Tolbooth for non payment of this debt when 'Lieutenant Grant violently endeavoured to stop them [the Town Officers] from Proceeding, and being joined by Colonel Alexander Penrose Cumming, Captain John Grant and the other defenders...they insisted that Thomas Duncan was their soldier...carried away the Prisoner Thomas Duncan to a backroom...to attest Duncan...Duncan was attested accordingly...and taken under the protection of the military...and the pursuer has not heard of him since.[93] If substantiated this action was clearly in contravention of Section XI. of the Articles of War which stated that 'No officer shall protect any Person from his Creditors on the Pretence of his being a soldier.'[94]

The officers vehemently denied the accusation stating in their defence that they were 'so unwilling to do anything illegal or oppressive that Colonel Cumming and Lieut. James Grant went immediately to the Town Clerk to have his opinion on the matter, who assured them decidedly that they were in the right. The Defenders positively deny that any of them used any force or violence...Duncan being attested...left the house together with Grott

42

[Town Officer in Forres] and walked down the street towards the house of Duncan's mother'.[95] There is unfortunately no record of the final outcome of this dispute.

* * *

On July 19th the regiment showed the first signs of mutinous behaviour. The Lt Colonel explained to Sir James the unfortunate incident which occurred that day:[96]

> The people of the Town have been infamous Instruments in seducing the minds of the men, to whom I have explained that it was not for a foreign enemy we were raised, but merely to keep such rascally spirits as every town in Scotland were full of, in order – we had this morning a very disagreeable riot & mob about the meal, owing to bad advice from the same people – we marched them to the field, read the articles of War to them, explained all matters and convinced them that we meant nothing but their good, their welfare & their credit We parted on the best footing & in token of their being thoro'ly satisfied with the conduct of their officers in every point they gave three Huzzaas & God Save the King – How long this calm may last, with such spirits I cannot pretend to say.

and on the following day he wrote again to Sir James:

> everything is quiet...there is every appearance of satisfaction & content, mixed as I am informed with contrition, for their folly; as the most of them see & acknowledge they were led into error by the malicious Inhabitants who they see led them on, for their own rascally purposes – The Meal is explained to their entire satisfaction & I have found it necessary that what you have procured, shou'd be distributed to the soldiers only & the Inhabitants keept from any part of it – a few bad spirits who must be watched, were the bane of the whole & those were men from whom you wou'd least have expected it.

On the same day Lt John Grant junior gave his version of events to Sir James:

> In my opinion if I may venture to hazard one upon the subject they proceeded from a witless Serjeant, Kilgour, having misunderstood or executed improperly the orders he received, and

once the minds of men are raised 'tis not so easy to convince them of their error, besides that they find many things to make a handle of – It is pleasing however to relate that immediately after matters bore the worst appearance yesterday at 10 we marched to the field rainy as the day was, and after a proper explanation of matters the whole were so much pleased that they joined in one cheer & Huzza and since nothing but peace & happiness is to be seen among us – our Adjutant poor man is more lucky than could almost have been expected for when the orders of I may almost say all were held cheap his was not only immediately obeyed but he was also cheered.

The statement to the men by the Lt Colonel that 'it was not for a foreign enemy we were raised, but merely to keep such rascally spirits as every town in Scotland were full of, in order' is very revealing and shows how close the government felt the country was to revolution. Fortescue reinforces this when he states that 'the home army...was not designed primarily for defence, against foreign enemies, but simply and solely for the purpose of domestic police'.[97]

* * *

On July 27th Private James Stevenson, a twenty year old shoemaker from Edinburgh, who was so well educated that it is surprising to find him serving in the ranks, wrote from Forres to his parents in Edinburgh:

Our Regiment now is almost Clothed, and whenever the Clothing and necessaries are completed we will march from Forres, we believe Either to Aberdeen or Edinburgh Castle, we are to be mustered on the 6th September, and shortly after we will go – During the time we have been here provisions has not been dear – but the manner of living among the Inhabitants of this place is extremely mean and poor, – if it were not for the fresh fish that comes in from Findhorn they would have nothing but Potatoes all the year round three times a day...

I gave my watch the other day to be cleaned by a watch-maker in this Town, and a Lieutenant in our Regiment happened to see it, and fell so much in conceit with it that he Employed the watchmaker to Bargain with me for it, so I sold it, and made my own of it – A watch like her is not to be seen in this Country and

44

many here never saw a watch since they were born – Robert Sutherland who listed with us and deserted on the Road arrived here from Glasgow being found and brought here a prisoner, you perhaps have forgotten him – he was a Comrade to me in the West port – He was tried by Court Martial and received a hundred Lashes which were very sore – his sentence was 400 But the 300 were remitted being the first offence – we have had three tied up to be whiped for small offences.[98]

Unfortunately, the regimental court martial book[99] is incomplete but it confirms that Robert Sutherland was sentenced to 400 lashes for desertion on July 15th and that only 100 of these were inflicted. The first soldier in the First Fencibles to be flogged was Archibald MacDonald who received 200 lashes on July 1st for 'unsoldier like behaviour & having debauched a young woman under the pretence of marrying her & telling lies to the Captain of his company'. On the same day Michael Anderson received 50 lashes for being drunk & threatening expressions against the officers of the Regiment & repeatedly making disturbance in the street'. On August 16th when the scars on his back can scarcely have healed Anderson received another 300 lashes for 'unsoldier like behaviour in attempting to stab Isabell Robertson an inhabitant of the Bourgh of Forres with his bayonet'.

There was no limit to the number of lashes that could be awarded. It was not until 1812 that regimental court martials were restricted to a maximum of 300.[100] However, in the First Fencibles, although as many as 400 lashes were frequently awarded, and in one instance as many as 650, in practice no more than 300 were ever inflicted. The usual army practice was for the flogging to take place in front of the whole regiment, with the 'cat o' nine tails' on the bare back of the offender who was tied to a triangle of sergeants Halberds. The lashes were administered by relays of drummers who in many instances were not much more than boys.[101] The regimental surgeon was on hand to ensure that the culprit was fit enough to endure the punishment but despite this in many cases the punishment continued until the offender lost consciousness. Occasionally, soldiers died during or after a flogging.[102] The flogging was either carried out as quickly as possible or by 'beat of drum' in which ten taps were beaten on a drum between each blow in order to prolong the agony.[103] There is no record of which method was employed in the First Fencibles.

There are not many first hand accounts from soldiers who were on the receiving end of such a punishment and as it was such a common occurrence in the army of the day it is worthwhile quoting at length from the description given by Alexander Somerville, a private in the dragoons, of the flogging he received in front of his own regiment.[104] After he had been tied up the punishment commenced. He wrote:

> I felt an astounding sensation between the shoulders, under my neck, which went to my toe nails in one direction, my finger nails in another, and stung me to the heart, as if a knife had gone through my body. The sergeant major called in a loud voice 'one'. I felt as if it would be kind of Simpson not to strike in the same place again. He came on a second time a few inches lower, and then I thought the former stroke was sweet and agreeable compared with that one. The sergeant major counted 'two'. The 'cat' was swung twice round the farrier's head again, and he came on somewhere about the right shoulder blade, and the loud voice of the reckoner shouted 'three'. The shoulder blade was as sensitive as any other part of the body, and when he came on again on the left shoulder, and the voice cried 'four', I felt my flesh quiver in every nerve, from the scalp of my head to my toe nails. The time between each stroke seemed so long as to be agonizing, and yet the next came too soon. It was lower down and felt to be the severest. The word 'five' made me betake myself to mental arithmetic; this, I thought, is only the fortieth part of what I am to get. 'Six' followed, and so on, up to 'twenty five'. The sergeant major then said 'Halt!'
> Simpson stood back, and a young trumpeter who had not flogged before, took his cat and began. He had practised often at a stable post, or a sack of sawdust, and could handle the instrument as scientifically as anyone. He gave me some dreadful cuts about the ribs...The pain in my lungs was now more severe, I thought, than on my back. I felt as if I would burst, in the internal parts of my body...I had resolved, that I would die before I would utter a complaint or a groan. I detected myself once giving something like a groan and to prevent its utterance again, I put my tongue between my teeth, held it there, and bit it almost in two pieces...It now became Simpson's second turn to give 25. Only fifty had been inflicted, and the time since they began was like a long period of life: I felt as if I had lived all the time of my real life in pain and torture...the poor fellow was

slow, from aversion to the task; I do not know if he gave the strokes more quickly; they all seemed to last too long.

When the other youngster had reached, or nearly, his second twenty, I felt as if I could yield...I prayed to God to put into their minds to stop, and pardon me the remainder. When this five-and-twenty was completed, which made a hundred, the commanding officer said, 'stop, take him down, he is a young soldier'.

Haythornthwaite[105] comments that the 'cat' was dreaded by all but the most desperate of malefactors and he cites the cases of a corporal who committed suicide by swallowing four ounces of vitriol rather than suffer a flogging and of a private who shot himself rather than receive 300 lashes. Some men were able to withstand the ordeal better than others. Rifleman Harris[106] recalls a deserter who received 700 lashes in one day 'and never uttered a word of complaint during the infliction'. Alexander-Gordon[107] tells of a private of the 93rd Highlanders who having received 50 lashes nonchalantly put his shirt back on again and turned to the Lt Colonel saying in a loud voice so that all might hear: 'Dae ye ca' that a flogging? Hoots! I've got mony a warse licking frae ma mither.' Alexander-Gordon was adamant that 'there was not the slightest trace of that feeling of "degradation" which according to the sentamentalists...overwhelms not only the man who is flogged but also his comrades'.

According to Richard Glover[108] despite sporadic outcries against flogging in parliament and the press 'flogging lived on because responsible British legislators dared not limit the use of what was regarded as the surest means of controlling an army so largely drawn from the criminal classes'. It must also be remembered that flogging was effective. The French Army dispensed with flogging only at the cost of making much more use of the death penalty. Flogging was also supported by many in the ranks. Rifleman Harris[109] wrote 'although I detest the sight of the lash...I am convinced the British Army can never go on without it'.

Non commissioned officers were seldom flogged when found guilty at court martial, instead they were reduced to the ranks. According to Richard Glover[110] there were two ways a soldier sentenced to be flogged by a regimental court martial could try to evade it. Firstly, he could appeal to be tried by a general court martial. There were dangers in this course of action as the court could not only confirm the sentence but might also increase it. Despite this, appeals were quite frequent as they temporarily postponed the infliction of the sentence. Secondly, he could appeal to the commander in chief to have his sentence commuted to one of service for life in some overseas garrison. The Duke of York*, when he succeeded Lord Amherst** as commander in chief, seldom turned down such appeals.

* * *

Another soldier, less well educated than James Stevenson but one who could nevertheless also read and write wrote to Lady Grant, Sir James's wife on August 9th:

> From Jeams Grant in colonell Sir Jeams Grants Own Company. Forres Aug 9th 1793
>
> To Lady Grant
>
> I am Bold to axe the feavor of your Ladyship to Ask the Feavor of Sir Jeams of an farlof to me to go to Fort Welam for the speace of five or six wieks to settle some Afears...
>
> As I did Gitt non of the money Due me If Sir Jeams would be so good as feavor with four pouns str I hope I shal peay him Honerably I also want my Bounty money Promesid me By Mr Mcdonale of Gleanco ten Pounds sterling[111]

This letter is a prime example of the phonetic way of writing adopted by the less well educated. The highland lilt can readily be heard in this letter. What the men were promised, or thought they had been promised, was often very different from the reality.

Another private soldier, John Fraser wrote to Sir James requesting leave:

> Honoured Sir
>
> I have been endeavouring to obtain a Forloe to Elgin – that I might converse with your Honour – but it would not be granted me – My health is broke and the thoughts of my wife and destitute Babes are ready to sink me altogether - being a stranger here I cannot expect any person would trust me so far as to

---

Footnotes:

*His Royal Highness Frederick Augustus, Duke of York (1763-1827). Second son of King George III. Appointed Field Marshall and Commander in Chief February 1795. Generally regarded as a good administrator who did much to stamp out corruption in the purchase and sale of commissions and to ensure that promotion went to those who deserved it.

**Jeffrey Amherst (1717-1797) A Regular Soldier. Lt Colonel 1756. Created Baron 1776. General 1778. Commander in Chief 1793-1795. Field Marshall 1796

advance my bounty money for me - But if your Honour would favour me with a Forloe to Perth I make no doubt of obtaining it, and would not pretend to a Discharge from the service untill it was paid - Dear and Honoured Colonel, be so good as consider my Case - and order me to have liberty to wait upon your Honour at Elgin - or if a Forloe to Perth can be granted me as may seem to your Honour most proper - and pardon this trouble from

Honoured Sir   your most humble Sert.

Forres 21st June 1793   John Fraser

P.S. Be so good as favour your poor servant
with an answer.

This request caused the Lt Colonel much annoyance and he wrote angrily to Sir James:

The adjutant show'd me a Card from you this morning desiring him to send Fraser to Elgin, for two days – If you insist upon it he shall be sent...this man was positively refused a pass from me...I did it under the firm belief he was a malingerer...there was a manifest...dishonesty in his saying he was not able to do his duty, & yet be able to walk 24 miles in two days – The Surgeon's mate & every officer are of the same opinion with me, that nothing is the matter with him & that his only plan is to touch your feelings to get a discharge.[112]

This was not the first time that Sir James had interceded on behalf of Private John Fraser for on May 1st he had noted in his Letter Book 'wrote to Mr Geddes at Perth particularly concerning the wife & family of John Fraser enlisted by him – beg'd he would enquire about them & not see them in distress – trusted he would not let them suffer want of meat or lodging 'till such time as I rec'd his report concerning them'.[113]

The factor pleaded on behalf of John Grant, taylor in Grantown and Lady Grant's recruit, now in the Grenadier Company 'for a furlough for two or three weeks to put his house in Grantown to rights, to dispose of his Furniture & settle some Outstanding Accts that Cannot be done without himself'.[114]

Whilst the regiment was stationed at Forres Sir James made use of some of the men on his estate. On August 10th David Laing and three other private soldiers from the First Fencibles were paid £2. 2. 3 for cutting hay at Castle Grant. They were paid 1/6d per day, three times their military pay. David Laing it is recorded stayed 11 days at Castle Grant.[115]

On August 6th Lord Adam Gordon instructed Sir James to march the battalion to Aberdeen 'without loss of time – in two or three divisions – as you judge best'.[116] Sir James interpreted 'without loss of time' fairly liberally for on August 13th he joined his officers for a mess dinner at Mitchells Inn in Forres. There were 41 officers there. The meal, apart from drinks, cost £3. 1. 6 which was 1/5d per head. The drinks were quite a different matter for the party consumed:

    3 dozen bottles of claret
    14 bottles of port
    6 bottles of white wine
    1 bottle of whisky and 1 bottle of rum
    28 bottles of porter
    32 bottles of ale

The wine bill came to £10. 15. 2 and there was an additional charge of 2 shillings for 4 broken glasses and a 5 shilling tip for the maids[117] but the alcohol consumed at this dinner pales into insignificance when compared with that drunk at a mess dinner described by John Peebles in the American war. On that occasion thirty one officers drank seventy two bottles of claret, eighteen of Madeira, and twelve of port, together with some porter and punch. John Peebles often complained of officers drinking too much and of their being 'Fou' [drunk][118] including himself.[119] Haythornthwaite[120] tells us that 'the culture of hard drinking was just as entrenched in the officer class [as it was in the ranks]' and according to Howard[121] alcohol consumption was an integral part of British military life and was not discouraged by the military authorities or even the Army's medical officers. A prevalent view amongst military men, and even some doctors, was that alcohol gave a degree of protection against the various lethal diseases that affected the army but it was also known, even in those days, that excessive drinking was associated with cirrhosis of the liver.

Shortly after this mess dinner the regiment did march out of Forres in three divisions, the men being billeted in some convenient town or village each night. One division went to Peterhead and two to Aberdeen.

Just before the regiment left Forres, the Lt Colonel wrote in his Order Book:

    As several of the men have fired away their Ramrods at exercise owing to shameful carelessness & inattention the Commanding Officer expressly forbids such behaviour as he is determined to try by a Court Martial any who may be guilty of doing so in future & they will be punished for disobedience of orders

The Lt Colonel wanted the men to look at their best on the march and ordered that:

> The Commanding officers of companies are to receive from the Quartermaster a proportion of feathers which they are to distribute to their Men...The officers are to have them put in their new bonnets, on the first halting days; so as that they may march into their new quarters in a decent manner.

Not much notice seems to have been taken of this order for he again wrote in his Order Book at Aberdeen on August 27th:

> The commanding officer is very sorry to observe that so little attention has been paid to a former order for having the Bonnets properly cocked & feathered, he now positively Orders the Commanding officers to have this order fully complied with

* * *

Meanwhile two of Sir James's children had died. His twelve year old daughter Christina Terresa died on July 16th. Sir James had returned to the regiment shortly after her death, possibly because of the riot over meal, and the Lt Colonel wrote to Lady Grant on July 28th:

> As I know it will be a satisfaction to you, I have much pleasure to inform you, that my worthy friend Sir James is as well and happy as cou'd possibly be expected under the late melancholy event – we do what we can, to beguile his sorrows, & I flatter myself it is not entirely without effect – His mind is employed by our little cares & manoeuvres, from deeper thought, & we are happy to observe he enters in to our little bustle almost without knowing it.[122]

Sir James's youngest son, Alex Hope, died of a 'malignant fever' on August 23rd. Sir James, by this time had returned home. The Lt Colonel sent his condolences in the following terms:

> To speak comfort to you on the melancholy tidings of this day is not in my power – as you are seperated, for a time, from a most delightful little Angel – The power who has bruised you, can alone make you bear it, as God tempereth the winds to the shorn Lamb – and bruised indeed you are, for you have lost two of the sweetest cherubs – It is not for them, I grieve, but their afflicted parents – and may that power who only can do it, enable you both to bear

it...I...look upon it as but a seperation for a time, & that we shall ere long be united, in a place where sorrows reach not[123]

Nor were these Sir James's only family tragedies. His eldest son and heir, Lewis*, newly elected Member of Parliament had contracted syphilis in 1791 at the age of 24 for which he had been overzealously treated with mercury. This left him, although physically well, mentally disturbed. His memory was impaired, he was irritable, unable to concentrate and he suffered from delusions of persecution. At first there had been hopes of a recovery but these were now fast fading.

* * *

The Lt Colonel had fixed views on corporal punishment and discipline but was happy to temper them if it was thought they might send out the wrong message, for on August 30th he wrote to Sir James:

> however highly deserving he was of it, I did not punish Gilbert Wright, who stabbed the Inhabitant at Elgin – He was brought here under sentence of Court-Martial & was an old offender, but I did not chuse to let the natives here see us so soon begin such business.[124]

but later whilst on leave in Forres in October he informed Sir James who was now commanding in Glasgow:

> I had the pleasure of seeing a Deserter of ours go past under Escort a few days ago – It is Capt MacDonell's little Piper who left them at Nairn and I hear he is a very wicked little Dog – However disagreeable it must be to punish, I wou'd suggest your not passing him, as well for the crime as for the example of the people of these countries from whence he comes – we can never have a better opportunity of showing them what must happen from breeches of discipline...in the present temper of these people it is fortunate you have such a fair opportunity.[125]

On August 29th the Lt Colonel issued strict orders that:

> no man is to be excused from parades or any duty who is not in the Surgeon's Sick List & any man absenting himself from any duty is to be immediately confined
>
> The non Commissioned Officers are expressly prohibited from

Footnote:

*Lewis Alexander Grant (1767-1840). Elected M.P. for Elgin 1790. His illness abruptly terminated what had promised to be a brilliant Parliamentary and Legal career. Succeeded his cousin as 5th Earl of Seafield in 1811.

drinking with Private Men & if they are found they may depend upon being reduced into the Ranks –

no man is to appear on the Street, at any time but with his coat hooked, his Bonnet properly on his head & his hair smoothly Combed.[126]

On August 31st the regiment held a field day outside Aberdeen and the Lt Colonel was able to tell Sir James:

We are just come in from a field day with the Colours & Powder; the men behaved uncommonly well & fired like an old Regt. We were much praised & admired, the more so, as it had been industriously circulated that we were the worst Corps in the Service & a set of Rafs.*[127]

On September 7th the Regiment held another Field Day which gave the Lt Colonel even greater satisfaction as he told Sir James:

Major Imrie came here last night, called on me this morning & requested to see the men under arms – we had a field day with powder; they behaved uncommonly well at everything – He was quite suprised at seeing us, and said he shou'd make a most handsome report to Lord Adam – He said that he had not the most distant notion we cou'd have brought them so forward in such a short time.

In the afternoon of the same day he wrote again to his brother in law:

I wrote you this morning; by Nelly's letter just recd. my Infant is rather easier; tho' I think his fate is sealed - I feel it a duty to wait tomorrow morning & monday morning's post, to receive Lord Adam's answer, which ought not to be but favourable - if it comes not, I shall set out, as I feel an impelling power beyond any consideration in this life, to be enabled to pay the last duties to what I fondly thought might have been one of the props of my declining life - I know twill pain you to hear your friends distress, it's an anguish that none but a parent can feel - may we be enabled to support & bear, what our maker pleases to inflict.[128]

The new born infant was having '2 or 3 fitts every day' and was not expected to live, so both Sir James and his brother in law now had distressing family problems.

Footnote: *Roisterers. Boisterously behaved people.

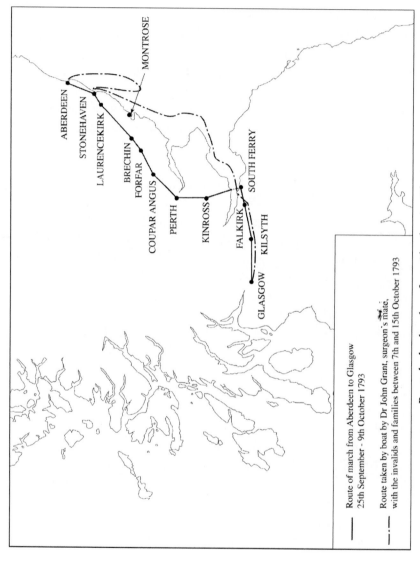

ABERDEEN
STONEHAVEN
LAURENCEKIRK
BRECHIN
FORFAR
COUPAR ANGUS
PERTH
KINROSS
FALKIRK
SOUTH FERRY
KILSYTH
GLASGOW
MONTROSE

Route of march from Aberdeen to Glasgow
25th September - 9th October 1793

Route taken by boat by Dr John Grant, surgeon's mate,
with the invalids and families between 7th and 15th October 1793

Route by land and sea from Aberdeen to Glasgow.

Chapter Two

Glasgow

'a post of too much importance to be left without a very responsible man'

The regiment remained in Aberdeen for only a short while. It had always been Lord Adam Gordon's intention to send it to Glasgow for the winter. It was ordered to leave Aberdeen in two Divisions, the first Division marching from Aberdeen to Stonehaven on Wednesday 25th September, to Laurencekirk on the 26th, Brechin on the 27th and Forfar on the 28th where it stayed for two nights. On September 30th it marched to Coupar Angus and on October 1st to Perth. It reached Kinross on October 2nd where it stayed for two nights. On the 4th it reached South Ferry [Queensferry], having crossed the Forth by ferry, and on the 5th it reached Falkirk where it again stayed for two nights. On October 7th the first Division reached Kilsyth and marched into Glasgow on October 8th. The second Division followed it in to Glasgow the following day.[1]

Because of the threat of civil unrest Glasgow was considered to be an important posting by Lord Adam and so he instructed Sir James that either he or the Lt Colonel should be with the regiment when it arrived in Glasgow:

> I do request that Either your – self – or yr Lieut. Col. – marches into Glasgow – with the 1st Fencibles – and reports to me your arrival there – for, it is a post, of too much importance, to be left without a very responsible man – at the Head of any Battalion quartered Here...I have wrote very much to this purpose to Lt. Colonel Cumming – But wishing there may be no misunderstanding, about it – I think it safer, to write to yourself[2]

Sir James informed Lord Adam as 'the Situation of Colonel Cumming's family & private affairs requires his remaining there [at home] for some little time I have resolved myself to march into Glasgow with the Regiment'.[3] This arrangement satisfied the Commander in Chief who told Sir James 'if you join at Perth or Stirling and march into Glasgow, with yr Battn. I shall be satisfied – and Lt. Col: Cumming may remain at Home – till ordered to relieve you – at Glasgow' but he added the proviso 'I shall expect you to remain there – untill he arrives'.[4] The Lt Colonel had gone home anyway, on September 14th leaving Major John Grant of Glenmoriston in command.[5] The Lt colonel did not show much gratitude to his brother in law for his generous and understanding offer, simply confining himself to commenting on October 4th from home 'I hope this will find you safely arrived at Glasgow – I am happy to think that you have had tolerable dry weather which wou'd add greatly to the comfort of the march'.[6]

* * *

Private John Fraser who had incurred the Lt Colonel's wrath by going behind his back in writing to Sir James requesting a furlough whilst the regiment was still in Forres was now granted one by Sir James despite the Lt Colonel's protestations. On September 14th Fraser wrote to Sir James:

> Your Petitioner got a Furlough from Aberdeen by your Honours order for the space of a fortnight only at the expiration of which your Petitioner is under the necessity to join his respective Corps either at Aberdeen or upon the March, upon his arrival there found some of his Children in the Small Pox & His wife by reason of fatigue much distressed...Though your Honour is a Stranger to Adversity Hopes your none to Humanity & Humbly supplicates you will have pity & Compassion...and condescend to take whatever your Honour thinks proper for my discharge.

and he enclosed a note signed by two ministers of religion confirming the truth of the contents of his letter:

> That what is asserted in the above Petition is true is attested by
> Dun. McFarlane Minr.
> James Scott Minr.

Little can Fraser have known about the recent death of Sir James's son and daughter. Even Sir James would not go so far as to grant Fraser his discharge but noted 'Could not discharge Fraser but allowed his wife 2 shillings a week'.[7]

* * *

On September 25th Private John Grant, whilst on leave in Strathspey, wrote to Sir James asking for back pay. He must have been desperate for money as his request was somewhat presumptuous, the men only being paid every two months:[8]

I John Grant private Soldier in His Majesty's First Fencible Regiment of Highlanders & in Capt Robert Cummings Company, Intimate to your Honour there is due me of my pay from the Eighth day of Aug. to the 25th Sept. – which is 48 days being 24 shs. sterling I being much strait of money have no better way than to Inform your Honour while in the Country to Solicit your favour with regard to this small sum which will be a great help to me at present.[9]

Another private soldier, Donald Grant, was discharged on September 24th as unfit for service 'being unhealthy and consumptive'. He was aged 18 years was 5' 7" tall, came from Banff and was a musician by trade. Lt John Grant junior, who sent his discharge papers to Sir James explained:

He is to get three weeks pay to carry him home besides arrears of Bread money amounting in all to 16 or 17 shillings and the Dr thinks he will get perfectly well once he is some time in the Country...Donald's father came here today & is to move home tomorrow or next day.[10]

* * *

The families and the soldiers who were unfit to march went to Glasgow by boat and were under the command of Ensign Dr John Grant the surgeon's mate, who wrote to Sir James on October 7th:

It will no doubt occasion considerable surprise that the Invalids have not arrived at Glasgow before the marching Divisions but we were detained by contrary winds untill Saturday Evening when we got aboard & set sail Sunday morning at one o'clock the wind was pretty favourable untill the afternoon of that day when it became boisterous & contrary – we were nearly opposite Montrose but were obliged to even back to Stonehaven where we landed about 4 0'clock in the afternoon – we were in great danger the sea washing over us several times but we at length fortunately effected a landing here...we were by far too much crouded there being about 120 in the hold of a small vessel the Soldiers wives & a great many of the Soldiers themselves say positively they will not set foot aboard the vessel – however I shall endeavour to persuade them tomorrow if the wind proves favourable.[11]

His powers of persuasion were evidently up to the task for he was able to write again to Sir James:

Falkirk Saturday 12th October

This night about six o'clock we arrived at Grangemouth at the entrance of the Canal – altho' not strong, we had, all along a favourable gale since we left Stonehaven and have all been in good Spirits – It will be Tuesday night before we reach Glasgow, because it is not Customary to go up the Canal upon Sunday – Many of the women are in a starving condition – The little that their Husbands left them at their departure has been expended long since – I have advanced many of them small sums to purchase the necessaries of life. The Captain of the vessel has been very kind & humane to them having distributed daily to the most necessitous a portion of what was made ready for the crew – I have enough to do among them as I was never in such a situation before.[12]

* * *

Whilst in Glasgow Sir James and his officers dined frequently at the Star Inn. The price of a standard dinner was one shilling per head exclusive of wines, which more than doubled the basic cost of the dinner. They mainly drank port, sherry and porter. When Sir James left Glasgow, the regimental paymaster picked up the bill for his accommodation which came to seven pounds for lodging and the maid was paid ten shillings and sixpence.[13]

Sir James appears to have ignored Lord Adam Gordon's strict instructions to remain with the regiment until the Lt Colonel came to relieve him. According to Lt John Grant junior he left for Edinburgh on October 19th[14] but it was October 29th before the Lt Colonel wrote to Sir James from Stirling 'here I am, after a disagreeable tedious journey – I propose being at glasgow tomorrow by late dinner'. In confirmation of this Glenmoriston, once again temporarily in command of the regiment wrote to Sir James on October 31st: 'Altyre arrived last night and from some information he gave me respecting my wifes Health I left Glasgow this forenoon'.[15] So for the eleven days between October 19th and 30th neither the Colonel nor the Lt Colonel was with the regiment.

Sir James Grant of Grant of Castle Grant, Bart.

Lady Jane Grant, wife of Sir James Grant

Major John Grant of Glenmoriston

i

Captain Alexander (Alasdair Ranaldson) Macdonell of Glengarry

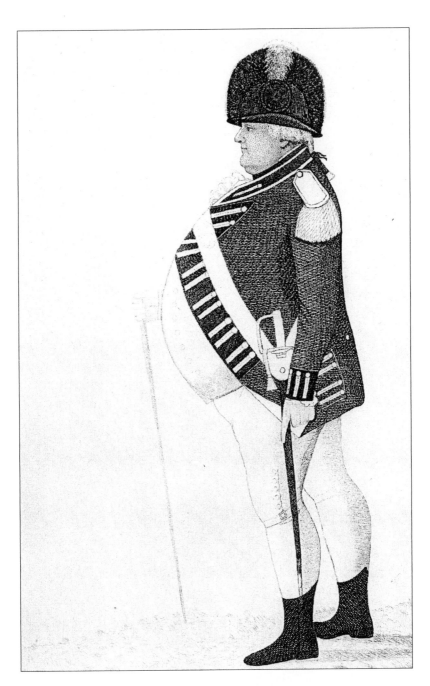

Captain John Rose of Holme

Henry Dundas, 1st Viscount Melville

Frederick, Duke of York and Albany

Dr John Grant   Lord Adam Gordon

Recruits on the way to Join. A romantic view of recruitment, from 'The Life of a Regiment: The History of the Gordon Highlanders'

Sir James Grant addressing soldiers of the First Fencible Regiment

Linlithgow Palace and Loch where the first mutiny took place

Dumfries from the Dock where the regiment was dismissed immediately before the second mutiny

* * *

The regiment settled in well in Glasgow and for a short period they seemed satisfied with their uniforms, the adjutant writing to Sir James on November 3rd:

> With Respect to dress I sincerely hope we are making Great Progress – we had a General Parade this morning and Colonel Cumming was very well satisfied with their appearance – notwithstanding we are still in want of some Triffling appointments – that will add much to their appearance on the whole.[16]

The Lt Colonel also expressed satisfaction with the men under his command writing on November 10th to Sir James 'the men are behaving with great propriety, sobriety & getting into cleanliness'[17] but not all the men met with his approval as two days earlier he had requested that 'I wish you would make us free of the other Macdonell, calling himself the volunteer; I have been obliged to discharge him from appearing at the parade, as he was nasty ill dressed & dirty beyond sufferance – He is nothing but a beggarly eat-meat on the Regt'.[18]

Young men of a good family but without other resources often took service in the capacity of volunteers. Volunteers who saw action hoped that they would so distinguish themselves in the field that they would then be rewarded with an Ensignancy.[19] Volunteers carried muskets and took their place in the ranks, but they messed with the officers.[20]

On November 13th the Lt Colonel was reporting:

> We have got a sad rascal in the guardroom – old macdonell of Grant's company, married a poor Hussey at Forres – She has her belly to her chin & yesterday the daughter of his other wife who is living at Edinr. came to claim him – He is mutinous drunken & worthless, and painful that it be, he must be punished.[21]

Sir James, who had an inborn aversion to harsh punishment, wrote to the Lt Colonel on November 14th: 'I am sorry you have to flog any one especially @ Glasgow – as old McDonells is a crime [Bigamy] cureable by the Civil Law it would be much better & a punishment that would affect him more to give him over to the civil magistrate – I am told in all such cases the Northern Fencibles adopt that method.'[22]

In reply to a query raised by Sir James the Lt Colonel elaborated:

The Macdonell who you wanted to know, is one of the major's fools, a Lad with an open mouth & thick lips, but a good enough person. He may do for some time yet, & notwithstanding me writing you yesterday to mention to Lord Adam the discharging the vagabond volunteer, I think we need not ask him a favour about the matter, but I'll dismiss the vagabond & keep the fool, who is the best man of the two – The other has lost his Bayonet, Knapsack & many other articles & is a most worthless subject – Lt Mcdonell must pay for all – I am also to give him the wicked Campbell from the Light Company in lieu of a very fine Strathnaver Lad 5 feet 9 high & eighteen years of age – Campbell is one of the worst & most unprincipled men in the Regt. so I hope you will approve of my doing both.[23]

The problem with Private Macdonell was not quickly resolved and the Lt Colonel eventually took the matter up with Lord Adam, writing to him on January 6th, 1794:

The worthless infamous Macdonell of Capt. Grant's company an old man upwards of fifty & the worst looking without exception, in the Regt has married two women; has deeply diseased both so much so, that one is in danger of her life; The whole officers join me in requesting that in addition to any other punishment, you will allow us to have him drummed, with infamy out of the Regt.[24]

Private Macdonell was not the only one spreading venereal disease amongst the camp followers for the Lt Colonel told Sir James on December 20th:

I saw your letter to the Paymaster about Shaw...he was told when he was about to be tried for Mutiny, that the only chance he had for your applying Lord Adam Gordon to discharge him, was by doing his duty & behaving well – this he promised at that time to do – but I understand the Pox has broke out on him again, & He is in Hospital – He is a worthless infamous wretch, injured his wife & killed his child – at the same time I candidly believe he'll never do any good with us, as he's as bad a man as ever I knew.[25]

But Shaw did not behave well. In a terse note shortly afterwards the Lt Colonel told Sir James:

The man you enlisted for the Dancing master has deserted, and I am rather afraid the rascals Shaw & Grott have done the same.[26]

The behaviour of the men towards the citizens of Glasgow was generally very good, but there were occasional lapses, a Mr Jackson of Charlotte Square complaining to Sir James on December 9th:

Mr Jackson presents Compts to Sir James Grant, or the Officer commanding his Regt.; Requests of him to be informed, that last night between 11 & 12, a Young Lady & Servant, with a Lantern coming from the College, to his house in Charlotte Street, were attacked by a highland Soldier, nearly opposite to Bell's Wynd: Without speaking a word, he gave the Lady a blow on the head, which luckily slanted upon her cheek; he then ran across the street, to 2 other highland Soldiers, and spoke to them; he afterwards returned, pulled the lantern from the Servant and dashed it to pieces on the street, and afterwards ran after the Lady to repeat his blow but their cries by this Time, had alarmed the Street, and a Gentleman from a Window, also cried out for assistance: Fortunately a man came up, when the 3 Soldiers run off.

Mr J. hopes that Sir James Grant or the Commanding Officer, will endeavour to discover these Soldiers, and have them punished as they deserve.[27]

Sir James, who was again back with the regiment, took this complaint seriously and replied on the same day that he 'will this evening in front of his Regt. offer a reward of one Guinea to the person or persons who shall discover the guilty persons'. There also exists an account dated March 13th, 1794:

To paid for three advertisements in the Glasgow Newspaper offering a reward of 5 guineas for discovery of a soldier who had struck a lady in the street – £16 6.[28]

If this account refers to the same complaint, then Sir James was certainly pursuing it with vigour and persistence and regardless of cost.

* * *

The general health of the regiment at this time appeared to be reasonably good. The return for the week ending November 15th recorded 8 sick in hospital and 36 sick in quarters and no deaths. A typical sick report was that for the week ending December 13th which read as follows

Ulcerated Legs	4
Diarrhoea	1
Rheumatism	2
Sore Eyes	1
Severe cold	7
On Recovery	1
Fever	1
Obstinate Cough	1
Slight Fever	1
Better	4
Bruised shoulder	1
Cough	1
Bruised Foot	1
Strained knee	1
Convalescent	2
Swelled neck	1
	30

(signed) P. Grant Surgeon[29]

Firfty-six men had been allowed home on leave during the week ending November 15th[30] but the thrill of getting leave must have been somewhat tempered by the hazards of the journey, the Lt Colonel recording 'we are informed by black Ewan Gillies...that another of the men returning here from furlough, has been murdered, but not robbed, in the Black Mount – I have not yet learnt the particulars'.[31]

Soldiers who were no longer fit to serve in the army as a result of injury or illness could apply for a Chelsea pension. Sir James described one such case to his London army agent, James Fraser of Ainslie and Fraser:

Inclosed I send part of a Letter to me from the Lieut. Colonel accompanying a Discharge and recommendation to the Chelsea Pension in favour of one John [?] a Soldier in our Fencible Regiment who doing his duty as a Soldier fell and broke his Thigh Bone so as to be perfectly unable to do for himself – I beg you recommend him with my most respectful Complts to Sir George Howard and the other members of the Board – The poor fellow bore his painfull confinement with the utmost fortitude and had it not been his uncommon good and patient Temper he must have fallen a Vetran as his fever rose to a great height after the fracture do not let the poor fellow want for anything till he has passed the Board.[32]

By December 2nd 1793 it had been recorded that 24 men had been discharged from the regiment, three had deserted, five had died and two corporals had been reduced to the ranks.[33]

Although the physical health of the men may have been reasonably satisfactory their spiritual needs were poorly catered for. The Rev James Grant had, by the Colonel's authority, been allowed a prolonged leave of absence from 2nd October 1793 until 1st December 1794.[34] This lack of spiritual guidance must have caused concern because John Grant, the paymaster replied to an enquiry from Sir James:

> Mr MacIntosh the Galick preacher, who very readily agreed to give the Regiment a discourse once a fortnight, as he gives his Congregation two preachings every Sunday he could not engage to give the Regiment one every Sunday, I signified to him you wished to make him some allowance for his trouble, but he would not make any demand, but I make no doubt he will expect a present when we leave here.[35]

* * *

James Grant of Corrimony* in Urquhart, wrote to Sir James on December 2nd 1793 concerning a tenant and relative of his:

> I had a letter yesterday from Duncan Grant soldier in the Grenadier company acquainting me that his wife was lately delivered of twins, & that her situation is such as to require his personal care & attention to his family – when I went to Urquhart with the view of promoting the recruiting service in that country, I found that the people were impressed with the belief that when your regiment should be levied, the men were all to be sold to the east India Company, it was of importance to remove that erroneous belief, I applied to Duncan to inlist in your regiment,

Footnote:
   * James Grant of Corrimony (1743-1835). Called to the Bar 1767.

in order to show the people they were mistaken, as I would not advise my tenant & relation who had a family, to engage in any regiment for foreign service, but only for the defence of Scotland. When Duncan engaged I told him I should apply to you for his discharge when his affairs at home made it necessary for him to quit the regiment. He said he was very willing to serve in your regiment as long as it was at all convenient – I approved very much of his sentiments, and as now the situation of his family requires his presence I must beg the favour of his discharge, he says he can provide a man in his place – I have writen to Capt. Cuming Logie who I presume will speak to you on the subject.[36]

Duncan Grant was allowed leave but was not given an immediate discharge. The next we hear of the matter is from the chaplain who wrote to Sir James on March 27th 1794:

Mr Grant of Corrimony desired me to send you Dr Robertson's & my own certificates, anent Duncan Grant's case. Corimony is very anxious that the man be discharged – and every circumstance in the case, makes it highly expedient. His pursuing of a military life will be the ruin of his family; besides that joining till perfectly cured might be the cause of the vile disease spreading.

and this was the enclosed medical certificate:

From James Robertson MD

25th March 1794

That Dun. Grant private in the Grenadier Company 1st Fencible Regt. has for some time laboured under that variety of the Venl. disease called sivens; That tho' he is now better the disease does not seem to be completely removed; he still complains – & besides being at present unfit for Duty, there might be danger, in his being the source of infection.

Certified by

Ja: Robertson M.D.[37]

Contrary to a body of medical opinion at the time sivvens or sibbens as it was more commonly spelt was not a venereal disease although it was caused by a bacterium similar to that causing syphilis and was highly contagious being found in poor hygienic conditions. It was characterised by red spongy skin lesions which frequently ulcerated. It also commonly gave rise to swollen lymph glands particularly in the groin. Good hygiene and treatment with mercury was usually beneficial.[38] Sibbens was believed to be a disease peculiar to the West of Scotland, especially Galloway, Dumfries, Wigton & Ayr.[39] Sir James was better informed than Dr Robertson for on April 2nd he wrote to Lord Adam Gordon: 'I recd the inclosed Letter from Mr Grant Minr. of Urquhart, & our chaplain, relative to Dun Grant...lying in infected Blankets in Glasgow, Aberdeen, or Forres (for the man seems to be doubtful which) he caught that terrible of all complaints the sevens, and became so ill that his life has been in imminent danger – it is doubtful whether he will ever get free of it – he has a farm & family & is really a good respectable man – he came in merely to encourage others from Urquhart – considering the State he is in, I believe it wd be best in real truth to discharge him.'[40] There is no record as to whether Duncan Grant was discharged, but it is likely that he was, in view of Sir James's strong support.

* * *

Other men, if their stories are to be believed, were not treated so well. On November 27th James Wardrobe sent the following petition to Sir James:

Unto the Honbl. Sir James Grant Baronet commanding his Majestys 1st Fencible Regiment of Highlanders presently in Glasgow

The Petition & Representation of James Wardrobe late Private Soldjer in said Regiment. 27th November 1793

That in the month of Aprile last Petitioner enlisted to serve in said Regiment that he accordingly joined the same and continued to do his duty as a soldjer untill fourteenth day of september last, when it pleased almighty God to afflict Petitioner with a shaking Palsy, by which means he is rendered an object and unfitt for any Duty, the surgeon of said Regiment having exhausted his skill on him finds him incurable. - That upon friday the Twenty second instant Petitioner was lodged a Prisoner in the Regiments Guard House and there remained untill Tuesday evening the Twenty third inst. During which time no Crime apeard in the report of the day against Petitioner no was he allowed any pay to subsist on

That on Tuesday evening aforesaid Petitioner was striped of his Coat, waistcoat, Plaid, kilt, stocks, Bonnet & knapsack, and a

Discharge from said Regiment put in his Hand without on sixpence of pay to Carry him any distance whatever, That this manner of Discharging British soldjers, is without example even to a common vagabond, far less to one who is now become an object of compasion

That before further application Petitioner is advised to make his misarable situation known to your Honor, Humbly requesting that your Honor will cause such persons to be brought before you as can verify the Truth of this matter and the same being found of Truth, that you cause Petitioner be put on equall footing with Soldjers Discharged from there Regiments.- That Petitioner is ashamed to go out to Beg his Bread having nothing to cover his nakedness only an old Peticoat of his wifes. That if Petitioner is not speedily releved out of his misarable situation he must with his family unavoidably perish for want.

Your Petitioner therefore not only Beseeches but also solicits and in the most Humble manner Implores your Honor to consider his miserable and unexampled Case and to order him such reliefe as to you shall seem proper, and Petitioner shall ever pray etc

James Wardrobe.[41]

* * *

These were difficult times in Strathspey and factor James Grant wrote to Sir James on December 10th 1793:

I am doing everything in my power to get in the rents – I have already had seven collection days and am to have one tomorrow but as yet the Rents have come in very slowly owing I truly believe to the great scarcity of Cash in Circulation.[42]

At the years end the Lt Colonel was far from happy with the state of his regiment. Many of the non commissioned officers were drunkards and others were fraudulent. He had some good officers but also some that did not pull their weight, in particular Alexander Macdonell, the under age chief of that clan and Sir James's ward. Additionally, some of the officers were not settling their accounts making it necessary for the Lt Colonel to write in Regimental Orders 'A Demand having been made upon the Paymaster & Quartermaster, of a Sum of Money which they have already paid; & which in justice & honour must be immediately replaced in their hands – The Commanding Officer feels himself called on, to request that the whole officers will before the 23rd current clear their accounts with both these Gentlemen'.[43]

The quartermaster was making money on the side by selling property belonging to Sir James and the regiment for his own profit. On November 8th the Lt Colonel reported to Sir James 'The Quartermaster put into my hands on Saturday his accot agst. you & the Regt. there are some terrible charges in it, which if not attended to in future, will cut up your profits...I propose ordering a Court of enquiry...to examine & strike off all over or improper charges & when that is done to seperate what is properly your's from what is the Regts'. To compound matters Gloags of Edinburgh were, he believed, supplying shoddy goods and he continued 'As our bonnets are so very bad I think no time shou'd be lost in your ordering the next years set that we may be satisfied of their goodness & have them all properly & uniformly cocked'.[44]

Mr Gloag's partner, Mr Livingston replied to a complaint from the quartermaster regarding the uniforms on December 4th:

> In Mr Gloag's absence who is presently confined from business on account of his mother lying a corpse...
>
> with regard to the articles that are proposed to be returned I take the liberty to observe, that if they are, it will fall exceedingly hard on Mr Gloag, with respect to the Shoes, one pair has only been served out to each man, whereas two pairs are distinctly marked in the order given to him by Sir James Grant and Captain Grant, as are two shirts, which were afterwards Countermanded but the Shoes never were...with regard to the Hose Tartan the number of pairs to be sent are not mentioned in the order in consequence of which Mr Gloag just sent what is commonly allowed viz 4 pairs each man.[45]

On December 19th Sir James replied to this defence with some irritation: 'Sir James Grants Compliments to Mr Gloag. He was in the right as to the Shoes ordered, but Certainly not as to the Hose,' and added: 'The Regiment complain of almost every article Supplied by Mr Gloag,' but thought better of it, crossed it out, and continued in a slightly more conciliatory vein: 'Sir James is inform'd that the Duke of Gordon Sent back from Aberdeen the first Clothing sent to his Regiment as he did not approve of it – Whether this is true or not Sir James does not know.'[46]

The following day Mr Gloag, not wanting to lose the large and very remunerative order for supplying uniforms to a whole regiment, replied to Sir James:

> If any of the other Fencibles were furnishd lower at the same time Mr G. contracted with Sir James He will most readily conform to their prices and as to this years Clothing He will most chearfully agree to the lowest prices in the comparitive accts. He can freely add that had an Estimate been ask'd from Him it would be in every article fully as low as any of them As to the quality of his furnishings he is possessed of vouchers stating that they were much better than some got from another House, He can sincerely say that it was his anxious wish to [?] that the first Fencibles should be provided on the best possible Terms
>
> As to Hose Mr G. never said there were more than two pairs in His agreement as also two pairs Shoes & two Shirts But in his verbal Instructions He was desired to put them on the same footing as others.[47]

On December 29th, the Lt Colonel again took up the cudgels not only against his quartermaster but also the poor mourning Mr Gloag telling Sir James that:

> It is unfortunate...that I have allowed Mr Sutherland to go to Stirling, where he has a chance of getting free of his own shirts, & Mr Gloag's bad Shoes – the quality of everything Mr Gloag furnished your Regt. is shamefully bad – I hope you will guard against a second imposition.[48]

The regiment as a whole was certainly chronically short of uniforms for the Lt Colonel later replied to an enquiry from Sir James 'you say nothing about the slop cloathing for the Recruits; something must be done as many of them are in raggs & the bad rascals who are discharged won't part with their coats'[49] and later he complained 'As some of the discharged men were necessarily discharged with their cloathing, we have none for our recruits, who are almost naked – I think it will be cheaper for you to have a sort of slop jackets made for them to last till the new cloathing is ready, than to be at the expence of giving them new Regtals'.[50]

The Lt Colonel concluded his letter with the comment that:

> I am afraid the major is not very desirous of playing me fair as he mentions his intention not to join till the end of next month.[51]

This last remark was rather unfair on his second in command because Glenmoriston had just 'lost both his Wife and his Father by Fevers, in the short space of 10 days'[152] and was surely entitled to a period of compassionate leave.

* * *

At the beginning of January 1794 the Lt Colonel requested Sir James to 'write to your Factor to give no prolongations of furloughs, which he has got into the trick of, but desire him to send up every man whose furlough is expired'. Sir James did as he was asked and the factor replied: 'I really have not taken upon me to prolong any mans furlough,' but that was exactly what he had been doing and he probably recognised the fact, for he went on to explain: 'Many of them were at me asking it & representing their bad state of health etc., & that they were unable to travel, all I told them was to set out as soon as they were at all able, & if their Furloughs were then run, that I would give them a Pass – This indeed I have given to severals of them, & if in this I have acted wrong I shall not do it more.'[153]

At the same time as he was complaining about the factor prolonging furloughs, the Lt Colonel was reporting the very bad behaviour of some of the senior non commissioned officers to Sir James:

> I shall be reduced to the disagreeable necessity of having two of the first description [two sergeants] before a Court-martial immediately – Forsyth of my company is this afternoon, confined for being brutally drunk on guard – a crime of such a nature, & in such a place, cannot be passed over without giving up the discipline of the Regt...The other is serjeant Fraser of the Light Company who I have ordered to be relieved from Largs for leaving his post without leave going to and remaining at Ayr for several days and letting out men of his party to go to voyages to the Highlands & Islands.

> The Sergeant Major has been behaving very badly – he got himself drunk & so beat that he is not fit to be seen; his face disgracefully marked & has not been able to attend a parade this week.[154]

The behaviour of some of his commissioned officers was also causing the Lt Colonel concern, for on January 12th he had to report to Sir James:

> I have been reduced to the disagreeable necessity of putting the

two oldest Lieuts in arrest this morning, the first for being again drunk on guard, the other for coming drunk to the guard in the middle of the night, striking the Serjeant on duty & being himself unfit for duty at guard mounting.[55]

If this account is true and some of the junior officers as well as the senior non commissioned officers had really been behaving in this fashion, then the morale of the regiment must have been at a very low ebb.

* * *

The Lt Colonel now started a long campaign to rid the regiment of Captain Alexander Macdonell. The young man had been on a series of prolonged leaves of absence but arrived in Glasgow in the middle of December. The Lt Colonel reported to Sir James on December 18th:

> Capt. Macdonell arrived two nights ago – the first sight I had of him was yesterday in Mr Dunlop's Court, on horseback in coloured cloaths – He never came near the mess but has taken up his abode in the Salt-market wt the Priest* – Finding he kept away from us, I directed the Orderly Serjeant of the company to go to him with my Compts. & to desire he wou'd read all the orders since he left the Regt. – He was at the same time put in orders for picket this day – He did not come to the parade and the enclosed is the answer I got...I answered him by hoping he would confine himself to the house till he got well...I am convinced as are all the Regt. we never shall have pleasure or satisfaction in him & for God's sake take the first opportunity of letting him resign.

and this was the enclosed answer:

> I this moment rec'd your message with Serjeant McDonell desiring me to attend for duty – which I regret being under the necessity of putting off at present on account of Indisposition...I have never got rid of a severe Cold I caught a bout the tenth of

---

Footnote:

* The priest to whom the Lt Colonel refers was Father Alexander Macdonell who went to Glasgow in 1792 and worked tirelessly on behalf of the destitute Highlanders until the raising of the Glengarry Fencibles in August 1794 when he was appointed chaplain to that regiment. When the Glengarry Fencibles were disbanded in 1802 many of the soldiers emigrated to Canada and Father Macdonell went with them. He became the first Roman Catholic Bishop of Upper Canada. He died on a visit to Scotland in 1840.

June last – & that I have had Medical advice seriously, to attend, to keeping free from damp feet, & wet of all kinds – & also ordering me to wrap in flannel, as the only way of getting free of my Complaint in addition to the Medicine prescribed.[56]

Sir James made no attempt to comply with the Lt Colonel's request to persuade Alexander Macdonell to resign his commission but confined himself to writing to Macdonell 'It gave me great pleasure to be able to transmit the Report of your having rejoined the Regiment to Lord Adam Gordon, as your absence made me liable to great censure'.[57] Nor did Alexander Macdonell confine himself to his quarters as ordered by his commanding officer for the Lt. Colonel wrote to Sir James on December 24th that 'Lt Urquhart saw him [Macdonell] drink seven glasses of whiskie after a deal of Port with major Cameron at Stirling – In short we are all of opinion he is shamming'.[58] On January 14th Alexander Macdonell finally reported for duty and the Lt Colonel reported to Sir James: 'Capt. M. has at last appeared at the parade but wrapped in a great Coat which he seems to have little occasion for – he has a cursed trick of laughing & speaking to the men, which does much harm, but I hope we will cure him of it by degrees.'[59] In a further letter to Sir James he noted: 'I am convinced that Auchterblair* is the best officer in the Regt. for them [the Macdonells] & that the real good men of the company prize him; & that there is not another in the Regt. who can fill his place...the young cub is by no means fit to manage them.'[60]

* * *

By the beginning of 1794 the Lt Colonel was becoming increasingly anxious to get home on leave not only to attend to his estate affairs but also to see his family and give support to his wife as several of their children were ill. He was still waiting for Glenmoriston to relieve him and he wrote to Sir James:

> I am surprised the Major is so very long coming, or shy of answering our letters – if he does not relieve me soon I shall be put to inconceivable inconvenience – beside my private affairs, several of the children are ill of colds & poor Jane alarmingly ill with a bad cough.[62]

By January 7th he was fully aware of the serious nature of his children's

---

Footnote:
  *John Grant, Auchterblair and John Grant, Rosefield are one and the same person.[61]

illness writing 'All my children are ill with the hooping Cough'[63] and again on January 8th:

> The day after the major arrives I go, as I need hardly explain to you, the miserable unfortunate situation in which I sit. I have almost made up my mind, to see poor John no more.[64]

At last on January 17th he was able to hand over command of the regiment to Glenmoriston writing to Sir James:

> The major is just arrived, which is an ease to my mind – I shall send away my horses tomorrow, & follow on Sunday...
>
> I have been in Dunlop's green for an hour, making a farewell ovation to the men, thanking them for their good behaviour & giving them good advice – I explained to Macdonell's Company their misconduct & they are sorry for it – I believe I am pretty much in all their good graces.[65]

There was a surprise in store for the Lt Colonel on his journey home to Altyre regarding the behaviour of his second in command as he explained to Sir James:

> I left Glasgow the 19th ult. & arrived here with difficulty the 23rd as the snow came on the night I was at Aviemore, & it was with difficulty I got down the Hill – But that was nothing to the Saturday and Sunday following in which several perished. I found the family well & John much better than I expected; I hope he'll now make out as he has stood so much...
>
> I mentioned the major being in such spirits as surprised us all; indeed nothing could equal my astonishment when I found on the road he had carried up a girl with him who he had made an appointment to meet with at Aviemore – He was so fond of this piece that he only travelled one or two short stages a day, by which means he did not come to us till the 17th...and by his damned delay had very near occasioned my perishing in the snow – the Inns on the road are quite scandalised at him – nor can I with any patience, myself, think of a man so devoid of all feeling and heart, as so soon to forget such an amiable and worthy wife.

In the same letter, from his home in Forres, he had another go at the Macdonells, and not only the clan chief, but also his cousin Ronald continuing:

> I had a letter from the Paymaster yesterday telling me Macdonell

is going on in his accustomed folly, such as coming to the parade in brown breeches, plain Hat, Sash & Gorget, & when reprehended for it, saying he didn't like the duty & would resign, if he could only be allowed to name his successor – I rely if he offers to resign to you, that you will not refuse him, for the Regt. will never be quite the thing while he is in it...

I propose when I return, to the Regt. to lay little Ronald's age, appearance etc, etc, before Lord Adam to have him set aside, as he is not fit to be trusted with a guard or post & on an emergency might be the ruin of the Regt.[66]

* * *

Whilst the Lt Colonel was journeying as fast as he could through the snow, Captain John Grant of Achindown was writing to Sir James painting quite a favourable picture of the state of the regiment 'the men are every day improving in their dress, Great pains are taken with them'[67] and again on January 24th 'the officers and men of your Regt present and all well & the men continue to behave very well' but he also had to inform Sir James that 'two of Captain Rose's serjts have been sent up here last week prisoners for most scandalous practises, getting drunk fighting, giving in false Returns of the company'.[68] They were court martialled on January 28th and on the same day Lt John Grant junior informed Sir James of the verdict:

I am just come in from a Court martial which had sat for two days upon Serjeants James Ross and John Chisholm...we found them guilty...of making false returns...and of exacting money for their own private use...these facts being proved we were under the disagreeable necessity of reducing them to the Ranks.

You will I daresay have different applications for being appointed in their stead...John Shaw from Grantown, and Dond. Grant from Abernethy...are the two most deserving Candidates the adjutant says...two corporals to be appointed – Thomas Stuart...and Lewis Grant...an exemplary good man... are the two that Mr Watson says are the most deseving of promotion...I mention these names, which I hope you will forgive, chiefly from the Adjutants approbation of them and partly from the good opinion I have formed of them since they became soldiers, as being <u>Sober attentive well behaved men</u>...and I am confident their appointment will give universal satisfaction among the men, which is at present in my humble opinion a matter to be attended to.[69]

This last comment indicates that at least one officer was very well aware that all was not well with the regiment and two days later he told Sir James: 'Our Drum major Weddell is such a Drunken man that we are much plagued wt him and often disappointed – we all wish much to be free of him if another would be got.'[70]

* * *

There was a strong republican element in Glasgow and some of the population were ripe for revolution. The officers were acutely aware of this. The Lt Colonel had written to Sir James just before he left Glasgow for home:

> From anonymous letters, & the evil spirit of the lower class of the people, I have been induced with the Provost's approbation to serve out loaded Cartridges to the guard.[71]

On January 30th Glenmoriston wrote to Sir James:

> I arrived here the 17th of this Month and Altyre left it the 19th following we are all queite at present, but we had several reports and anonimous Letters mentioning that the Democrates here were to assemble attack our Guard take their firelocks from them & knock down our men as they came out of their Billets or Quarter, but I would fain hope there is nothing in it, however it makes us be upon our Guard, in consequence all officers and Soldiers of the Regt. are ordered to remain at Head Quarters till further orders.[72]

At the same time he tried to tighten discipline in the regiment, stating in orders that he was:

> sorry to understand that many of the Non Commissioned Officers & Privates have made a practice of being out of their Quarters at untimious hours, he positively assures them that if any such practises are carried on in the future that he will be under the necessity of punishing any Non Commissioned Officers or privates that are found on the Streets after 10 o clock at Night.[73]

* * *

On January 10th, William Hope of Craigiehall, the Commissary of Musters had written to 'Lt. Grant':

> I received the Muster Rolls with your letter and certificate yesterday - The last of these examined attentively, and finding the Dates annex'd to the real and erroneous names to be exactly the same, I did not think it worthwhile to make any alteration that would have disfigured the Rolls to no purpose except drawing a censure on the defect...the practice that I am informed prevails among the Highlanders of changing their names for readier distinction from each other has been partly the cause of this confusion, and your Corps or Clan must have given much into the fashion, for exclusive of the officers I cannot find above four score Grants in the whole Regiment.[74]

Here commissary Hope explains something that must have puzzled many, namely why there were so many families in Strathspey so soon after the clan system was disbanded who did not have the surname of Grant. The gentlemen and men of substance retained their surname but to avoid confusion called each other after the names of their farms i.e. Heathfield, Lurg, Dalrachny etc whilst with the same aim in view, according to Hope, the common men changed their surnames. Sir James must have been concerned by this practice for he wrote to his factor on January 9th:

> I should be glad you get me three or four young men of the name of Grant, not under five feet five and sufficiently stout & well made for the Regiment as we discharged three very bad penny worths Mr Jno Grant the D master. Donald his Brother and Peter Grant Rothymoon...I wish the name to keep its ground in the Regt. and having permission to discharge some bad men from the Regt. wish to fill their places wt. good men from the Clan.[75]

* * *

In February 1794 the First Fencibles, along with the other Scottish Fencible Regiments, were augmented. Sir James received his authority from Sir George Yonge on February 21st 1794:

George R.

Whereas we have thought proper to direct that each of the Companies of Our Regiment of Foot under your command shall be forthwith augmented with 1 Serjeant 1 Corporal and 25 Private Men & that 2 companies each to consist of 4 Serjts. 2 Drummers & 100 Private Men shall be added to our said Regt. These are to authorize you by beat of Drum or otherwise to raise so many Men in any County or part of Our Kingdom of Great Britain as shall be wanted to Compleat the said augmentation. And all Magistrates, Justices of the Peace, Constables, and other Our Civil Officers whom it may concern, are hereby required to be assisting unto you in providing Quarter, impressing Carriages & otherwise as there shall be Occasion.

Given at Our Court at St. James's this 21st day of Feby 1794 in the 34 year of Our Reign

By His Majestys Command

[signed] Geo. Yonge

To Our T. & lvd. Sir James Grant Bart

Col of Our Strathspey Regt. of Fencible Men.[76]

This was a very substantial increase, the regimental establishment now being over a thousand strong. In addition Sir James also wished to either raise a second battalion or a new Regiment of the Line. Lt John Grant junior in a letter to Sir James makes it clear that the authorities preferred the second course of action. He then went on to mention some possible names to fill the senior posts in the regiment:

By the agents letter it would appear to be more the wish of His Majesty that you should undertake to raise a Regiment of the Line than another Battalion of Fencibles...

Our present major who is a popular man among the Highlanders wd make a most excellent Major or Lt. Col...Mackay of Bighouse* if you accepted of him could raise a considerable number & even if he declined the service himself he wd raise the men for his friends...it would be an essential measure to be at liberty to take men from your Fencible Regt. as chuse voluntarily

Footnote:

*George Mackay of Bighouse (1737-1798) was appointed Lt Colonel of The Reay Fencibles when this regiment was raised in October 1794. He was by this time 57 years of age.

to enlist, as they could be very easily replaced wt. men that wd. not be so fond of the marching Regt. It would certainly be a creditable thing to have a Regt. of the Line and a Fencible one at the sametime, and wd give you a very great patronage...

We are all well and peaceable here and shd the anonymous information sent us be followed by attempts to execute the acts therein mentioned, we are in such a state of preparation as will enable us to make our evil wishers feel that we are not to be triffled with – The Major is in as good spirits as can be expected.[77]

Sir James took Lt John Grant junior's advice and offered the second majority to George Mackay of Bighouse. Mackay was very dubious about the prospect of military service and wrote to Sir James on March 12th 'I fear I am now too stiff and rusted for the business'. The Lt Colonel was much more forthright about George Mackays suitability for the post writing to Sir James 'a company is attached to the 2d Majority – as to a Drill Officer Bighouse never was or will be one, but he is a worthy man'.[78] Nevertheless, this did not stop Mackay taking command of the Reay Fencibles when they were formed later in the year.

No wonder the major was in good spirits despite the recent loss of his wife. His thoughts were now on the 'piece' he had picked up at Aviemore.

The Regiment of the Line or Marching Regiment which Sir James now undertook to raise was the 97th Regiment of Foot. He now had to recruit men for this regiment as well as for the augmentation of the Fencibles. This placed him in a bit of a quandary as he felt that Strathspey had lost quite enough of its fit young men to the war effort as evidenced by a letter the factor wrote to Captain Forbes of Curr on March 2nd:

I have had a letter from Sir James of date at London the 18th February ordering me to prevent recruiting by every means in my power in Strathspey...James Gow a smith at Bridge end of Curr in your name was yesterday and till this morning in Grantown giving all the trouble in his power endeavouring to trepan* some there I therefore request you will be so good as order him to desist....Drinking and Trepanning is not the best way to engage men – Bonny words and fair means will have a much better effect...I am exceedingly happy you are to be in Sir James Grant's

Footnote:
    *Trap or Cheat

Regt. and I hope and trust you will make up your Quota easily without giving trouble to any in this Country.[79]

The dubious recruiting practises of Captain Forbes of Curr also came to the notice of Simon Fraser the Sheriff of Inverness* who complained to the factor on March 8th:

> One Lauchlan MacIntosh a poor fellow on a part of Sir James Grant's Estate, has just now informed me of a violent outrage committed on his son James, who was an appprentice at Cluny, by a party who were drinking on the evening of the 27th ulto. and by the accounts he gives it wd seem doubtful if the young man will survive it and will at any rate be a cripple all his lifetime, and in either of these Events it becomes certainly my duty to investigate this matter, and I have therefore to request that youll take the trouble of letting me know how the facts Stand, as I am certain was Sir Jas in the Country he wd put a cheque to such proceedings which do a manifest injury to his Majesty's Service as it will inflame the minds of the common people agt recruiting...it was most wanton in this case as I am told that the Lad attacked had formerly enlisted with Grant Fencibles and had been discharged as unfit for service.
>
> The story told me is that Capt. Forbes of Curr with some of his servants and dependents, having with this Lad gone into the house of one King at the bridge of Curr – after drinking a good deal of whisky & offering enlisting money to the Lad dragged him out of the House and handled him so roughly that his best knee has been dislocated (the other having been formerly hurt) and that he is now in such a state as not to be able to turn himself in bed.
>
> If so it is such a shameful act in a Civilized Country as justly to merit the attention of the Civil Magistrate.[80]

Fortunately, there seems to have been a happy ending to this story for the factor wrote to the sherriff on March 24th:

> Immediately upon receipt of your much esteemed favour of the 8th instant per Lachlan McIntosh as to the Maltreatment of his son by a recruiting party belonging to Capt Forbes of Cur at the

---

Footnote:

* Many years later, in August 1810, Sheriff Simon Fraser was tragically drowned whilst bathing in the Moray Firth.[81]

Bridge I immediately wrote by Lachlan to Mr Grant of Kinchirdy as a Justice for the County of Invs. to come to Grantown on Monday last to precognise those Lachlan had to adduce for proving the treatment his son had met with and I ordered William Grant in Grantown a Constable to call those Lachlan would name to appear that day which William accordingly did On the Saturday preeceding this diet Capt Forbes came & told me he had agreed & finally settled the affair with Lachlan MacIntosh & he told the same to Kinchirdy on his way to Grantown Monday last – Kinchirdy and I stayed all that day at Grantown upon this business but neither Lachlan nor any of his witnesses appeared nor have I since heard any more of that affair I therefore expect there will be no more about it I hope that the concern you was so good as to take in this matter will make other men more Cautious in future – nothing can be more hurtful to recruiting than such conduct – the lad Lachlan's son is now going about with the help of a staff. I hope he will soon be able to follow his business – I did not hear a syllable of the affair till within two days of the receipt of your letter – Nothing.[82]

* * *

The Lt Colonel communicated regularly with Sir James whilst on leave at his home in Forres. He wrote on February 27th first giving his advice on the regiment 'In consequence of the augmentation...for any sake appoint only men who can be relied on' and then went on to impart bad news about his family 'all the children are ill with the Chin Cough* – I rely on your getting me leave to stay for 3 or 4 weeks'.[83] Much worse was to follow for he wrote again to Sir James on March 12th: 'Our poor little fellow is interred, & it's to be hoped time will bring us to submit to these heavy dispensations with patience – To another I might dwell on the loss of my three Sweet Boys, but you are my Brother indeed, in such an affliction, & to you I must yield the palm of misery...We are now most anxious about poor Jane, who has the disorder to a more alarming degree than the rest – Four of them are moved to Altyre.'[84]

Footnote:
 * Whooping cough

At this time Capt-Lieutenant John Grant of Rippachie who was recruiting at Forres was asked by the Lt Colonel to come and see him at Altyre. On February 28th Rippachie sent the following account of their meeting to Sir James:

> When I set out from Forres I thought Altyre had something agreeable to inform me respecting the Fencible Regiment But I was sadly Balqued and mortified when I was told I was to be Superseded and that the Majority was offered to Mr McCoy of Bighouse on the footing that he would bring a number of men to the Regiment – if he accepts and engages to raise men for the Commission I have no doubt but he will be successfull – but I would humbly suggest that it is not altogether a good reason for superseding an older officer, who has the undoubted right, if the general usage of the army establishes such a right to succeed, unless there was objections with regard to Character.
>
> Nothing can hurt the feelings of a good and deserving officer more than having one put over him and I am confident that you who has as much feeling and Sympathy as any person whatever will view it in the same light.[85]

On March 11th Rippachie, still smarting over having been passed over for the second majority, called again on the Lt Colonel who informed Sir James 'he is much hurt & mortified & calls his supercession a reflexion on his military character which I deny – I rather think that if neither of the Commissions falls his way, he will quit, which I shou'd much regret, as he is one of the best we have'.

The feeling of injustice aroused in the breast of Rippachie was to linger on like a festering sore for the next eighteen months during which time the First Fencibles were to mutiny twice.

* * *

With the depopulation of the Highlands the poorer Highlanders, a large proportion of whom were Roman Catholics, were flocking to Glasgow. As a result there was high unemployment, growing distress and discontent and sedition was rife. To counter this towards the end of February 1794 the government proposed raising a Catholic regiment under the command of Alexander [Alistair Ranaldson] MacDonnell of Glengarry. The knowledge that their chief proposed leaving them, a Catholic company in a Protestant regiment, may account in some degree for the serious disorder that was shortly to follow at Linlithgow.[86]

Chapter Three

Linlithgow

*'the mutinous fellows huzza'd & immediately flew to the Storehouse
& took possession of the ammunition'*

By February 1794 there was a real fear of a French invasion and the Government understandably felt that the proper place for the Scottish Fencibles was on the south coast of England.[1] Lord Adam Gordon proposed that four of the Fencible regiments should each provide 500 men who would be sent by sea to the Nore. He stressed that the men were not to be sent against their will for he was very well aware it was a breach of the terms of their enlistment which were that they would only be called upon to serve in England in the event of an actual invasion.[2] However, in early March while the Strathspeys were still in Glasgow rumours, accurate as it turned out, began to circulate that 2000 men from the Fencible regiments were to be sent to England.

These rumours taken in conjunction with orders for detachments to return to headquarters and all officers and men to return from leave led Glenmoriston to write excitedly and rather incoherently to Sir James on March 6th:

> From the sudden orders we had to call in our outposts and all
> absent officers and soldiers I suppose we will soon leave this, there
> are reports in town from Edin. that we are to march for England
> in case of any thing of that kind becoming known and as it would
> be pleasant and necessary to know it as soon as it transpires to a
> certainty, we have a great deal to do before we could well be ready
> for a long March I trust youl inform me how soon you can Learn
> what is to be done.[3]

The following day Sir James replied to Glenmoriston with the first definite information regarding the proposed call for volunteers to go to England:

> There is no doubt that it is in contemplation, and I believe certain
> that 2,000 men are to be sent to England from the Fencible Regts
> but in what proportion from each Regt. we do not know as yet –
> It is proper however that every Regt. be in perfect order &

preparation and that all the officers and Furlough men join – I shall be uneasy untill I hear the officers are all come in.

Altyre has got leave to remain till he gets another letter on account of the illness of his family and his friend Sir William Gordon.[4]

The previous day Sir James had written to Achindown, the regimental paymaster 'you must clear the men of the Regt. of all their arrears and everything else due to them that there may be no room whatever for complaining'[5] and on March 9th Adjutant Watson wrote to Sir James: 'We are as bussy as possible paying the men all just demands to the 24th December Last.'[6]

This letter to the paymaster would certainly suggest that Sir James was well aware that trouble might ensue if the men were asked to march for England in contravention of their terms of engagement and that he was taking all possible steps to ensure that there was no other cause for complaint. It would have been much more sensible if the authorities had from the outset informed the men directly that they were going to be asked to go to England rather than leave them to learn of the proposal through rumours in the press and half truths by word of mouth. On March 10th 1794 the First Fencibles were ordered to march from Glasgow to Linlithgow and Sir James joined them on the march.

Other Fencible regiments experienced problems in persuading their men to go to England but despite some protestations 500 men of Colonel Montgomerie's 3rd West Fencibles embarked at Fort George at the end of March and arrived at Chatham Barracks in mid April. 181 men of the Earl of Hopetoun's 7th Fencibles volunteered to accompany their commanding Officer, Lieut. Colonel Napier by land or sea into England. On March 12th the Gordon Fencibles at Edinburgh Castle told their officers that they would not embark, their Colonel the Duke of Gordon writing to his uncle Lord Adam Gordon: 'If my Regiment, or 500 of them, had been asked to march into England they would readily go, but whether they will boat is more than I will answer for.'[7] In the end he did manage to persuade his regiment to embark at Leith. The Sutherland Fencibles and the Breadalbane Fencibles both refused to go to England but the Argyle Fencibles reluctantly sailed to England from Dundee on the 19th June.[8]

Meanwhile, some of the officers wished to transfer from the First Fencibles to the 97th Regiment which was now being raised. Watson was one of these, but the Lt Colonel was determined not to lose him, writing to Sir James 'if you take Watson from the Fencibles you give <u>them</u> their death stroke'.[9] Sir James agreed with his Lt Colonel and informed Watson on March 7th: 'As we consider you as necessary to our existence in the Fencibles you must not be Surprised, that I do not agree to the Representations of some of your friends who propose my having you as Adjutant to the Invernesshire Regiment.'[10]

Dr John Grant the surgeon's mate was another who wished to transfer to the 97th and asked Sir James for 'a continuance of your goodness by granting me an Ensignancy in your new Regiment'.[11] The factor was also keen to further his son's military career and wrote to Sir James on February 13th:

> As I hope & trust there is now no doubt of your Honour having got the raising of a new Regt. on the British Establishment; allow me request the favour that if Dr Peter Grant is appointed surgeon of it, you will be pleased to appoint my son John to succeed him as Surgeon to the first Fencibles, or if Dr Peter Grant prefers continuing as he is, that you will be pleased to appoint John to be Surgeon of the Regt to be now raised.[12]

On March 9th Dr John Grant wrote to his parents from Glasgow to let them know what Sir James had offered him and with some regimental news

> Dear Father and Mother
>
> I this day received a letter from Sir James Grant informing me of my being appointed Ensign and Surgeon's Mate in his new Regiment upon the condition of raising 22 men with the levy money or 15 without the levy money – I returned an answer that I could determine upon nothing untill I heard from you – Sir James mentioned in his letter that he had written to you concerning it – he did not say one word concerning the Surgeoncy whether it was or was not disposed of – I have not heard of any yet appointed – I think it would be a preferable plan to have a promise of the first vacant Ensignancy rather than raise such a number of men and at such high Bounty – being a new Regiment & several entering into it with no other view than that of enabling them to attain a higher rank it is probable three or four months

went past without a vacancy taking place – at least it is generally the case in such Regiments – This day we received orders to march for Linlithgow from whence it is supposed 500 will go for England – being one of the <u>staff</u> I will remain behind – That is to say if the whole Regiment does not go – however it is only conjecture yet – we march the first Division off upon Thursday the 13th currt. so that when you write you may direct under cover to Sir James Grant at Linlithgow or elsewhere – Mr Grant the Minister of Abernethy's son goes to Bombay so I think it would not be amiss to write by him notwithstanding our writing before – the Parson is here just now recruiting he has got about 14 or 15 – he has 19 to raise – they call him Capt. Grant the Minister – Capt. Grant Achindown's son is to be a Lieut. in Sir James Grant's Regiment provided however he gets him gazetted as Ensign in some other Regiment. I expect to hear from you on receipt concerning the offer made by Sir James Grant. Sir James will be here tomorrow or next day – I shall speak to him on the Subject – I shall write when we set out or when we arrive at Linlithgow – My compts. to all friends.[13]

The mention of Bombay and sending a letter there by the hand of the Minister of Abernethy's son is explained by the fact that John's eldest brother, Lewis was stationed there as an Ensign in the East India Company.

On March 13th factor James Grant wrote to Sir James:

Till this evening that I recd a letter from my son John I did not know that to get in as Ensign to the Invernesshire Regt. he must raise 22 men with the Levy money or 15 men without the Levy money. These being the terms upon which he can get in I must decline his accepting & have by this post wrote to himself to that effect – Could I afford to sink the money that would at this time by fair means raise that number of men I think it would bring him yearly near equal to Ensign's half pay without trouble – I have therefore desired him remain continued as he is in the first Fencibles if your Honour would be pleased to appoint him a Lieutenant in it would enable him in some time hence with what assistance I could give him to purchase an Ensignancy.

Last year John brought 12 to the Fencible Regt which I think no other Ensign in it did.[14]

This placed John Grant in a bit of a quandary for he now wrote to Sir James: 'My Father...seemed to disapprove of my entering so much into a military line of life – both as it would hurt my Education and would attend with an Expence to him he could ill bear...it would hurt me much to take any steps contrary to the wishes of my Parents.'[15]

This correspondence between father and son highlights the system whereby commissions in the army could be purchased by young men of means either by raising recruits or paying army brokers to raise them for them. The more recruits that a young man could raise, the higher the rank he could purchase. A story circulating at the time alleged that 'one proud parent, requested leave of absence for one infant Lieutenant Colonel, on the grounds that he was not yet fit to be taken from school'.[16]

* * *

On March 14th Lt John Grant junior wrote a long seven page letter from Kilsyth to the factor railling against some of the iniquities of prevailing army practice and giving some regimental news. The following is an extract from his letter:

> I hope never to deserve the name of being a Democrat but I cannot help thinking the riding system now so fashionable a very absurd if not an odious and despotic one I now do and always did understand that your son was not to be ridden longer than till the Gentleman Rider had obtained an other commission and I am now well informed that his present Commission as Ensign in Col. Cunningham's Scotch Brigade is dated so far Back as the month of July last and if I recollect right the 6th day of that month, so that according to the understanding of the agreement for the ride the rider should have been paid by the ridden to that date only, and I do wish you to say something to me on this Head in course that I can make use of in support of such other materials as I may be able to adduce – our first division marched from Glasgow yesterday morning and are this night at Falkirk, and tomorrow at Linlithgow where we are to wait for further orders which will be according to what I can learn independent of the Newspapers to ship on Board transports at Leith for the South of England, where it is expected some sport may soon take place...we are now

Heavans be thanked free of Glasgow and I had much rather go to the Plains of Flanders than return to it, altho' we have certainly been singularly lucky in not having one single material quarrel with its inhabitants – I did not nor wd not believe that there were such places as Glasgow and Paisley in Scotland before I saw them...There are 1 Lt. Colonel 4 Captains & 15 Subalterns of us ordered wt the 500 men for England, but we can get none of our absent officers to join, and this days post brought a Letter from Rippachie, setting further his being dangerously ill and signifying his Resignation, altho' he was but a few days before at Edinr. soliciting a Majority – I hope the period is now arrived that will convince the Chieffs & shew them clearly who will & will not stand by them in the Hour of danger...

I have seen Mrs Grant's recruit for the new Regt. – He is a fine boy and will do very well...

Your son John properly speaking should raise 22 men but both he and I must go to England and how can we raise men...

There is talk but I hope without foundation that the Fencible soldiers are determined not to embark particularly the Gordon's who have wrote many improper letters to our men.[17]

He wrote again on March 16th this time from Linlithgow:

The Bounty and Instructions for the First Fencibles are the same as before, but we must not be so very nice about the men -

our first Division arrived here last night and I marched with the second yesterday amid a heavy rain from Kilsyth to Falkirk where they lie this day Sunday which place Sir James & I left this morning & came here to breakfast.

We are all in excellent spirits and altho' we have not yet made a formal proposal to them of going to England I have no doubt they will unanimously agree unless poisoned by the Gordons who have already done very improper things...I have already secured a majority of voices for the Paymastership and wrote to Capt. Forbes Curr sometime ago but have not yet heard from him – I also wrote to him that if he declined the Capt. Lieutenancy which at his time of life & all the circumstances of the case considered I should imagine no object for him but I hoped he would let me have the first offer of it – do speak to him of this – I had a letter today from [?] in answer to one I wrote to him upon the same subject and if Capt. Forbes declines I have no doubt but I shall be the Capt. Lieut. – you will see by the newspapers that there are to be vast new livings. Col. Hay of [? Barnes] is to have the raising of a Corps – Ld. Caithness is to be Sir Jo Sinclairs Fencible Lt. Col. & Culdihill Major.[18]

No reference can be found in the army history books to the 'Riding System' but it would seem that this was a system whereby an officer purchased a commission in a given regiment and let another, who could not afford to buy one, serve in the regiment in his place so long as the salary was paid to the officer who had purchased the commission in the first place.

It is interesting to note that the second Division marched from Kilsyth to Falkirk amid heavy rain, for John Prebble let his imagination get the better of him when in his account of these events he wrote: 'The second Division came through the dust of the Stirling road.'[19]

This reference by Lt John Grant junior to his seeking the Captain-Lieutenancy refers to the newly formed 97th and not the Fencible regiment where the indignant Rippachie was still the Captain-Lieutenant.

* * *

On March 17th the whole regiment paraded at Linlithgow and in an attempt to persuade the men to go to England Sir James read them the following address which he had penned that very morning:

Linlithgow Monday morning 17th March 1794

To the non commissioned officers and men of the 1st or Strathspey Regt. of Fencibles.

My Friends and fellow soldiers,

You know that we are come here in consequence of a call from His Majesty to go to the South of England, where in the present exigency of Public affairs he thinks our aid of most consequence -

I can with truth assure you that it proceeds from his high opinion of you as a Regiment, the confidence he has in you, and the name you have deservedly acquired by your conduct ever since your establishment – you may believe it gave me great satisfaction when last in England to hear every person speaking of you in the most flattering terms of approbation. -

88

His Majesty taking into consideration the length of the march by Land and the loss of time has ordered Transports and a Convoy to Leith to receive you – The Transports and convoy have already gone to Inverness, as I am informed to receive those of the West Lowland, Hoptoun Fencibles, who are likewise to go to England and we may expect their return soon to Leith to receive the Gordon and Strathspey Regiments – five Hundred men Rank and File including Corporals with a proper number of Sergeants, officers and staff, are to go from each. – they must undoubtedly be the chosen men of the Regiment, for abilities, good looks, vigour, youth, and strength of constitution – come forward then my friends – Let every Brave man and lover of his country, step forth & vie with each other, who shall be the first in so noble a Cause – Be assured you have not your own welfare, and Happiness at heart more than I have. – You will find England excellent Quarters – the soldier lives much better there than he can do here, and however well you look at present, I expect every one of you will look ten times better before you have been a month in England – The voyage is nothing with good Transports, and a good convoy – Let me once more beg you to prepare, with as much spirit, and alacrity as possible – As to myself you know I have much to do before the tenth of May, but if you wish it I will go with you. -

The King wishes this to be a voluntary act on your part, and I trust I shall have it in my power to declare your readiness and spirit on the occasion – let me once more say I go with you if you wish it. – His Majesty looks upon going by sea the least fatiguing, least expensive and most expiditious method of going, which it certainly is, but will not be insisted upon unless you prefer it. -

I remain
My friends and fellow soldiers,
Your faithful friend and Colonel,
Ja: Grant
Colonel First Fencibles
Linlithgow
Monday morning 17th March 1794.[20]

No volunteers stepped forward in response to Sir James's request which rather made a mockery of the view expressed by Lord Adam to Sir James 'when your people are assured, that no force was ever meant, or intended to be used – & that they certainly, never will be compelled to embark – I should think – they would sett satisfied'.[21]

Despite the absence of volunteers Dr John Grant, in a long letter to his parents written the following day made it clear that he still thought the regiment was going to England. At the same time he took the opportunity to give them an update on his own career prospects:

Dear Father and Mother

About a fortnight ago I wrote to you concerning the Ensignancy & Mateship offered by Sir James Grant and mentioned it as my opinion that it would be better to wait a vacancy than raise such a number of men – Since that time I have seen Sir James Grant from whom I understand I must go to England with the Fencibles on account of the scarcity of officers – he at the same time added "as you go there I can't expect or desire you to raise men for the new Regiment – you are sure of the Mateship & an Ensignancy – and if my application to Lord Amherst to get you and some others gazetted Ensign in other Regiments be successful, you come in Lieutenant and mate" this is very generous of Sir James Grant and deserves my utmost Gratitude – Altho' not exacted, it would be best making a proper return to raise a few men especially if they can be got at a small Bounty – Before I left Glasgow I got two men at 10 guineas each – if I can get two or three more at such Bounty I hope you will have no objections to my taking them – I know that my exertions would please Sir James and might be a means of inducing him to extend his favours especially as it would be a voluntary act it might make a greater Impression on him – Before I left Glasgow I settled with the Paymaster – he produced my receipts of £8 for the Quartermaster and £6 for college fees – I gave as much out of my monthly pay as I could spare – the remainder I was under the necessity of drawing upon you for – it amounts to £12-18 – As I did not know of any other way of managing the business I took the liberty of drawing upon Mr Adam Stewart at Edin. convinced that his Friendship would pardon this freedom – Mr Cumming received six months Pay which includes subsistence & everything else – Bellintomb has got above 60 men Achindown's son 26 the minister 16 Sir James 50 or 60 all in the Town of Glasgow – I heard Sir James say "it is thought at Edin. we are 600 strong but I don't believe that – we are about 300" – however Sir James is very delicate & would not assert but what he was <u>sure</u> he had tho' <u>probable</u> conjecture might make the number much greater – I am sorry that William is so slow and inactive – I once thought that if he was not bright he had perseverance – I shall take advantage of the first leisure moment to write him on the Subject – I just now received your Letter of the 13th – I can assure you that I am by no means so much attached to a military life as to make me lose sight of my professional pursuits – if they are both compatible good and well – if not adieu to the sword – how long we may remain here is uncertain – by what I have mentioned in the beginning of the letter I hope you will no longer object to my accepting Sir James' offer – I can't draw Pay from the two Regiments what I draw now from the Fencibles I must refund out of my other Pay – My complts to all friends Dr Father & Mother

I remain

Your afft. son

John Grant

Linlithgow 18 March 1794.[22]

Sir James must have been referring to the 97th Regiment when he mentions a regimental strength being about 300, as the Weekly State of the First Fencible Regiment of Highlanders at Head Quarters in Glasgow on February 22nd was given as 620 Rank & File.[23]

The pay that Dr John Grant refers to would be his pay as surgeon's mate. His pay as Ensign 'including subsistence and everything else' will have gone to Mr Cumming his 'Rider'. There were now so many regiments being raised that prospective recruits could hold out for a Bounty of £10 or more. As the recruiting officers were only reimbursed three guineas by the government relatively poor young men like Dr John Grant could not afford to make up the discrepancy out of their own pockets.

The 'William' Dr John Grant refers to was his younger brother who did not join the Fencible regiment until May 1797.

By March 20th Lord Adam Gordon was still hopeful that the First Fencibles would agree to march to England and wrote to Sir James accordingly:

The 6th Fencibles have all agreed, to go to England by Land or by Water – which their Colonel has signified to me officially – I now wish to know officially from you – if your Battn. / not a detachment / have any objection to march bodyly into England – leaving such men & officers only – as you may think requisite, to carry on your augmentation, in Scotland – if / as I hope / your Regiment agrees to march – no time shall be lost – and the season is in their favour – But if they do not – no compulsion is to be used – and it will be offerd to another Battalion –

P.S. – The non commsd officers and privates will each receive a Gratuity of a guinea – when they arrive at their destination in England – I wish to see you here as soon as you can satisfy yourself on this business.[24]

Before he had received this letter, Sir James had written the following letter to Lord Adam dated 21st March:

My Lord,

I have the infinite satisfaction to be able to acquaint you, that the Strathspey men shocked at the idea of their not having presented themselves the day I spoke to them, all resolved next morning to express their sorrow and their resolution to go to England in any way I saw proper – accordingly yesterday every man of them declared it, and in the Evening immediately after the Parade, The Light Infantry led by Captain Fraser, their Captain came in a body to my quarters and declared the same resolution – my own company whom I had just parted with desiring them to come forward next morning at the Parade immediately recollected & joind the Light Infantry, it became too dark to collect the other Companies but individuals from the Lieut. Colonels Capt. Grants and Capt. Roses declared their companies would all do the same – I trust this morning will bring forward the Grenadiers and all to the same expressions of obedience – I cannot however be so sanguine as to the Macdonell Company, whose animosity to the measure, & proceedings, supported by some of the Grenadiers, and heightened by the Reports and Letters they received as to the other Regiments, had made the whole so seemingly backward – Capn. Macdonell of Glengarry regrets the conduct of his company, & says he hopes they will likewise come forward this day he says their having heard of his intention of offering to raise a Regiment and so leaving them had deprived him of his former Influence amongst them – I must do the whole the justice to say that the Contagion came latest to them, & was of the shortest duration & I trust in God they will resume their former good Conduct and behaviour, and that His Majestys Commands as to going to England will be completely obeyed.[25]

As Lord Adam wished to know immediately whether the First Fencibles were willing to march to England, Sir James did not send the above letter. Instead he once more paraded the regiment and asked for volunteers for England to come forward, but none did and then quite spontaneously men from the MacDonell, Grenadiers, Colonels, Lt Colonels and Majors companies broke ranks and took possession of Linlithgow Palace.[26] At 6 o'clock that evening Lord Adam Gordon, having been informed of these events, sent a note to Sir James in reply:

I am hurt beyond description at the contents of your letter – and at Capt Grant's report – But I see nothing to be done – but to be cool, & temperate – to tell those who are well affected – that nothing has, or will be expected of them – but good order – and that no man will be desired to march out of Scotland – without his consent...I hope – the report you must send me tomorrow – may bring accounts – that disorder is subsiding.[27]

* * *

During the course of the next few weeks Dr John Grant, the Rev. James Grant, Adjutant Watson and Lt John Grant junior all sent accounts of the mutiny to the factor at Grantown. The first to write was Dr John Grant on March 22nd, the day after the mutiny:

Dear Father & Mother

I wrote two days ago mentioning that the Strathspey Fencibles might be considered as on their way to England and I thought I was to go along – but the face of affairs has greatly changed since

93

that time – Upon Thursday night the Light Infantry to a man & most of the Colonel's turned out for England – this gave us hopes that all would go well – upon the Friday forenoon the Regt. was drawn out colours flying etc. & the Proposal made – the mutinous fellows huzza'd & immediately flew to the Storehouse & took possession of the ammunition – they were about to march thus prepared against those who remained firm, when luckily the Adjutant went among them – he was at first threatened but by intreaty & request he prevailed upon them to desist & return – C. McDonell & Dr P. Grant who is Lieut. in his Company which acted the principal part then went among them – they kept them all three Prisoners – at last they let out the Doctor with a letter to the Colonel desiring that he would assure them on his word & honour that they would never be commanded to go out of Scotland except in the Terms of their Attestations and that he would read Lord Adam's letter to him – this was granted and they became pacified but still refused to go except in case of <u>actual</u> Invasion – all is now quiet – their number at first was about 120 – but towards Evening many of these who stood out in the forenoon joined so that the whole at last amounted to about 300 – as the proposal was made in Terms that would admit of a refusal, that is, it was by no means a <u>command</u> but a <u>proposition</u>, the idea of going to England was dropt Lord Adam got Intelligence & Rippachie who was the Bearer spoke of our getting in to garrison such as Edin. Castle The answer was that Troops that behaved as ours did would not be intrusted with any important post at least this is report – it is not known where we go next – The Gordons I see by the Paper have all agreed – Altho' not spoken as yet about it yet it is supposed Kinchirdy's son & I will get home to see if we can raise some men for the Invernesshire Highlanders – I shall write again soon
I am Dr Father & Mother
Your afft. son
John G.
Linlithgow
22 March 1794
  P.S. Excuse inaccuracy as it is almost the post hour.[28]

On March 29th the Rev. James Grant the chaplain, now on leave from the regiment, wrote to the factor from Inverness giving his views on the causes and consequences of the mutiny:

you would hear of the very disagreeable mutiny, among some of the Fencible men on the 21st at Linlithgow. As all was peace, on the 23rd when my last letter was written, I wish to hope that all is over; but it is a most unpleasant scene, & coming under promises to Soldiers – only to be done from necessity. Sir James is much distressed by it & no wonder. It appears to have originated in the Glengarry Co. and I am sorry to find there were several from Urquhart, Glenmoriston & Strathspey, who joined them. I wish this conduct may not bring about a reduction in the Fencible Regt. The Montgomeries have embarked & latterly behaved wonderfully well – blamed the consels of this Towns people for their irregularity – as do our own Fencibles – the inhabitants of Glasgow Linlithgow etc, for misleading them.

The chaplain also expressed his views regarding the terms on which Sir James was prepared to offer the factor's son an Ensignancy in his new regiment:

I had no kind of idea, that Sir James would have ever thought of burdening your son, with a single man, for the Ensignancy & Mateship – on the terms offered, there was neither advantage nor obligation. I hope however that matters might come round yet, and that he gets both appointments gratis – and after all I consider the favour as very moderate, every thing considered.

He ended by expressing his views, shared by most of the officers of the regiment, on the Macdonell company:

I wish Glengarry & his men had been in Botany Bay when they joined our Fencibles, they have been the source of every evil.[29]

On the 11th April the factor replied to the chaplain:

My wife and I return our best thanks and are much obliged by the favourable accounts you are pleased to give us of John I sincerely wish he may continue to conduct himself with propriety & be deserving of the countenance and esteem of his superiors and equals.

I had a letter from him the 22nd March the day after the mutiny in general terms saying that to the amount of 300 or so of the men had refused going to England by sea or even by land but in the event of an Actual Invasion – I have another letter from him dated 31 March saying they are all quiet & orderly – that tho' the rout had not then come it was known for certain that they were to move soon from Linlithgow & that there headquarters were to be at Dumfries. Then he tells me that in consequence of the augmentation to the Strathspey Fencible Regt, Auchindown was that Day appointed Major, Rappachie Capt, & Paymaster, Lt. Grant Auchterblair Capt. & Wm. Grant Lettoch Capt. Lieut. This is all his news – he always writes short letters & gives no news almost never the particulars of anything respecting the Regt. I am exceedingly sorry at their mutinying in the manner they did. They might have stood firm to the terms of their attestation without breaking into the stores & taking possession of the ammunition.[30]

This criticism of his son's letter writing seems a little unfair as John's letter of March 31st was both long and detailed and is set out below:

Dear Father and Mother

I this day received yours of the 25th currt. – the Letter to which it was an Answer did not contain an account of our irregular behaviour when the proposition of going to England was made – I suppose by this time you will have an account of it from others as well as me – We still remain in this place and are all quiet – altho' the rout has not yet come, it is known for certain that we move from this very soon and that our head-quarters are to be at Dumfries – the Gordons go off Wednesday first – various reports are in circulation regarding them – some say that the Colonel promised they would go no further than Berwick – others that Lochell's Company had retracted – the first of these one of their men told to some of our officers yesterday in this Town – the last I heard from a Robt. Adam who was with a Wright in Strathspey – he says he heard it yesterday from one of their Serjeants at Edinburgh – you say my Mother has enlisted a Drummer or Fifer – I have no doubt that he will be among the very first of the Regiment – but as it is probable Sir James will reserve the Drummers Fifers & as many of the non commissioned officers as possible for himself, it is best to proceed cautiously – I am as yet uncertain whether I go to Dumfries or not – as there have been a good many new officers joined I think I might now be spared – but the longer I am detained the better as there will be fewer men expected of me – There has been a good number of promotions in our Regt. today – Rippachie who is Capt. Lieutenant & Auchterblair who is oldest Lieutenant come in Captains – Lieut W Grant Lettoch is Capt. Lieut. Capt J Grant Achindown is Major – all these appointments are in consequence of the augmentation – Rippachie who as Capt. Lieut. ranked wt. the Captains and as half pay officer was likewise the oldest Captain would have come in for the majority but he preferred being Captain & Paymaster & Achindown preferred the majority to his present situation – if I mistake not, Glengarry will soon resign which will give my friend Lettoch a Company & make Advie Capt. Lieut. – I am truly very sorry to hear that Mr L. McGrigor is getting no better – he was but weak when he left Glasgow I thought however the country air would soon make him well as his Complaint was of such a short standing – I am afraid his Spirits are affected by it at least he seemed dull & melancholy in Glasgow Two days ago I accidently saw an old fellow student passing thro' this on his way to London – upon Enquiry I found he was going to Bombay which you may be sure made me very happy – he only staid to take a hasty Breakfast I had not time to write a letter I gave him a short memorandum mentioning we were all well etc. he goes out as Hospital mate wh. I am informed is a very good berth – Have you heard of Ballintomb passing thro' with his recruits – he had great difficulty in getting 47 from Glasgow & was obliged to leave some there whom he could not find – Mrs Grant & his family followed soon after – Auchterblair has about 17 or 18 in Glasgow – Lewis Grant from Tomintoul is at last appointed Corporal and Lewis MacGrigor from Grantown they are both very deserving as they have a better hand of write & better Education than most of them while their behaviour is always very regular – I heard lately from my cousin John at Edin. he was very well – about a week ago we had Dr Gry. Grant Mr Isaac Grant Mr Alexr. Grant & Sir James's Family out here on a visit – Lurg was here some days does he come into the new Regiment – there is nothing more new here – my complts to all friends

I am Dr father & Mother

Your afft. son John Grant

Linlithgow 31st March 1794

Chas Grant the Hatchet man* is anxious to hear about his wife & family he wishes to know if his son got redress of the Saw miller.[31]

When John wrote that Rippachie preferred the Paymastership and Captaincy to the majority he cannot have been aware of Rippachie's letter of February 28th 1793 to Sir James when he was 'balqued and mortified' at not being offered the majority. [see chapter 2]

* * *

On the same day Adjutant Watson sent Sir James his views on the current mood of the regiment:

Honoured Sir,

I was duly favoured with Letter this morning by James Grant – at the time of his departure I had not time to Spare it being a busy hour with me owing to parade -

and still in anxious waiting to see if a Little time would have brought about such a good worke as a Reformation amongst the men the day being unfavourable for field movements gave me a Little Time to consult with some of the Ringleaders of the unfortunate business that happened Lately amongst us.

However I am sorry to say that all my Endeavours both at this time and every other opportunity since you left us has proved inaffectual to bring about the Desired Effect – still it would be a great presumption of me to despair – of the measure as yet notwithstanding the Backwardness of some of their dispositions to come forward in such a Laudable undertaking. The McDonells are still obstinate to the Last degree and tho I am the only person that speaks to them on the subject they still affirm that the Gordon's will never Embark in the business either by Sea or Land any further

Footnotes

*peat digger

than Berwick upon Tweed, this was declared amongst them yesterday by one of there own <u>men</u> who was here yesterday from Edin. Castle to see a Brother of his in Capt. McDonells company, this I consider to be Like many more of there wild Ideas, but it was Circulated here with some degree of confidence particularly amongst the Black Sheep who is at all Times Ready to receive such doctrine however ill founded, on purpose to exculpulate <u>themselves</u> from the well grounded <u>Charge against them</u>.

I have endeavoured to abstract the ammunition from those that I was confident had large proportions of that article but I have been hitherto very unsuccessfull – however I hope in the course of time they will see the impropriety of that illicit practice a few of the moderate ones have surrendered to their Serjeants a certain proportion of ammunition – but whether they have even delivered the whole or not is very doubtful to say.

I sincerely hope that no bad consequences will arise from what is in there possession at any Rate.[32]

On April 4th Watson found time to sit down and write to the factor with a lengthy account of the recent events at Linlithgow:

From the Enclosed narrative you may easily conceive what a state I am in for there I have actually wrote more than I have had time to Read – or examine – <u>however</u> my dear ffriend you will I am certain except of the will – for the deed. with Respect to my aunts situation – I am trully sorry for but as you have justly observed that I would lay the weights upon your shoulders – to provide for her in some degree for the present – I hope in God you will untill this Blast Blow over – untill it is in my power to write to you more particularly on that subject.

With Respect to my inseperable friend and constant companion your son John I cannot find words strong Enough to sound his praise – both as an officer in the field and his <u>Practice</u> in the Regimental Hospital – or where his presence is necessary – in a word he is universally Respected in both and in other Respects everything you could wish him to be, however flatering this report may seem to you it comes far short of what merit he has acquired in both his professions he does not Know anything my writing to you at this time – and suffer me only to observe for the present that he is well and hearty; and I hear him say that he meand to write you soon – However, I presume if England goes against us, for the present, that you will soon see him in the north but at present it is scarcely possible to say what turn matters may take in our favour, and I hope in god that the next news you may hear of us – that we are Like Brave ffellows on purpose to Repell – & take our share of the Laurels that may be bestowed on those that show themselves the best soldiers in Repelling – the threatened <u>Invasion</u> of olde <u>England</u>, should this be the case I make no doubt of their Being as forward in the cause as their neighbours who embarked yesterday at Leith – I mean the Duke of Gordons Fencibles. I cannot help taking notice of the MacDonell's, on occasion that lately happened – they have been a curse to us from the beginning but particularly conspicuous on the last unfortunate business of which I have already said so much about for they to a man – mutinied and our foolish Strathspey men unguardedly and unthinkingly adhered to them so much so as to be lost to all sense of Gratitude to their worthy Colonel and patron – I shall only mention two names to you that was the most voilent of the Strathspey men one of them you Recommended to me last year. I mean <u>Solomon</u> Stewarts son, the other gentleman was Alister Dow some distant Relative of the family of Burnside, I am informed and lately a servant to belentomb – many others I could mention but the above were most outrages particularly to me in the <u>ardurious</u> Task I had amongst them but for the choice <u>Glengarry</u> Company any Description in my power to give of them would come far short of the mutinous disposition they showed on the 21st of March which is certainly a memoriable day if commited to the <u>annuals</u> of the present age History – against the 1st or Strathspey Fencible Regt. – my best respects to the Minister of Cromdale and family and inform him I have had it in my power some time ago to get Thomas Stewart promoted to corporal. I make proffer of my best compliments to Mrs Grant accept of the same and believe me to be at all times my Dear Sir

Sincerely yours in haste

James Watson

Adjt. 1st F. Reg.

I meant to copy and correct but has not so much time to spare at present. I dare say you have had this business detailed by abler pensmen than me but I have simplified it in giving you the Real Transactions as they really happened – JW

ATTACHED
Linlithgow Apl. 4th 1794
Dear Sir,

Nothing but the Emergency of our situation of Late could warrant me to withhold an answer to your kind Letter Recd. by my cousine Corpl. Grant now Serjeant the man that you have often wrote about has come on at last for he was made Corpl. in Grants place many other promotions by augmentation too Tedious to mention – at present Woes me my Dear ffriend I have something more at Heart than promotion amongst them I am truly sorry and with Deep Regrate – that I mention to you that there has been a great deal of commotion amongst us to our utter Disgrace I am affraid – but at this moment I still Expect that they will Come forward Like men yet – altho it was this very day fortnight that the unfortunate business happened, Sorry am I to say that your Trusty Strathspey men were very active in this affair So much indeed that they galed the Hearts of those that was Connected with them with ties of the strongest nature – Still all consideration of that kind was laid aside and nothing but the utmost disorder prevailed for a length of time too shocking to Relate at present which clearly convinces you what an Extraordinary Creature man is when he gives way to his inordinate passion wihout allowing the smallest Rays of Reflection to take place and believe me my Dear ffriend this was exactly there situation for they had wrought themselves up to such a Degree of anger and Revenge without the smallest occasion whatever that they thought it was necessary to give way to their wild Ideas in purpose I suppose to exculpulate themselves in future from any charge that might be advanced against them Something desperate must be done in this affair and certainly the devil himself never devised a more desperate matter after their officers had said a good deal to them on the propriety of Embarking in this laudable undertaking but at the same time with such mildness and Precaution that they were not to go unless they choosed to do it cheerfully – in the clap of a hand disorder commmenced and about 150 of the most desperate Left the field to the great astonishment of all present, only consider for a moment the situation of our ever Respected Colonel and his amiable Lady and some of his offspring around him to witness this fatal <u>scene</u> which I may justly call it for I will make bold to say that nothing ever came over him in my opinion that shocked him more – if leaving the field had been all notwithstanding that being of itself a very Irregular proceeding for soldiers to leave their cowlours – still we might have got over the odium of the aspertions against us but unfortunately they had more in view for they Reppaird to a strong Hold which would have done them credit as soldiers had it been a post of honour they had to defend but woes me to Live to see the day that they should have taken such a stronghold and commited such outrages for the purpose of mutiny and sedition I really thought my very heart would have broke upon the occasion – in the first place, to consider that I had served my King and Country so long both at home and abroad to come in amongst my very blood Relations to be Deceived in such a manner was giving me such a home stroke at once as <u>almost</u> sank my feelings which a soldier never be divested of, at once to the deepest sorrow, and Rendered me at one time Regardles of life which in fact I was like to pay very severely for my attachment to my King, my Country and my Colonel placed me at once in a very Delicate situation for in a short time they had made <u>themselves</u> master of the ammunition belonging to the Regiment which was at that time very considerable owing to our last station, I mean that cursd place Glasgow which has been our utter Ruine at the time when the magazines were attacked I suppose we had about 12 or 13 thousand Ball Cartridge in it fit for any service whatever, taking the most moderate calculation besides powder and flints in proportion – the field was a considerable distance from the stronghold already mentioned – in fact <u>being</u> the <u>ancient seat</u> of King James the sixt of Scotland no person Dreamd that they had such desperate measures in view however they soon declared themselves masters for in a very little time they shewed themselves in different places Ready for action by firing several pieces in different directions which convinced us without doubt of their having made themselves master of the <u>ammunition</u>, who to restrain those men from committing acts of outrage which was certainly there intention, was the next thing to be considered on however by this time with grief I had absolutely Resigned myself to anything and I was ordered of from the main body single handed to go in amongst the insurgents which was at once a novel undertaking and not at all likely to succeed – at least not without Loosing the Life, in the attempt however as God & his Goodness and unbounded mercy had determined otherways I made my appearance at the gate accompanied by no other person at that moment when I was accosted by the Sentinels which were by this time numerious what my business was – I told them I came as a <u>friend</u> and if they would admit of me amongst <u>them</u> I would Endeavour to do them a service after a council of war being held in the inside I was admitted after making such concessions as you may be assured hurt me much particlary one, that no other officer was even to make his appearance amongst them but myself not even the Colonel – whom I thought at the time to be their ffather besides an Indulgent Colonel and Commandant who never wish'd to make himself disagreeable to any man; and particulary them who had at all times and in all situations shewn them his <u>Countenance</u> however this was the impulse of the <u>moment</u> and I could not possibly say anything to counteract there opinion – and at the same time I must acknowledge I feeld myself very awkwardly situated not withstanding their pretensions and in fact it shews you clearly to what a pitch they had wrought there Tempers to before I arrived amongst them that they were Determined to sally out and Repell force by force to those who would not join them what a Blessing of God it was that they were in some measure prevented from this rash and unwarranted act of <u>voilence</u> as had it taken place god only knows where it might have ended, however after a great deal of altercation amongst them I had the good fortune to Establish a little order – and I proposed that falling in and Exercising would shew the world at once that they meant no <u>harm</u> to any individuals who was not of their way of thinking – this they at last agreed to altho god nows neither my heart or Inclination was Equal to the Task – at that time however I did the best I could and had the good fortune to Divert their minds from commiting any more outrages and altho every man's [?] was properly flinted and most part loaded there was not the smallest accident happened and I Exercised them untill they said they were tired and wish'd to Rest themselves this motion I of course agreed to as I was tired enough myself still I did not wish them to know that – however towards the evening after many couriers had pass'd betwixt them and the Commanding Officer they agreed that I should go for him for they wished to speake to him – this was the only moment I was <u>suffered</u> to be out of their sight from the first commencement of the unfortunate Blockade as I may very justly call it – the Colonel came – honest man with a heavy heart and Granted them all they wanted they then insisted on marching out with flying <u>culars</u> which was also Granted and they have in some measure Remain perfectly Quite since – we are all still in hopes of there Repenting and taking the Right side of the Question yet, god Grant it may be the case & that they will Remove the stigma from their unsullied characters Previous to this date – and as there is only one method for them doing it I hope it will soon be <u>Done</u>

Yours most affectionately

James Watson.[33]

Although Watson's letter is long winded, repetitive and somewhat disjointed his devotion to the regiment and utter dismay at the behaviour of the mutineers is apparent. His letter also gives us some insight into the the minds of the mutineers.

* * *

On April 10th Lt John Grant junior gave his account of the mutiny to the factor. Inside the cover of the letter he wrote: 'Ever unlucky I am now to be opposed in the Paymastership as to which more particulars in my next meantime do me all the good you can.' As previously mentioned this was a reference to the paymastership of the 97th Regiment.

Dear Sir, Edin. 10th April 1794

I was this morning favored with your kind and much esteemd letter of the 6th inst. and as I have only a few minutes to write shall say all my time will permit in answer to it and refer another letter of yours I have unacknowledged 'till I have more leisure which I hope will be soon but my hopes have often been blasted.

Despite the protestation of lack of time, Lt John Grant junior went on to write a twelve page letter!

Instead of applying the word Mutiny to the conduct of a very considerable number of our darstadly Fencibles if the words open Rebellion had been used I think it would have applyd much better according to my understanding of these words & their conduct. –

Be Assured My Dear Sir I would not have missed a post in acquainting you of this business as I know well you will and must always feel interested in the fate of Strathspey men even where the tie is not so strong as in the present case, but I certainly thought John wd have detailed every incident to you much better than I possibly could did my time permit. – To be brieff then as we had acquired merit enough to make Government wish to have us in England our worthy Colonel after taking in conjunction wt all the Officers every necessary preliminary precaution put the question fairly to the whole Regt. on or about the 17th ulto. at Linlithgow by asking who wd follow him & the officers to England when to his & you may believe our complete mortification not one man expressed his readiness to go -

We represented fully that there was no force, it was to be only choice but all to no purpose – we then dropt the question and I came express to town to acquaint the Commander in Chief of this very unexpected event – a few days thereafter however late at night we were flattered wt the Light Company (Frasers) to a man were coming forwd. and after drawing up in proper order before the Colonel's window unanimously expressed their readiness and willingness to follow him & their officers anywhere – The Cols own Company joined & were almost unanimous in doing the same as were a great many of the majors – you may believe we now thought matters wd come round as we wished and next morning at 10 we marched to the field of exercise near Linlithgow and after drawing up the companies seperately as usual began wt putting the question to the Grenadiers when we found we could prevail on a very few only to join the colours and those who declined in a darstardly manner broke from their Ranks run off huzzaing and being immediately joined by the Black Sett the Macdonells & many others put the whole Regt in confusion & run into Town broke open the store and after siezing upon the ammunition & made up Ball Cartridges several of the Rascalls came to the opposite side of the Loch betwixt us and began to fire upon the men & officers who had remained in the Park – In this situation you may imagine but I cannot possibly describe our feelings and to make the matter worse if possible at this very moment Lady & Miss Grant came into the park. Sandie Grant & Isaac were also present. This scene having lasted for about 10 minutes we got those that remained wt us put into some order and after taking a list of the present & absent marched Back to Town laying our account for being fired upon by the Dastardly Rascalls as we marched past them, but they thought proper to decline that -

At first there would be a little more than 100 who left us as I have described and took possession of the Old Palace of Linlithgow but how soon we dismissed those who had remained wt us in the Field but declined going to England immediately joined the Rebellious Rascalls in the Castle till at last they were full 300 strong with plenty ammunition and excellent musquets to defend the old castle and themselves.

Capt. Macdonell and the Adjutant immediately on the fellows leaving the field being the officers of the MacDonell company followed in hopes of getting them prevailed on to return, but they no sooner appeared than they were seized as Hostages and the Macdonell Company repeatedly threatened to put him to death if any the least violence was offered to be done to them & positively refused to let him or the Adjutant go out without the walls of the Castle – Luckily the Adjutant who has a very strange & uncommon knowledge of the minds of the lower order proposed that as they were idle they should fall to their exercise and that he would drill them which strange to be told they to a man agreed to do, and in that state they continued for near two Hours till at last they said they were tired and wished to do no more – All this time they had their centries posted at every hole and corner of the Castle and on one pass they had no less than 12 men posted and they began to make new posts of Defence as they expected every moment to be attacked by the Dragoons -

Doctor Grant who is the Lieut of the Macdonell Devils had been in wt them soon after they took possession of the Castle and he found them so violent that it was to no purpose to confer wt them. He about 4 o'clock returned and after long reasoning they agreed to return to their duty if they got a letter from the Col. (Sir Jas) promising they wd never be asked to go to Engld. and as it was never meant they shd. go agt. their will an answer was sent verbally to that effect, but wt which they were not pleased as it was not in writing – however they at last agreed to return to order if the Col. & Major came & promised them what they asked and they then marched in great good order to the usual place of parade & after they were dismissed gave three cheers and however sorry I may be for their conduct I am happy to say they behaved most obediently & exemplary ever since – I am perfectly satisfied that if it had not been for the Macdonells we would not have had a dissenting voice at least to make a head or produce any disagreeable consequences, but the Macdonells being all unfortunately from the beginning in one Company & as one man enabled them to make a head and many of the soldiers had told me that they had arranged their Black plan so as to threaten the first man that consented with instant death which intimidated many young Boys & gave room to those who inclined it to join them.

With regard to names you may believe I cannot be particular just now, but I can assure you from my own certain knowledge that none were more active than your cousin Malcolm McCoiloig and he was the first man that broke the powder barrells – Luke Dickson tho' not so active did by no means behave well – John Grant, Wm Grant your Ground officers Son in Law altho' he did not join in the castle yet he run off like a coward as I believe he is from the field – Adam Gordon the lymers son behaved very well indeed –

Many very many I am sorry to say of the Strathspey men behaved exceedingly improper but none more so than those two Rascalls James Mitchell & James Rattray* who were in a great measure brought up upon Sir James's kitchen -

These are the outlines of our misunderstandings – once their brain was afloat thousands of ideas each wilder than the other gender'd in it – one among the rest was that Capt. Frank had brot. a stand of the Duke of Yorks Colours along wt. him & that they were all to be sold and sent to Flanders, What gave rise to this was that our Regimental embroidered Colours were unpacked that day and displayed for the first time – we had only the temporary Painted Colours before that -

You may easily conceive how much our good Colonel has been cast down by this return which he so little expected or deserved.

Notwithstanding all this by all accts from Linlithgow there are not at this moment 100 men in the Regt. who have not signed papers expressing their regret at what had happened and their readiness to go to England, and I do not yet despair that the whole may go – But let them after what has happened do what they may I thank my stars that I am to be free of them – I have no doubt but evil designing people had put mischieff in their Heads for when they were at their worst at Linlithgow some Democratical Towns Rascals encouraged them crying "there is the Brave fellows who will not be blinded"

There is vast promotion in the Fens. Achindn. is to be 2nd major, Rippachie is to have a company & be payr. – Rosefield is to have a Company and Lt. Wm. Grant is to be Capt. Lieutent. so that Advie and I are the two oldest Lieutenants – Carmichael Geddes is to be Quartermaster in the Fens. and the Inverness Regt. Green Horns are to be saddled wt. Sutherland.

I dare say you know the names of all our officers for the Inverness Regt. The Lt. Col. is not yet named – Capt. Cochrane of the 78th Regt. a brother of Ld Dundonalds & quite a young inexperienced officer is to be our major – The Capts. are

Footnote:
*James Rattray [or Rattrie] was recruited by Dr John Grant on March 6th, 1793.[35]

Bellintomb, Auchterblair, Capt. Stuart, Francis W. Grant, Baillie nephew of Dochfour, Lamont younger of Lamont, Colquhoun younger of Luss who excepting the three first are perfect Boys and Curr you know is our Capt. Lieut. – The subalterns are not all named and the 1/4 of those that are cannot raise half their quotas of men – Sir James desires you will immediately order up the man you enlisted for the Fens. (mentd. in your letter to me) to join at Linlithgow or where the Regt. may be – you must give him a pass as Justice of the Peace – I differ wt you in opinion as to your John – He will be 1st Mate & Ensign which will secure half pay at the Redn. – I certainly hope Sir James will not count strictly wt him or me seeing the manner in which we are nailed down at present – Jas Grant the Provost's son is to be surgeon & Effingham Grant, Carsons son 2nd mate – Mr Roy whom you saw wt us at Forres is to be Ensn. & Adjutant and will I hope answer our purpose – it was no small difficulty to get him at this <u>crisis</u> from the artillery – He and Lt. Harry Cumming set out yesterday and the day before for Inverness wt. near 80 Recruits of Sir James's etc. for the Inverness Regt. – Our Recruiting goes on everything considerd far beyond expectations -

Philips son has I think justly declined an Ensigncy in the Fencibles – might he not buy in the Inverness or any other – He can get an Ensigncy now at £250 st.

I have got your John's business with his [?] settled to my liking & will write ostensibly my own on that head – Logie & Mr Jas Grant Glenmoriston set off yesterday for the north – Logie was long dangerously ill and is not yet quite well -

I forgot to tell you that yesterday eight days the Gordons to a man shipp'd on the Board Transports at Leith in the most peacable manner equally so as if they had been stepping into Church – The Duke was the first that went on Board the boats that carryd them to the Transports and the brave fellows crowded after him into the hold where he led them, and all went off amid the shouts of thousands – at the same time that I liked the sight & thought it <u>a grand day wt the Duke</u> I felt it a degrading one to myself and those I feel so immediately connected wt. & I really could not help tearing upon the occasion – The Gordons having shipp'd has had a wonderful effect on our lads as the Gordons and they were in League & corresponded before.

Had the Gordon's not been in garrison their conduct which at first was not the best wd have been equally ill as ours – Sir James was at Linlithgow two days ago when a joint Letter from the Adjutant and your son came which I sent by post rather than keep it to be franked when Sir Jas returned. – I suppose it wd mention some particulars relative to an affair where John behaved like a Hero and to the entire satisfaction of all his Brother officers in the Corps one only excepted whose approbation is in no case to be counted more especially where he is a party concerned.

He is gone to London and may he never join us say I.

Burn this long incoherent scrawl when you read it.

Remember me wt affection & gratitude to Mrs Grant & Believe me always to be My Dear Sir most faithfully yours
John Grant.

Owing to the Equinoctial Storm and easterly winds the Transports in which the Gordons are Still remain in Leith Roads which I am truly sorry for as the Highlanders will not like their situation more especially as the sea runs high.[34]

The anguish and shame felt by the officers at the behaviour of the regiment is apparent in this letter. The factor did not burn it as instructed. He folded it neatly and filed it away with the rest of his correspondence.

* * *

On Saturday March 22nd the Lt Colonel wrote to Sir James to let him know that he was leaving home to rejoin the regiment but added: 'I go tomorrow, tho' with an heavy heart as Jane & some of the rest are extremely ill.' He had not yet heard of the mutiny at Linlithgow but it would come as no surprise to him as he was well aware of the disorders that had occurred in other regiments. He concluded his letter to Sir James: 'The 3d Regt have played hell at Inverness, mutinied, seized on the ammunition & set all order at defiance – they are determined not to embark, but say they will march anywhere, it is said the 7th at Banff have adopted the same resolutions and we hear the 6th in the Castle are of the same mind – I hope our Lads will escape the contagion but I rather wish than expect it.'[36]

As soon as he reached Linlithgow the Lt Colonel realised that the best way of disposing of the vast quantities of ammunition available to such potentially mutinous soldiers was to fire it off. On March 28th he ordered that 'The Colonel's Majors and Captain Cummings Companies, are to parade to Morrow morning at 7 o' clock properly flinted, on purpose to fire Ball – Captain Mcdonell's Captain Rose's and Captain Grant's Companies are to parade at 10 o'clock, the Lieutenant Colonel's & Captain Frasers Companies are to parade at 1 o'clock in like manner for the above purpose'.[37] This order was repeated on March 30th and 31st and on April 2nd and 3rd 'on purpose to fire ball at the target'. Many of the men still retained large quantities of the ammunition so illicitly acquired in Linlithgow Palace for the Lt Colonel stated in Regimental Orders on April 4th: 'A Complaint having been made by the Provost & Majistrates to the Commanding Officer that several of the Men have been going on in a very unmilitary Practice of shooting in the Country & Firing through the hedges to the great risque of the lives of the country people. He expressly forbids such conduct in future.' Despite this strict order he was forced to repeat it on April 21st: 'The Commanding Officer is sorry to observe the very improper conduct of the men this forenoon after being dismissed from the field in firing their pieces repeatedly in the very streets of the Town...in future no such unsoldier like practices can possibly be looked over.'

The Lt Colonel was acutely aware that his men might mutiny again and he wrote to Sir James on April 10th: 'Twill be obliging if you will get the Commander in Chief to send us out some flints, as we have three barrels of powder which I wish expended for many reasons & we have hardly a single flint to send with a command, having only rec'd 1200 bad ones since our embodying.' On April 16th he wrote again: 'I have sent serjt. Jack for the ammunition & desired him to leave some of the Boxes of Ball at your house, as we shall not have immediate use for them nor need they be about our hands, more than we absolutely require – The English expedition keeps their minds in an unsettled state, which I wish was put an end to, as till it is entered into, or given up, there will be two parties which never will assimilate – & from what I can learn the whole are now like the sea, subject to every blast & liable to every impression.'[38]

The Lt Colonel's innate reaction to the mutiny was to tighten discipline and on April 1st he wrote to Sir James: 'I hope you'll have got our men secured, & that you'll get them immediately tried by a General Court Martial & punished in the Castle,' and again on April 3rd: 'I...entreat that you will not allow of MacLachlan being released for some time, for if these miscreants arn't frightened into better behaviour, there is an end of all discipline...as to their ever agreeing to go voluntarily to England, I wou'd not have you indulge the idea, for that company [MacDonell] by all I can learn are determined never to do it – Their Capt. positively denies giving MacLachlan leave, & his having no pass shows it to be a lie.'[39]

Soon after his arrival at Linlithgow, the Lt Colonel informed Sir James that Glenmoriston 'is this morning gone upon an whoring expedition to his piece at Glasgow – he promised to be back tomorrow,' and added: 'If Sunday is a good morning I shall probably be in to breakfast with you,' and concluded: 'I think what I mentioned before wou'd be the best plan to give Achindown the Majority & Rippachie the company & Payship. Achterblair as a steady good officer is very deserving of the other company.'[40]

* * *

Despite the mutiny, efforts were still being made to try to persuade the men to volunteer for England, Glenmoriston writing to Sir James on April 9th: 'Since yesterday morning we have been doing all we could among the men & I think almost the whole except the MacDonalds [*sic*] who have not yet been spoke to have agreed to go to England by land...I wish Lord Adam would defer reviewing us till some other occasion our clothing etc being in bad order.'[41]

On the following day the Lt Colonel spoke to the men in a further, and as it turned out, fruitless attempt to get them to serve in England. He sent his report to Sir James who forwarded copies to Mr Dundas and Lord Adam Gordon:

Linlithgow 10th April. Thursday evening.

After evening parade I went up to the palace with the Major, Adjutant, Doctor and Capt. MacDonell's company and after putting sentries at the Gate told them that I had called them together to speak to them as their Commanding Officer and friend – that I shd treat them as I had ever done with civility and kindness – that I had a few propositons to make to them and that I expected and relied that what I had to say to them would be listened to respectfully and meet with a cool and civil answer – That I had it in command to inform them that a very considerable part of the Regiment sensible of their late misconduct, had come forward and offered to march to England with their officers – That if they would handsomely and voluntarily do the same, that the whole of us would esteem it as a mark of affection and attachement, that you would be much flattered with it, and that it would go far to reestablish us in the publick esteem in which I was sorry to add we were at present very low – as I went on with the different sentences the other officers translated it literally to the circle – They unanimously expressed very great concern for what had lately happened, and said it was the madness of a moment which they did and ever should regret – that they would by their future good behaviour endeavour to do away with the folly of that day and would in every respect as far as their engagements went in future behave as good soldiers, but that it was their unanimous and fixt resolution that they would not march out of Scotland unless there was an actual invasion and in this they would remain determined – this was and is their fixt determination without a single dissentant voice – The business was carried out with civility and good humour, and they expressed every regard for their officers who they said had always treated them kindly; the leading speakers among them said they were happy to have this opportunity of assuring me that they were willing to seal it with any oath, that Capt. MacDonell was unjustly traduced by the suspicion of it having been said that he had any hand in their declining the expidition, for he had used his utmost influence and exertion to bring them to do it, and by his doing so, had got the ill will of the whole.

I have a satisfaction of making the report of this latter part of the transaction to you on Macdonell's account who certainly suffered (it appears now unjustly) in the general opinion – I mentioned his being gone to England on the idea of promotion in another Corps, which they bore with unexpected sang froid, and seemed to think they could be as well with any other officer – It is but justice to the officers to add that they have every inclination and Exertion to carry your wishes into execution – Excuse this hurried account of the matter as I am afraid to miss the post.[42]

When the Lt Colonel states that 'the other officers translated it literally' he is referring to the fact that many of the men only spoke Gaelic. Their inability to understand English might well have been a factor in their believing that they were going to be sent to England against their will.

The Macdonell Company may well have regretted 'the madness of a moment' and promised 'future good behaviour', yet only a fortnight was to pass before they mutinied again. Sir James gave the details to Lord Adam on April 25th:

> Upon going down to the Regiment on monday last, I was informed that some of the men, particularly the MacDonnell Company, had of late shown a mutinous disposition & behaved unbecoming Soldiers to some of their officers – that particularly upon Sunday last, when one of that company was ordered to mount guard, he told his officer he would not – on which the officer very properly confined him...the moment the rest of the regiment had gone to Church four or five of the most desperate rushed into the guard room, and took the prisoner saying he was confined for nothing at all, and they would not suffer it – The rest of the Company being ready to aid their Companions, in case of opposition...a meeting of the officers was called, when it was resolved to lay the matter before your Lordship for your advice & Cooperation...The officers are resolved at the risque of their lives to enforce obedience, and are of opinion that the sooner the regiment is moved from Linlithgow, whose bad advice is privately & industriously disseminated the better.[43]

Lord Adam dealt very leniently with this most recent and serious breach of discipline, confining himself to having his 'pointed censure' read at the head of the regiment:[44]

GENERAL ORDERS

By The Right Honourable General Lord Adam Gordon commanding His Majesty's Forces in North Britain

From the various reports made to Lord Adam Gordon of the very unsoldier like behaviour of several individuals of the 1st Fencible Regt. and of the want of subordination to their officers, so Essentially Requisite in every well disciplined Corps, it is with the greatest reluctance and concern he finds himself under the necessity of taking this publick method of expressing his disaprobation of a conduct so disgracefull to themselves and Injurious to the service – His Lordship is well informed that the number of those who had exposed themselves to this pointed censure, bears no proportion to the rest of the Regt. who upon every occasion behaved themselves to the satisfaction of their officers and to their own credit -

His Lordship therefore flatters himself, that Influenced by their good example, those who had hitherto been Refractory, will be ashamed of their past misconduct and endeavour to blot out the Remembrance of what is past by their exemplary Conduct in future – But should they still persist in their Error It will be then his indispensible duty to lay the whole circumstance before his Majesty, as such Contempt of good order and discipline cannot be passed over with impunity.

Edinburgh. 25th April '94
Signed: A. Gordon, General.[45]

* * *

Earlier, on April 4th Dr John Grant had been ordered by Sir James to proceed post haste to Inverness as there was no surgeon or mate with the 97th, or Inverness-shire Regiment, as it was commonly called and he wrote to his father:

I yesterday received a letter from Sir James desiring me to go north to Inverness with all possible dispatch as my presence there as mate was much wanted. I intend to set out tomorrow – I go first to Edin. to get Sir Jas's Commands & then proceed the highland road thro' Perth Blair in Athol etc I expect to be in Strathspey by Friday or Saturday first where I can stay only about one day as Sir James's letter is so very pressing – however when matters are properly settled there and the Surgeon and other mate come up I hope I will get leave of absence for a few weeks – our Regiment still remains here tho' a movement is daily expected. Those who go to England will have a route soon. The Hopetouns to the number of 300 are at Kinross on their way to England – it is said the remainder would willingly go now were they permitted. I hope that will be the case with the Strathspey Fencibles – a few days more will determine...

Mate's arrears are £5-6 & Ensigns which I now have some expectation of getting at least from the date of my Commission £8 some Shillings – Some time ago when Sir James Grant was in town he told me that I would recover Ensigns pay from Mr H. Cumming from the date of my Commission until the time I commenced pay in Glasgow as he being appointed Ensign in the Brigades drew pay from July – the Bargain with Capt. Cumming was 6 months pay or untill he commenced pay as an Ensign in another Regiment – I likewise suggested a plan to Colonel Cumming for securing me Ensign's & Mate's pay in both Regiments which he thinks will answer & which he intends to follow out viz I give in my resignation here in the usual form & am marked in the pay book & in the returns to Lord Adam resigned When I am to be gazetted in the Invernesshire Regiment it is not to be Ensn. John Grant from the Strathspey Fencibles as is usually done but simply John Grant Gent – so that they may have no suspicion that I am...gazetted in another Regiment...

the two recruits I got in Glasgow have gone to Inverness some time ago – I paid the one 5 & the other 3 guineas in part of their Bounty – which sum I borrowed from my Friends Lettoch & Delshangie besides a guinea to one of the bringers which I got from the former – if I should leave drafts for these respective sums with Lettoch and Delshangie I hope you will honour them – You'll have seen by the Papers that 3 frigates are taken from the French* – private letters state a very considerable victory over the French 5000 killed 8,000 prisoners and 50 pieces of Cannon.[46]

This order for Dr John Grant to proceed at once to Inverness must have been cancelled, as also would the rather dubious plan for drawing double pay, for on April 19th he writes to his mother from Linlithgow:

Footnote:
*This refers to a brief engagement between Admiral Howe's squadron and the French Channel Fleet.

Dear Mother,

I received my father's letter of the 13th by which I understand he was to proceed to Inverness and Urquhart upon the 18 currt – I have as yet received no answer from my friend Mr James McGrigor concerning the surgeoncy in the Breadalbanes – however favourable the terms may be I shall resolve upon nothing without your and my father's advice – the conditions must indeed be very good that would make me prefer it to my present Expectations – Our Regiment still continues quiet and orderly about ten days ago the Grenadier company turned out for England very few excepted – all the Colonel's company did the same, as did 36 of the majors, 30 of the Lt. Colonels, all C. Grant's, 45 of C. Roses, and the whole of the light infantry – not a man of C. McDonell's Company turned out C. McDonell himself has gone to England to propose raising a Catholic Regiment – what answer he will receive may easily be conjectured – it is thought he will get a flat refusal – This day week we were mustered and in a few days we are to be reviewed by Lord Adam Gordon – I would probably have got North had it not been for this but there are so few officers present that I could not be spared at this time – I can't say what figure we will cut before Ld Adam. I think that for our opportunities and time we do very well – Our winter quarters Glasgow were much against us we had not a fortnight's Exercise in it from the time of our arrival to the time of our departure this may leave us behind other Regiments in our progress but what we do is done with life and spirit & equal to any – notwithstanding our being so near Edin. I have not yet got in to see that City where I would find a good many medical acquaintances – when the Review is over I intend to ask leave for a few days...Has my Father got any Recruits for me – I could wish to have a few more before the 10th May which is not now far distant – I suppose that you have seen by the papers that Danton and his party are guillotined You may assure Mrs Ross that Mr Ross is perfectly safe – he was neither hurt nor was there any attempt made to injure him or any of the Regiment – the reason that Mr Ross did not write also to my father of the Strathspey men who would not go to England was that soon after they all agreed to a man.

Please make offer of my compts. to my Brothers & Sisters & all enquiring friends – I have nothing more to add.

I am Dr Mother

Your afft. son

John Grant

Linlithgow 19th April 1794.[47]

Dr John Grant was wrong in thinking that Alexander Macdonell's offer to raise a Catholic regiment would be rejected. As will soon be seen he was given the go ahead that very summer.

Even up to the end of April and beyond, there was still talk of part of the regiment at least, marching to England as Sergeant Major Donald Ross explained to the factor:

I wrote you some days ago what I hope has come safe to hand. Now again I thought it my duty to you to send you this few lines of information of what is going forward at present –

We are under orders to march but when I cannot tell you, some time this week the Regiment is to be divided into two divisions those that chuses to go to England is to march and those that will stay is to go to some place as Commander in Chief directs. I expect 400 at least will turn out for England. I have enclose you a copy of Lord Adam Gordon's letter which was publickly read at the head of the Regiment saturday last. Mr John Grant is well and desires his best wishes to you Mrs Grant and family.[48]

* * *

Alexander MacDonell of Glengarry resigned his commission on May 2nd writing to Sir James in the following terms:

I was favour'd with your letter of apl 25 of last month, to which I am sensible I ought to have returned a more early ansr. – The circumstance of my coming of age in Septr. next makes me desirous of withdrawing at present fm. a military life, that I may have the more leisure to examine in to the State of my affairs, & see in what situation they are – I therefore beg leave to offer the resignation of my comissn. which I hope will meet with your acceptance.[49]

Sir James replied on May 13th: 'I am by this days post informed by Lord Amherst that His Majesty has been pleased to accept of your resignation.' However, Macdonell did not withdraw from a military life for long for on August 14th he received a letter of authority to raise a Catholic regiment of Highlanders which was to be called the 1st (Fencible) Regiment Glengarry Highlanders. The terms of service of this regiment were that they should serve in 'Great Britain Ireland and the Isles adjacent'.[50] Macdonell was able to recruit into this regiment many Catholics already serving in other regiments and in particular the Macdonells serving in Sir James's First Fencibles who wrote to him from Stranraer on October 27th:[51]

> Most Honoured Renowned Colonel
>
> We the under written sergeants corporals and privates of your company, understanding a permission is given by government to soldiers in this and other Fencible Regiments of entering into yours, or any other new Corpse now rising to serve out of great Britain let you know it is our most earnest desire and ardent wish to follow you to any part of the earth his Majesty may order you to led us...we are kindly treated by our officers which makes our present cituation comfortable enough but our minds can never ben content separated from you...we expect to enjoy those possessions which our ancestors so long enjoyed under your ancestors though now in the hands of Strangers, as we do not wish that you should loose by us we shall give you as high rent as any of your Lowland Sheepherds ever give.

This letter was signed by 72 men who were mainly Macdonells and is of interest on two counts. Firstly, the blame for the mutiny at Linlithgow was firmly placed on the shoulders of 'that Black sett the Macdonells' by the Strathspey men but here we see the Macdonells only seven months later happily volunteering to serve anywhere in the British Isles. Secondly, it is clear that the men were fearful of losing their lands in Glengarry on disbandment – and how right they were to entertain such fears.

* * *

Following the augmentation, the senior officers of the regiment were now as follows:

Colonel [Sir James Grant of Grant, Bart]
LIeutenant Colonel [Alexander Penrose Cumming]
First Major [John Grant of Glenmoriston]
Second Major [John Grant of Auchindown]
Captains
Robert Cumming of Logie
Simon Fraser of Foyers
John Rose of Holm
John Grant of Rippachie
John Grant of Rosefield
William Grant, Esq;

Lieut. Allan Grant of Advie was promoted to Capt-Lieutenant in place of William Grant who had previously succeeded Rippachie in that post and was now promoted Captain. In addition, there were now no less than twenty one Lieutenants and eight Ensigns in the regiment. James Carmichael was appointed quartermaster in place of Angus Sutherland who joined the 97th Regiment now forming at Inverness. Dr John Grant also transferred to the 97th and on May 3rd was once again 'ordered to Inverness to take care of the sick there as the Surgeon is not yet arrived'. His place as surgeon's mate in the First Fencibles was taken by Dr Thomas Stephen.[52] Other officers who transferred to the 97th were Lt James Grant, Lt John Grant junior and Lt F. W. Grant, Sir James's son.

In early May Angus Sutherland set out for Inverness, but his journey took him longer than expected because, as he explained to Sir James: 'I cannot think of being at Inverness before Saturday having so Grate a load on one horse, my wife, daughter & myself & about one hunder weight of baggage with these the horse performs extraordinary well.'[53] It must indeed have been quite a remarkable horse!

By the middle of May it had still not been decided where the regiment was to be stationed or even if it was once more going to be asked to go to England, the Lt Colonel writing to Sir James: 'We are all in the agony of expectation to have our fate determined one way or another.' The regiment was still behaving badly for the Lt Colonel continued: 'We were driven in this morning by the rain – were under arms again between 1 & 2 but were prevented going out by numbers of them being drunk from the Breadmoney – we are to try it again tomorrow at 7 o'clock.' Glenmoriston had now managed to get his 'piece' pregnant for the Lt Colonel concluded his letter to Sir James with: 'The major is off to attend his lying in at Glasgow – indecent enough you will say, but he talks about it with the greatest ease.'[54]

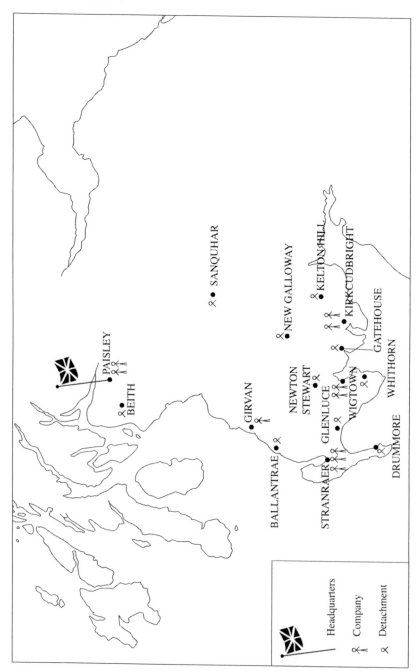

In May 1794 the regiment was widely dispersed.

Chapter Four

Paisley and Dumfries

'Comprehending three Irish vagabonds, who were a Terror of the neighbourhood'

O n May 16th the regiment finally got its marching orders. Sir James was instructed by Lord Adam Gordon to march to Paisley 'in such divisions and by such Routes as you shall find most convenient'. The first division commenced its march on Wednesday 21st. Three companies were to be stationed at Stranraer, one at Girvan, two at Wigton, two at Kirkcudbright and two were to stay at headquarters at Paisley. In addition detachments were to be posted at Drummore, Ballantrae, Sanquhar, Glenluce, Whitehorn, Newton Douglas [Newton Stewart], Gatehouse, Kelton Hill, New Galloway and Beith,[1] so the regiment was well and truly dispersed as is well illustrated in the map on the facing page. This was done for the purpose of showing how a military presence to the civil population in as many places as possible and on June 5th Glenmoriston wrote to Sir James:

> I have the pleasure to inform you that yesterday the King's Birthday passed over here tolerably quiete, the magistrates and principle people were much alarmed a prodigious crowd of the lower orders assembled they have been threatening mischief for some time but our appearance I think has had a very good effect in this place I do not think they can do any longer here without the military.[2]

and on June 14th Quartermaster James Carmichael informed Sir James:

> The Magistrates and Country Gentlemen gave us a great Credit for keeping peace and good order on the Kings Birthday and at all times in this Town There was a Mob of the lower Classes gathered near the Guard Room door and throwed some Bricks but they were soon dispersed by the Guard.[3]

Glenmoriston wrote again on June 25th:

> The principle Inhabitants were much alarmed before we came...they say there is no fear of the Democrates while there is a Grant remains in Paisley. you would be astonished at the numbers of that sort in & about this place.[4]

According to Mackintosh[5] friendly relations were maintained with the towns people of Paisley during their six month stay there but Watson, writing to Lt John Grant junior who had now joined the 97th Regiment, was much more circumspect:

> We are still continuing on a pretty good footing with the inhabitants of this place I make no doubt of our still continuing It was fortunate we keep them at arms length at first for now it is pretty certain that they meand in some measure to subvert us from our duty but in this they were cussedly mistaken Adml. Howes victory has d---d them most effectually At least for the present the dissatisfied creatures dare not stir I am trully happy to find that you will soon have it in your power to shew yourselves before those Rascals on the continent I have every reason to hope and it shall be my constant prayer that you will all of you distinguish yourselves when engaged as it is most likely you soon will have a Brush with them...with every good wish that can possibly attend you and sorry thrice sorry is Watson at not being one of the number.[6]

Whilst the regiment was stationed at Paisley a local budding bard penned some excruciatingly awful verse to commemorate their stay. The first two verses went:

> *There came the Grants into this Town*
> *They were all Stout and Gallant men*
> *Their Commanders were of high Renown*
> *As Ever came to Paisley Town*
> *Chorus with a Fa La La etc*
> *Major Grant as you may know*
> *In this Town made a Gallant Show*
> *He is a neat and clever man*
> *And from Glenmoriston he came*
> *Chorus*[7]

* * *

There is no doubt that the Lt Colonel was held in high regard by many of his officers even though he kept flitting backwards and forwards between home and the regiment with bewildering speed. Rippachie wrote to Sir James: 'By a letter this day from Colonel Cumming he is to leave home on the 23rd [June] and is to be here on the 30th. Major Grant is impatient to get home and I cannot say but that I am very happy to learn Altyre is to be so soon with the Regt. tho the major is one of the best men,'[8] and on September 8th Watson wrote: 'Colonel Cumming and family left us yesterday on their way to the North with universal Regrate on our part.'[9]

Whilst at Paisley on August 19th the Lt Colonel had a severe attack of colic from which he made a complete recovery writing: 'Yesterday...I was confined to Bed by a sudden and alarming cramp in my stomach, which threatened to number me with my fathers – I am thank God rather better at present, tho' very week; the pain having seated itself in my right side.' In the same month he commented to Sir James: 'It was the idea of Sir Ws.* death which from all accots can't be very distant / and not his <u>marriage</u> / that I was so anxious to get away.'[10]

The Lt Colonel was now toying with the idea of entering politics for in a letter dated 27th November to Mr James Brodie of Brodie Sir James wrote: 'Mr Cumming of Altyre has intimated to me his intention of standing Candidate for the County of Moray when a vacancy happens, yet I am convinced, if the recovery of my Sons** health should enable him to attend his duty in Parliament that Mr Cumming would still give way to him. You have certainly a perfect right to stand Candidate for the County tho' I cannot wish you success.'[11]

* * *

Watson was for ever anxious to help the private soldiers with their family problems and he wrote to the factor on July 20th:

> Inclosed is a Guinea note which John McIntosh seemed at – a loss – how to Get home to his wife when I found the poor man anxious I have taken the Liberty of troubling you with it – which I well know from the goodness of your heart you will apply it as directed...it will be proper that the woman on receiving the note should acknowledge it In the first letter she writes her husband who is a worthy Goodman and I hope we will have it in our power to do something for him soon.

Footnotes:

*Sir William Gordon of Gordonstoun, upon whose death Lt Colonel Cumming was shortly to inherit a large fortune.

**At this stage Sir James still had hopes that his eldest son Lewis would recover his mental health.

He then referred to the regimental establishment:

I suppose now all hands will be Employed to fill us up to Establishment this I presume will not be a hard matter for you to do as very few Strathspey men I understand want the new Regiment – I therefore trust and hope they will not be backward in filling up the notionall [Torn] as it will be a sad pity if a peace takes place Before we have it in our power to Return ourselves once complete to the Establishment propos'd you will no doubt have Red in the public prints that we still continue to hold forth to the world a Tollarable character in spite of the battle of Linlithgow which rather lays heavy on our stamochs as yet Still I hope we shall soon do away with that <u>odium</u> and be good Lads for the time to come.[12]

The factor had received his own instructions to assist in bringing the regiment up to establishment from Sir James's clerk:

Sir James Grant desires Mr Grant the Factor may fix <u>a day</u> next week for the Tenants in <u>each Parish</u> to meet him at Grantown by Eleven o'clock in the forenoon to assist in recruiting the necessary augmentation of the Fencibles – He should be sorry that the Strathspey Regiment could not be compleated.

Castle Grant

1st August 94

Three or four following days or one intervening as may be most convenient but the sooner the better.[13]

However, despite all efforts only 64 new recruits were obtained for the augmentation between June 17th and December 19th 1794.[14] During this period some men had been discharged for on May 13th the Lt Colonel had ordered that: 'The Captains & Commanding Officers of Companies will give in to the Commanding Officer...a List of such men as they may think proper objects to be recommended to the Reviewing General to be discharged by infirmaties...The Surgeon will also give in a Return of such men of the Regiment, as he actually knows to be unfit for any further Service, owing to incurable sickness.'[15]

Recruiting was marred by another unpleasant incident. On September 19th George Grant of Ballifurth complained to the factor about the behaviour of one recruiting party:

The boy himself I understand like a man some years ago in

Lochaber... was made a Volunteer, by the Sergeant Major and his associates, he says that...he was very ill used most unhumainly by drageing cuffing and throwing at him, and the sergeant himself – threatening to bind him neck – and heel, sending him directly to Fort George in order to put him in a ship, so that he says he was glad to agree to what they pleased for fear that they would Murder him or put him aship bound where he would never see any person belonging to him Consequently that he took a shilling of money from the sergeant in the King and Sir Jas Grant's name.[16]

As well as being short of recruits the regiment was still lacking in much equipment, Rippachie writing to Sir James from headquarters at Paisley on May 30th:

We have Drum Boys here idle for want of Drums – it will be necessary for Drums to be immediately ordered if not already done as also Halberts Swords & Sashes for the additional Serjeants.

Arms will also be necessary soon at present the non commissioned of the two additional Comps. with the Recruits are supplyd from the spare arms of the other companys – white Belts for the non commissioned Offrs & Privates shd be ordered here by the first vessel from Londn.

P.S. a very fine young lad of the majors Compy. was drowned this forenoon as he was bathing in the River after Parade.[17]

* * *

The men at Paisley were in camp but new barracks were being prepared for them, Quartermaster Carmichael writing to Sir James: 'I am very bussie fitting up Barracks here for your companies...the rooms will be ready for your men in a few days,'[18] and Watson wrote to the factor: 'We are pretty well settled here their is Barracks preparing for us with the greatest Expidition.'[19] In a further reference to these barracks, the minister of Abernethy received a letter from Sandie Grant, a Strathspey man currently living in Glasgow, in which he wrote:

You would be surprised how well the Strathspey Fencibles at Paisley look with their new cloathing & with shoulder belts – they live like gentlemen in their Barracks & are much liked by the inhabitants.[20]

This description of life in army barracks is somewhat at odds with the account given by Scobie,[21] who over a century later wrote: 'The newly built barrack rooms had few conveniences or comforts, and the accommodation was often extremely insanitary and bad. The men slept two in a bed. Sometimes there were no kitchens and food had to be cooked in the barrack room. There were no arrangements for washing and the men performed their ablutions in the open air under the barrack yard pump.' Haythornthwaite[22] gives a similar picture of barrack life writing: 'The barracks which resulted were thoroughly unpleasant...there was no sanitation save open tubs in the dormitories in which beds often had to be shared.' Veronica Bamfield[23] describes the barracks from the army wife's point of view: 'The wives and families of the Other Ranks were permitted...to live in screened-off corners of the barrack rooms. On the other side of the sacking lived anything up to eighty men. Sanitary arrangements were non existent and typhoid fever and tuberculosis endemic; the last brought about by the lack of any facilities for drying clothes when the men came in from sentry duty. The rough communal kitchens bulged with women elbowing each other for space in the greasy smoke-laden atmosphere.' Occasionally, wives were permitted to live in rented accommodation nearby[24] but no allowance was paid to a soldier in respect of either his wife or his children.[25]

Prior to 1792 the army had no barracks outside castles and forts. Troops either slept in tents or were quartered in ale houses. The soldier had to pay 4d a day to the Innkeeper out of his pay of 6d for which the Innkeeper had to supply him with food and beer.[26] With the rapid growth of manufacturing industries and the consequent appearance of revolutionary agitators the need for small bodies of soldiers in many towns became apparent. Pitt therefore appointed Colonel Oliver Delancey as Barracks Master to oversee the building of permanent barracks to house the troops but, according to Fortescue,[27] Delancey's buildings were more like large police stations and more suited to the maintenance of internal order than military barracks. As a result they were said to be less beneficial to the army than they should have been.

* * *

The government was still regretting the limited use to which the existing Fencible regiments could be put by their exemption from serving outside Scotland except in the event of an invasion of England. In October, Henry

Dundas now proposed that a new Fencible corps be raised in all respects on the same footing as the old one but with two important differences. Firstly, it was to serve in any part of Great Britain or Ireland or Jersey and Guernsey as well as Scotland and secondly, the new recruits were to have ten guineas bounty money instead of five.[28] This proposal was not well received. Sir James drafted the following reply: 'I would be extremely averse to making any new propositions to the private men in my Fencible Regiment, especially in the quarters they now occupy [Paisley] where they have gain'd so much credit by their behaviour, & where the minds of the people seem to be changed much for the better since they went there, great circumspection must still be required,' but on due reflection he did not send this note but instead wrote: 'The more I think of it the more I see the Delicacy & perhaps Danger of interfering with the Fencible Regts. in the manner proposed – I therefore must earnestly give you my opinion against it and when I do so, I hope you and His Majesty will be satisfied that it is from the purest motives of disinterested Zeal.'[29]

The Lt Colonel was of the same opinion as the Colonel and wrote to Sir James from Forres: 'I'm sorry for this 2d ill-judged attempt on the Fencible Regts. the first ruined our discipline, & I think this gives the Coup de Grace to that sort of internal defence in future – a man never now will enlist in the Fencibles but under the impression that means are to be used to break bargain with him – his situation ought to be as sacredly guarded as a militia man in England – and no such attempts have ever been made on them.'[30]

Rumours reached Sir James that one of his company commanders, Capt. Cumming of Logie, had been openly discussing these proposals. Sir James was terrified that the men would see this as another betrayal and would mutiny again. He immediately wrote to Cumming telling him in no uncertain terms to keep quiet on the subject:

> For God's sake never mention such an idea, as the present Fencible Regiments going out of Scotland – as you know Government has expressed no such intention – and it would be highly improper to start it
>
> The intentions of Government are to raise other Fencible Regiments to go to any parts of Great Britain or Ireland – I was very much surprised when Mr Carmichael told me you had taken up such a thought – I earnestly request that you may never again say a word about the matter but to contradict it.[31]

Eventually the whole idea was dropped and these new Fencible regiments were never raised.

* * *

Some shuffling of the companies now took place so that on November 1st four companies were stationed at headquarters in Paisley, three at Stranraer, two at Wigton and one at Girvan. Detachments were posted at various small towns and villages between Ballantrae and Gatehouse. The Lt Colonel had been granted extended leave by the Commander in Chief for the period September 1st 1794 until March 1795. Second Major John Grant of Achindown had also been on extended leave since May leaving the amorous Glenmoriston as the only officer of Field rank with the regiment which was only 606 strong, still 434 short of full establishment.[32]

The Lt Colonel was at home for the birth of yet another son and was able to write to Sir James on November 12th: 'Your sister was this morning safely delivered of a fine Boy*...both are in a good way.'[33]

Another officer on extended leave was the chaplain, the Rev. James Grant. He wrote to the factor from Inverness enquiring after his health and giving news of own:

> I hope you have got free of the Rose** in your face, which you complained of, when I saw you – & that Mrs Grant & the young folks are well. On Wednesday last I met with a little accident, which has confined me here since, at the west end of the bridge, my horse being smooth shod, came down all fours & my left leg under him. Providentially there is no fracture nor dislocation, but the knee and ankle considerably bruised – Dr Robertson immediately prescribed leeches & the affected parts are constantly kept moist with Goulard water. There is scarce any pain now – at least very little – except when I move or turn – but am obliged to lie continually in bed. The recovery however advances fast – & I hope I shall be able to get home in some conveyance or other during the week.[34]

Footnotes:
  *This little boy who was named Edward survived for less than a month.
  **Erysipelas.

On December 1st there was a mutiny in the Breadalbane Fencible regiment which was stationed at Glasgow. This had repercussions for the First Fencibles because a small fracas that had taken place a few days earlier in Paisley between some men of the First Fencibles and some local inhabitants now got blown up out of all proportion. A brief account of the Breadalbane mutiny will therefore be given here.

On the night of November 27th the sole prisoner in the guard house of the Breadalbane Fencibles was a deserter from the 68th Regiment of Foot. One of the guards, a private Hugh Robertson, by lack of attention, allowed the prisoner to escape. Robertson was then himself confined to the guard house to await court martial and an almost inevitable flogging. On December 1st his companions in the regiment, feeling that this would be an unjustly severe punishment, freed him as the court martial was assembling. For 15 days the mutineers held authority in defiance but then four of the ring leaders, John Malloch, Duncan Stewart, Ludovick McNaughton and John McMartin gave themselves up and offered to stand trial on behalf of all the mutineers. As they were being marched to Edinburgh where the court martial was to be held rioting broke out again and two officers were attacked. A loyal company of the battalion quelled the riot and the ring leaders, Alexander Sutherland, John Scrimgeour, and Donald McCallum were arrested and also brought to Edinburgh to stand trial with their companions.

At the court martial, which opened on January 6th and lasted until January 23rd, all seven were found guilty. Sutherland, McCallum, Malloch and Stewart were sentenced to death. McNaughton was sentenced to receive 1500 lashes, and Scrimgeour and McMartin to 1000 lashes each. Lord Adam whilst wishing to set an example and at the same time show some clemency confirmed the sentences and ordered Sutherland to be 'shot to death' at Musselburgh on January 27th. He then suspended the sentences on the others who were to receive a Royal pardon on condition that they enlisted in the 60th Royal American Regiment which was then stationed in the West Indies. McMartin, Scrimgeour and McNaughton preferred a flogging to service in the West Indies but, after each having suffered 500 lashes inflicted on two successive days, their resolve broke and they finally agreed to go to the West Indies.[35]

The First Fencible riot had been first reported to Sir James by Glenmoriston on November 18th:

> We had a very unpleasant thing happen here on Thursday last, a riot betwixt some of the Light Company and some towns people, there was a great Fair in town and drinks going on all sides, the sheriff has been taking a Precognition for some days past about it, and I am obliged to sign a Bond of Cautionry for the mens appearance at any time they are called for. I fear it may breed bad blood betwixt them and the Inhabitants.[36]

When he heard of this commotion Sir James instructed Glenmoriston not to leave the regiment until the Lt Colonel rejoined. Fearful that he would be recalled before his leave expired, the Lt Colonel wrote to Sir James on November 27th:

> I was electrified last night by a letter from Logie informing me you had ordered major Grant Glen morisson not to move till I joined – If that is the case he must of necessity remain with them a very considerable time, as from the situation of my family & affairs it is impossible for me to leave home...
>
> I hope therefore you'll see no impropriety in Achindown Commanding as he is now at Paisley & if I may speak my sentiments the fittest person of the two by far.[37]

These disturbances at Glasgow and Paisley thoroughly scared Lord Adam who sent an urgent note to Sir James on December 5th saying: 'In the unpleasant situation of things here – particularly at Glasgow and Paisley it becomes my Duty, to request your attendce & that of all officers in N.B. as soon as possible.'[38]

On December 7th Achindown wrote from Paisley to Alexander Grant in Edinburgh 'in the absence of Major Grant Glenmoriston who has gone to Stranraer':

> As to the Riot it is by no means of such a serious nature as it has been represented at Edinburgh, it was a drunken frolick, being a market day many of the disorderly kind of the Inhabitants got drunk and five or six of the Light Company being late out of their quarters, a scuffle ensued and some damage done in the house they were in, there was neither want of discipline or disobedience of orders, only

the men were not willing to go to Jail but to the Guard house where they remained till Bailled out by their Commanding officer – I have a letter from Lord Adam Gordon ordering a Court of enquiry and report to him, which I am to order tomorrow – I have just now received a Rout of March from here with the four companies at this place for Dumfries when the court of Enquiry is over.[39]

On December 16th Achindown was able to report to Sir James:

I did not know anything about the riot at Paisley till I came to Edin. on my way to join, it made a great noise there, owing to it being ill represented by the Sheriff Substitute of Paisley...I received a letter from Lord Adam ordering a court of enquiry...and report to him which I did and it turned out to be nothing more than a drunken affray betwixt a few of the light company...and some country people...who called the Soldiers Highland B – rs which the soldiers resented & they came to blows.

At the same time Achindown wrote to Lady Grant informing her also, of the incident at Paisley, but couching his letter in more genteel language: 'I...must now say something to Lady Grant about the Riot at Paisley...calling them Highland something which was resented by the Soldiers.'[40]

* * *

In December regimental headquarters moved from Paisley to Dumfries, the division at Paisley marching south on the 10th and setting up headquarters at Dumfries on December 13th.[41]

The journey from Paisley to Dumfries was undertaken in the most trying conditions. The road was in a bad state of repair and was in constant use. In addition it rained heavily throughout the four day march. Watson described the march to Lady Grant in a letter of December 13th:

We have this moment arrived here after one of the severest marches that Possibly has been Performed in this Country for many years – no less a distance than 89 miles in four days and the worst and Heaviest road in Scotland – However thank God we have performed it wonderfully well...to add to our difficulties we were obliged to Carry Rations along with us on purpose to Give the men at the different Halting Places.[42]

On December 16th Achindown also wrote to her Ladyship:

I arrived here with the first division...upon Saturday and Capt.

Cumming with the last Dn last night, we had a most disagreeable march, the stages were long, being obliged to come by Moffat, in order to avoid falling in with a part of the Hopton Regiment...we had continual rains all the way.[43]

* * *

Lt Colonel Cumming was still on leave at Forres. He had been exempted by Lord Adam Gordon from a General Order for all Officers and men to return to their regiments on account of the death of his newborn son Edward, although his daughter Louisa 'was recovering slowly'.[44] He was also involved in a prolonged legal battle to acquire the lands of Gordonstoun upon the death of Sir William Gordon together with a substantial portion of Sir William's fortune.

He wrote to the factor from Forres on December 31st: 'My friends in Strathspey won't be sorry to hear, that at a <u>certain persons death</u>, my chance is as good, as my friends cou'd desire – I was present there yesterday opening repositories.' The factor also received a letter on the same day from Geo. Cumming, a merchant in Forres, stating that: 'Sir Wm Gordons papers was look'd at yesterday & am happy to hear Altyre gets the whole Lands and no doubt a part of the cash of which I am told there is no less as £70,000.'[45]

The Lt Colonel, as well as attending to his estate and personal affairs, was also involved in recruiting for the First Fencibles. He was generous to the new recruits from Strathspey in allowing them extended Christmas and New Year leave, writing to the factor:

I am happy to have it in my power to oblige the Strathspey recruits by allowing them to remain till Xmas is over with their friends – I shall be perfectly satisfied if they are all here on Friday the 9th Jany. and were it not that I cannot say how soon an order may come for our moving, I would willingly let them remain till the Old New year is over – but that is impossible.[46]

The Lt Colonel was not too impressed with the calibre of some of the recruits, writing Sir James two letters on the subject on January 4th:

There are two men of Achindowns – one of Delshangies – one of Lt. Stewart's and a 2d. of Ensn MacDonalds (besides the man I rejected) which are a disgrace to the name or appearance of a recruit – Achindown has two or three upwards of 70 – Stewart has a sort of deformed idiot, & MacDonald's is a debauched Kings-eviled*, drunken, change keeper of Inverness near 70 – It is cheating government, the marching them south or keeping them an hour on pay.[47]

In the second letter he rather repeated himself:

What shall be done with 2 or 3 of the horrible fellows who are here – Ensn. MacDonald has another drunken old change keeper 70 years of age & terribly Cut with the Evil – Stewart has a deformed fool & Achindown 2 or 3 ten years older than himself – in short I'm ashamed to see them at parade.[48]

* * *

At this time there was some confusion with regard to the ordering of pistols, Glenmoriston writing to Sir James on New Year's day 1795:

I am just favoured with yours inclosing Lord Amhersts Letter about Pistols I am certain there never was any ordered for the men...I think it would be right to corr'spond with Coln. Cumming on the Subject...Pistols were ordered for the officers when we were in Linlithgow by Coln. Cumming.[50]

The Lt Colonel replied to Sir James's enquiry stating quite openly that the pistols were for the officers for their own protection in case of another mutiny. In this the Lt Colonel showed considerable foresight when he wrote:

I never could have taken upon me to give an order, in which your pocket was so deeply concerned without a previous communication, with you – The pistols never were ordered nor ever ought to be; they are an unnecessary incumberance...the officers getting pistols which I ordered by desire of the whole at Lithgow, was more for protection agst. their own men, than an enemy – The officers pistols were ordered from Innes the Gunsmith at Edin. Mr Mckenzie & Rippachie knows it & they ought to be served out to the officers immediately.[51]

Footnote:
*King's evil or Scrofula – tuberculosis of the skin and Lymph glands, particularly of the neck, was known as the King's Evil, as it was thought to be cured by the touch of the monarch.[49]

Rippachie, who had been passed over for the post of second major, still firmly believed that he ranked as the senior Captain and the matter came to a head on December 29th when he went so far as to write to the Commander in Chief on the subject:

> Your Lordships order for the 1st Fencible Regt. to furnish one major & one capt. for the Genl. Court Martial to be held in Edinr. Castle on 6th January...The order and Detail of the Court, Major Grant put into my hand & told me that the Eldest Capn behove to take that duty – I said it was what I expected...Capt. Cumming made ansr that as he was the eldest Capt...he insisted that he should be put in orders for the Court martial...The major ordered the Adjt to put Capt. Cumming in orders This happened in presence of severals of the offrs. – By this single order, My Lord, I am at once deprived of my Rank in the Regt...
>
> Major Grant can not deny that untill this moment on all Duty of Honor, fatigue I was the Eldest Captain...I beg therefore to mention to your Lordship that I think myself grievously injured by Major Grant...I must beg...your Lordship, at any rate will excuse my doing duty in the Regt untill the Question of Rank is tried.[52]

Sir James, as ever, tried to pour oil on troubled waters by writing an open letter to 'The Commanding Offr and Capts of the Strathspey or 1st Fencible Regt.':

> Gentlemen,
>
> That no confusion may arise in the Regt. in Conseq'ce of the dispute as to rank betwixt Capt. Grant late Capt. Lieutenant and Capt. Cumming on behalf of himself & other Offrs. standing before Capt Grant in the Roster or List of Captains –
>
> Ordered that Untill the question is decided by the Commanr. in Chief to whom it is now referred or by an other person or persons having power to decide according to the rules of the Army that Captn. Grant may hold the same precedency, as has hitherto been allowed him by the Offrs. themselves since the Establishment –
>
> Ordered that Capt. Cumming being appointed by the

Commanding Officer at Head Qrs. to attend the Court Martial in Edinr. in conseqce. of the Summons of one Major & one Capt. from the Regt. by the Commr. in chief and being now there shall remain & attend accordingly as Capt at the said Court Martial but without prejudice to Capt Grants claim of precedency.[53]

When informed of the situation the Lt Colonel sprang to Rippachie's defence with some withering comments on the abilities of Captain Cumming of Logie:

I was astonished this evening by a letter from Rippachie saying that Logie had claimed rank over him & had in consequence gone to Edinr. on the Court-martial – He does not mention the reasons for such an unprecedented step but says that the major ordered it, in consequence of Logies being the eldest Captn. of the Regt. at least that the adjutant told the major, Logie was such – It is a fact that Rippachie started with us as eldest Capt. & had he insisted on it, wou'd I have no doubt, been additional major – but he very wisely preferred the more lucrative office – what pretensions Logie can have, I cannot divine – He surely is not, nor ever will be fit to command the Regt. for I always thought a company was fully up to his meridian and if with those you have he ever was to become a field officer, Lord have mercy upon your Corps – I know not the merits of the business but sure I am that Rippachie is the best officer in your Regt. and that if you allow him to be put over or trampled upon by a man who is an ignoramus, & perfectly unfit for such a situation, you do injustice to yourself & the Regt.[54]

Letters then flew backwards and forwards. On January 15th the Lt Colonel wrote to Rippachie:

I am perfectly ignorant on what footing the three Capts wish to deprive you of the rank you have so long held undisputed...your waving being 2nd Major is also in your favour – I have written Sir James my opinion of it & think it must end to your wish.[55]

and he again expressed his views to Sir James in his usual forthright manner:

From what I know or can see of the matter Rippachie has the most undoubted right to be the eldest – His waving the majority too is entirely in his favour – over and above all this, I take the liberty in confidence, to tell you, that he is by far in my opinion the best

137

officer of the whole, and the only one fit to command the Regt. and it is for your interest & credit to keep him in the situation he started.[56]

Rippachie then wrote a long letter to Sir James from Dumfries arguing why he should be the eldest Captain, concluding:

> I hope to be able to show that Capt. Cumming in particular, as well as every other Capt in the Regt. knew that I was to be the eldest Capt. and acquiesced therein even before the list was given in, and on different occasions afterwards, in doing duty with the Regt. and otherwise Capt Cumming & the other Captains also acquiesced.[57]

Sir James, anxious to see matters settled amicably, called upon Captain Cumming of Logie at his Edinburgh home to discuss the matter and sent an account of this meeting to Rippachie on January 23rd, telling Rippachie that Captain Cumming:

> told me that he could not by any means give up his pretensions to precedency...but as I thought it improper to trouble Lord Amherst in these times, with discussions of that nature, that he was willing to let his claim lie over to a future, & more proper period – as therefore you enjoy the precedency in the meantime, I imagine this delay will be equally agreeable to you.[58]

and there the matter was to rest for a while but it was by no means permanently settled.

The court martial which Logie was attending in Edinburgh, was the trial of the Breadalbane mutineers. On February 16th, after Alexander Sutherland had been 'shot to death' at Musselburgh, the First Fencibles were paraded under arms at 12 o'clock at headquarters in Dumfries to have the sentence of the court martial read to them.[59] They can therefore, have been under no illusions as to the penalty for mutiny. Despite this they were shortly to mutiny again and for reasons very similar to those that started the Breadalbane mutiny.

* * *

By now Sir James's son Frank had left the 97th Regiment and had been promoted to the rank of major in the newly formed Fraser Fencibles and wished to recruit men from the First Fencibles for his new regiment in order to pay for his majority. Sir James was perfectly agreeable to this as long as they were the worst soldiers in the regiment! On December 26th Glenmoriston wrote to Sir James:

Mr Watson and I with some of the other officers have been considering the best method of inlisting the Supernumerary men for Major Francis, the Idea is that Mr Watson & Achindown or me should go to the different out posts before any thing more is said about the matter as Mr Watson is so well acquainted with the men that both you and all of us would wish to part with from the Strathspey Fencibles and as it is of no consequence to my young Friend the Major if he gets but numbers...we are so terribly dispersed and will have near one hundred and I believe fifty miles to travel that it will take up a little time before we can settle and see the whole...I hope youl send Altyre word to get as many of the worst of the Recruits in the Country as possible for the Major, the men you mention shall be sent to Col. Fraser in a few days.[60]

Accordingly Watson, Achindown and the young Major Francis set out from Dumfries for the various outposts in the middle of January in the most atrocious weather. On arrival at Girvan on January 22nd Watson wrote to Sir James:

We arrived here this day about 4 o'Clock from air [sic!] having found at Sanquhar that the Hill Road to this place was inaccessible owing to the intense weather that Lately set in...what I have yet seen of the Detachment here under the command of Capt Allan Grant of your Company looks astonishingly well as to their appearance and Dress...I am well aware that everything that may tend to their happiness you are interested in. It would indeed be presumptious of me as an Inferior officer to mention the name or Character of a Superior officer but Still I Cannot help observing that the uniform attention that has at all times been shown to the Company under the command of this Captain is and has been truely meritorious –

and then he added as if surprised at his own presumption:

- in my weake opinion.[61]

On January 25th Achindown wrote to Sir James from Stranraer which the small party had now reached:

We arrived here last night about 8 o'Clock all well after leaving the head quarters of your Company & must confess I was highly pleased with the mens appearance and the Character they maintain after being so long in the place, there was not a single Complaint from the Commanding officer, or from the Inhabitants or had the men any complaint but seemed all perfectly happy & pleased.

and then he rather contradicted himself:

upon my arrival here last night I found a Corporal Simpson confined in the Guard house by Captain William Grant for allowing a deserter escape.[62]

That night the men were given dinner at Sir James's expense. On January 29th the party reached Wigton and Achindown wrote again to Sir James:

I paraded the two companies here this morning & found the men Clean & well dressed, & their arms in a very good state, no complaints of any kind they behave very orderly...

Serjeant John Grant of my Company Miss Grants recruit, is most anxious to get in to a Regiment of the line, and he would be no discredit to any Regiment in the Service, he wished to get in Volunteer, but I advise him otherwise, as he could not support himself in that Cappasity any time, & his chance would be but poor, he is a very desent young fellow & much attached to your familie and if you thought it proper, to give him an Ensignancy in your Fencible Regiment when one was vacant he would by it be able to save some pence, to enable him to go a volanteer in a Regiment of the line with same Rank, if I did not think him a deserving young man I would not take it upon myself to recommend him.[63]

and on February 2nd Adjutant Watson wrote from Kirkcudbright:

The oldest Inhabitants in this Country Scarcely Remembers such an Intense Frost and Depth of snow which in some places of the Road we Came yesterday was nearly from 5 to 6 feet Deep – we had much ado to get forward with four horses.[64]

Rippachie was unaware of the scheme afoot to supply Frank with recruits from the First Fencibles to pay for his Majority in the Fraser Fencibles. Thus on February 1st Whilst Achindown and his party were journeying through the thick snow from Wigtown to Kirkcudbright, he was writing indignantly to Sir James from Dumfries pointing out to him that his plan to rid the regiment only of its worst soldiers was liable to backfire:

Inclosed I send you a list of the men aluded to in my complaint against Mr Carmichael's conduct recruiting here...which you wish to be transmitted to you – Before I had received any information respecting this business all the Men of ours which Major Grant /Commanding Offr./ wished to discharge in consequence of your instructions to that Purpose were all accordingly discharged & again inlisted for the Fraser Fencible Regt. the others which are not thus mark'd, as I understand, were never intended to be discharged, and I am confident that it was owing to their being tamper'd with, and being encouraged by a very high Bounty which they were told they were to receive that occassioned their ever thinking of quitting your Regiment, and if Recruiting Parties are allowed to adopt such measures, it will, in my humble opinion, occassion discontent, and make one half of our best men desireous of getting off to other Corps, and by that means Your Regiment will be reduced to a skeleton.

and this was Rippachie's attached list:

Capt Rose's Co.	Drummager Waddle
Grenadier Co.	Drummer Armstrong +
	Richard Holt +
	Robert Allan +
	Alexander Bruce +
	Thos McChesnie Discharged & inlisted again
	Robert Dewar Do Do
	John Forsyth /Reduced Sergt/
Capt Grant Senr. Co.	James Robertson +
	John MacKenzie +
	John Roccastle. Discharged & inlisted
	Willm Milliken +
	Jas Cunningham Do Do
Light Compy.	George Grott[65]

It was easy enough for soldiers to obtain a discharge if they had influence and more particularly money, to buy a suitable replacement. The Rev. Alexander Henderson wrote from the Manse of Echt near Aberdeen to Sir James on March 28th:

John Henderson a Nephew of mine who inlisted with you at Elgin in May Seventeen hundred and ninety three, and has since that time been in the First Fencible Regiment under your Command...He had been but a short time in the Regiment till he repented...and applied earnestly to his friends to see if they could procure his discharge...Colonel Cumming promised to grant his discharge on procuring a good man in his place ...His friends were at considerable expense inlisting a man at Aberdeen...The mans name is Donald MacDonald, said to be a very stout & handsome young man near five foot ten inches high.

On May 5th Lord Adam wrote to Sir James saying that he had 'no objections to his discharging John Henderson Soldier in the 1st Fencible Regt. He having found a proper man in his room'.[66]

It now became apparent that Quartermaster Angus Sutherland, who was by now serving with the 97th Regiment, had been involved in some dubious activities. Rippachie, in his capacity as regimental paymaster, wrote to Sir James on February 2nd:

> Respecting the account due by Mr Sutherland and sent to you by Mr Frater for payment...my own opinion which I venture to give here for your satisfaction and on your account only, is that I consider the claim made on you for Payment to be a gross imposition – I saw these Goods Come to Forres & lodged in your storemill Mr Sutherlands private Direction on them and not marked as the furnishings for your Regt were. In short this was a private adventure of Mr Sutherlands for profit and with which you have no earthly concern, unless you have given Mr Sutherland a letter of credit or that Mr Frater can produce your order for furnishing such goods – if you give in to the claims for which Mr Sutherland is bound there is no saying where it may end – For at Linlithgow Bannockburn Kilmarnock & Edin. he owes large sums you are by no means bound for.[67]

* * *

The senior officers of the regiment had at this time two main concerns. The first was that the regiment was scattered far and wide and they unanimously felt that it would be to their great benefit as a regiment if they could be all stationed as one unit at Dumfries. On February 15th Achindown, now in command of the regiment, in the absence of the Lt. Colonel and First Major, made a plea to Sir James for the regiment to be united at Dumfries writing: 'We will never make an appearance as a Regiment till we are two or three months together in one place. I sincerely wish you could prevail upon Lord Adam to order us all in here for some little time how soon the weather would permitt. this town would for a short time contain us all' and again on February 17th: 'The benefit that would derive from our being embodied once more in one place, were it but for two months...was that the case I do think we would turn out to be one of the best looking Regiments in the Service.'[68] The situation in which the regiment found itself in being so widely scattered was by no means unique as Houlding[69] comments: 'The playing of the police role...required that individual regiments be very widely dispersed and preoccupied for lengthy periods of time. Training in consequence, suffered very considerably,' and he later comments: 'Ill housed, and often wretchedly cared for, the army in general knew that any opportunity for advanced training in peacetime was a luxury.'[70]

The second concern was that the regiment had no doctor. This was particularly worrying as the winter of 1795 was a severe one. Glenmoriston, who had gone on leave in early February, wrote to Sir James on February 14th that he had just arrived home having journeyed 'through mountains of snow'. The surgeon Dr Peter Grant had left to join the 122nd Regiment of Foot. At the end of January Dr John Grant was still with the 97th Regiment in Guernsey, although his father, the factor, had successfully persuaded Sir James to appoint him to succeed Dr Peter Grant as surgeon to the First Fencibles. On February 17th Achindown told Sir James: 'There is a number no less than 17 sick, bad of colds owing to the severity of the weather, and is very ill attended, a surgeon is much wanted.' On February 21st Watson wrote to Pat Copland, Sir James's clerk: 'Can you by any means learn when our surgeon is to join us I can assure you the Sooner the better...it may be easlie conceived what a state we shall be soon in for want of that necessary staff officer.'[71]

By February 22nd Achindown had changed his mind and was now of the view that the local civilian doctors could cope adequately with the needs of the regimental sick. 'No attention shall be wanting,' he wrote to Sir James, 'which can be paid, on my part, to the sick men of the Strathspey Fencibles, whom I have considered as entitled, in a particular manner, to every attention I can show them – I have generally had four or five of them under my care in our Infirmary...indeed any of them who are particularly indisposed, are sent immediately to the Infirmary...some few are presently affected with coughs and sore throats, as people in all situations have been, from the severity of the season.'[72] On March 3rd Watson wrote to Sir James: 'I am sorry to say that the major and Rippachie has been very ill with a severe cold and cough for this Two days past many of the men are Likewise very poorly in the same state – I humbly take the Liberty to suggest to you that the sooner our surgeon was ordered to join us the better.'[73] Rippachie must have recovered pretty quickly for he wrote to Sir James three days later: 'Our men here you may rest assured is well cared for, so that you need not be in the smallest degree uneasy that we have no surgeon with us. Dr Gilchrist is not only attentive to the men, but to the officers.'[74] Achindown also held Dr Gilchrist in high esteem telling Sir James: 'I cannot help Mentioning the attention Dr Gilchrist has paid to us. he has been most attentive to our men when Sick & wrote letters to the Surgeons at the Different Quarters to do the same.'[75]

The Lt Colonel, writing from Forres on March 9th, told Sir James: 'We are all dropping down here...with the influenza, which I see will go thro' us all.'[76] On March 27th Watson wrote to Sir James: 'I am sorry to inform you of the death of one of the Light Compy at Kirkcudbright who died on the 20th Current in a Consumption which made such a Rapid Progress as to Baffle all medical aid his name was Donald McDonald* a handsome youth – of 20...Doctor Grant arrived here Late on Wednesday Evening however I am happy to say that we are now more Healthy than at any one period since we have been in this place.'[77]

So Dr John Grant, having left the 97th Regiment, arrived to take up his post as regimental surgeon on March 28th, writing to Sir James the day after his arrival: 'I beg leave to take the earliest opportunity of acquainting you with my Arrival at this place – I arrived last night late – I have seen the sick here who are very few in number and not at all dangerously ill – there are no Fevers – There is however one Lad of the name of Fraser in the Major's Company who is pretty far gone in consumption...I was under the necessity of waiting at London for more than a fortnight for the day of Examination – I got myself qualified Surgeon.'[79] Prebble[80] states that the effects of the

---

Footnote:

*There were no less than eleven men with the name of Donald MacDonald in the regiment. This young man was one of the original recruits and not the replacement for John Henderson. See Mackintosh.[78]

influenza epidemic 'would have been worse without the professional dedication of Surgeon John Grant', but the epidemic appears to have been over before Dr Grant reached the regiment.

Dr Peter Grant's departure from the regiment was associated with a good deal of acrimony. On April 28th he wrote to Sir James from Wells in Somerset: 'I observed in the Gazette of the 28th Ulto that I was Superceded in the 1st Fencibles – I saw it with regret, but it was only what I had to expect. From the manner, however, in which it was done it was evident my interest was not considered...I find that the agents...have now an idea of disallowing me some months Pay...I think it my duty to acquaint you, my dear Sir, that I mean to insist on being allowed pay etc. for the whole time which I was in your Regt.'[81] On April 14th William White, a civilian doctor at Girvan wrote to Sir James: 'Your late Surgeon Dr Peter Grant engaged me in my medical capacity to attend the party here...for 5£ p. year... Captain Grant...swears he will not pay it and as he is determinedly obstinate and ill natured...I pray therefore that your Honour will order Captain Grant to pay me my account.'[82]

The bad weather that winter prevented many of the men getting home leave, Adjutant Watson informing Sir James on March 10th: 'I have perus'd the several petitions for furlough, and after Consulting the major and the Rest of the officers present, they are of the same opinion with myself, that it will be attended with certain Ruine to the few that would be full hardy enough to go all the way to the north at this season of the year when it is more than probable that many of them would be scarcely Let down at their Respective Homes when they would be obliged, to Return again.'[83] Watson cannot have seen the word 'foolhardy' in writing. The Scottish accent can be heard in his phonetic way of spelling the word.

* * *

Sir James now, but for the only time in the six years of the life of the regiment, showed some irritation with his Lt Colonel writing to him on March 16th:

> The sooner Capt Rose, Lieut Reynolds etc come up with the Recruits the better as they are much wanted with the Regt. & Lord Adam Gordon says when others have gone North what is to prevent a little exertion on their part to come South, you are included in this observation

At the same time I suspect from what has happened at Gordonstown you will be obliged to remain at home till the further inspection of the papers & if so you should write to Lord Adam Gordon yourself.

and again the following day:

I have received yours with the <u>Return</u> comparing it with the <u>Return of the Strathspey Recruits</u> sent to me formerly...I find one man <u>omitted in the present return</u> who is mentioned in it viz one <u>James Potts</u> be kind enough to explain that.[84]

In Forres the Lt Colonel had over a hundred new recruits ready to march south to Dumfries to augment the regimental establishment and he wrote to Sir James on March 6th: 'When the weather becomes fit to march, which probably yet will take 20 days, you will recollect there is from 100 to 120 men, and that it will be necessary that some person of weight shou'd have the charge of them – Reynolds wou'd have done, but I am sorry to hear by a letter from him yesterday, that he is ruined by cautionary* & that he knows not what to do or where to go, & that he is afraid that he can't appear to march the men – but he is to let me see him soon & explain matters.' Unable to stop himself having a dig at the quality of some of the recruits he went on: 'There is one Strathspey recruit has a long & a short leg and Achindown has three unfit for us.'[85]

In Lt Reynold's absence the Lt Colonel had ordered Capt Rose of Holme to march south with the men but Reynolds managed to sort out his problems and on March 12th the Lt Colonel was able to inform Sir James: 'Reynolds has weathered the <u>storm</u>, is returned, & marches with the men, when the weather will admit of it – so they can do without Holme, as Reynolds is much fitter & will walk step for step with them,' but the fitness of some of the men concerned him for he continued: 'There is 2 or 3 here I am afraid will not be able for the march – Serjt. MacPherson's brother is threatened with a consumption & the Strathspey man, in the venereal, with perhaps one or two more – may I take any opportunity to send them to Leith by water, which wou'd be a great help to them.'[86] Even though Reynolds was now available the Lt Colonel still insisted that Capt. Rose and his son go along with the recruits, writing to Sir James on March 22nd: 'I am just now

Footnote:
    *cautionery = standing bail for, standing security for.

sending an express to them [Capt. Rose & his son] with positive orders [to join the recruits at Grantown], and if they disobey I will report them.'[87]

Although he was determined that his officers should obey his orders, the Lt Colonel was not so keen to obey orders himself which caused Lord Adam to write indignantly to Sir James:

Private   Abbey Edin = April 6th 1795

D Sir James

    Your Lt Col is most importunate, to remain absent – and I have been oblidged, to write Him – I cannot feel at liberty, to depart from H. My's <u>positive</u> order – for all officers, to be present – at <u>this</u> <u>season</u> of the year – & I give it to you, as my opinion – that It would be much wiser, for Him, to resign – and stay, to look after his immense – additional – fortune & numerous family, than to be at all times, asking leave of absence – which Both you, & He well know, has been – & will be the case – I remain My D Sir – at all times much and very faithfully – yours

                              Ad: Gordon G.

    Colonel

    S Jas Grant etc etc etc[88]

Despite this rebuke the Lt Colonel still prevaricated writing to Sir James on April 7th: 'Lord Adam has given me a peremptory order to be at quarters by the 10th...I have not said to him whether I cou'd or would be able to join by that time.' He then went on to inform Sir James of continuing troubles with the new recruits: 'The Fraser mentioned was...one of Logie's recruits – he has since thought proper to desert on the march from Grantown to Aviemore...I am resolved to get him and have him to our Regt. for the rascally manner he took to leave us,' and he went on: 'There is a rascal one MacPherson, the fellow with pox in his head, who told me he was able enough to march, shammed at Grantown & wou'd go no further – I wrote the factor to send him down here, to order him off by sea, as [Dr] Straith thinks little is the matter with him.'[89]

The new recruits reached Dumfries in mid April, Achindown writing to Sir James on April 20th: 'Captain Rose. Lieut Reynolds & Ensign James MacDonald arrived here Thursday last with about 104 Recruits. I am sorry to say the Recruits from Strathspey do not altogether agree with the high opinion I had of them.'[90]

* * *

The regiment was still having trouble with its uniforms and with Mr Gloag, Quartermaster James Carmichael writing to Sir James on April 21st:

> I find by a letter from the agents...that the cloathing of this year is to be made up in London, if they are made in such a manner as those that were sent by Mr Gloag from London last August...they are such (that what came) that they will hardly fit the Battalion men, and many of the Coats with small and with Large Buttons, and no white cloth Turnouts, nor Fringe on Shoulders, nor WhiteLace...
>
> The Recruits are arrived from the north, and we are making up slop jackets for them out of the Cloth that remained in Store, that we may be something uniform when we take the Field – The Taylors will be immediately idle for want of cloth, as I am informed by a letter from Mr Gloag's partner that he cannot send me any Cloth till he has an order from Mr Gloag.[91]

There were now expectations that the regiment would soon be reunited at Dumfries, as the officers wished. It was Watson's opinion, as well as that of most of the officers, that the Strathspey men, who were mainly in the Colonel's company, should be spread around in other companies as a steadying influence. He therefore wrote to Sir James on May 5th:

> I believe Colonel Cumming will readily agree that...what is absolutely necessary...is for you giving up the Strathspey Company now to Run their Chance amongst the Rest...as they are undoubtedly the best men in the Regt by dividing them as patteran [pattern] men amongst the whole will give every man an Emulation who [how] to excell in the Line of his profession.'[92]

Sir James must have agreed with this suggestion because on May 14th Watson wrote to him: 'I am happy that the matter I took the Liberty of suggesting has met with your approbation,'[93] but they were soon to be proved very wrong in their assumption that the Strathspey men would set a good example to the rest of the regiment.

Glenmoriston wrote to Sir James on May 10th from Dumfries: 'I am just returned from Kirkcudbright and went the Length of Wigtown found our people well every where I suppose we will soon be brought together which is much required after being so long and so much scatterd, we have the recruits drilling here and beginning to look very well when Altyre arrives which I think will be in the course of a few days we will have the Regt. to form anew and I suppose to mix the young soldiers with the old ones.'[94] The regiment was reunited at Dumfries in the middle of May and James Watson commented to Sir James on May 28th: 'We are Coming on in the discipline Remarkably well & we are constantly at it from morning to night without the Least Intermission.'[95]

* * *

The Lt Colonel, following his recent good fortune, had changed his name to Gordon-Cumming and had rejoined the regiment at Dumfries from where he wrote to Sir James on June 2nd regarding recruiting malpractices by Sergeant Major Donald Ross:

> You have heard of the disgraceful shameful manner in which the serjeant Major left the Regt. in my abscence – there appear to be many well founded claims agst him by several of the recruits – you will therefore (as he'll probably be ashamed to meet you) write the factor, by no means to clear with him, till you inform him all here are done justice to.[96]

On the following day Pat Copland wrote to the factor:

> Very great complaints have come to Sir James against Sergeant Major Ross for the manner he left the Regt. at Dumfries and the well founded complaints against him by several of the recruits – Sir James is very sorry that he gave ground for any complaint of this nature which he suspects must have proceeded from his going in to take too much liquor – Colonel Cumming writes to Sir James that you may by no means clear with him till you are informed that all the Regiment are done justice to as his intromissions were long and a good deal of money went through his hands – Sir James desires you with Mr Ross may make a full account Dr. & Cr. as soon as possible as Mr Ross wrote to Sir James he was to call on him at Edin. and has not done it – he suspects he has gone home in consequence of the allegations against him from the Regiment.

The factor replied directly to Sir James on June 8th:

> I am really sorry that Mr Ross should leave the Regt. without settling accounts with the Recruits. I saw his accounts...and they seemed to be exact. He has not yet come North. When he does I

will speak to him & endeavour to get matters cleared up but it cannot be final until a note of the mens claims against him is sent down from the Regt.

but the Sergeant Majors accounts were not exact for on the same day Watson wrote to Sir James:

I hope that the Claims now Remaining...against our late sergeant major will be But few for the very night before his departure, in the presence of Lt Reynolds I made him pay up several sums – the idea of settling with the Colonel as he went through Edin. I well knew this was a mere pretence – to the amount of £6 -15 – stg which he certainly meant to go off with.[97]

Earlier Watson had written an account of their last meeting:

His Late Conduct has absolutely gone beyond precedent, particularly towards the Recruits he brought to the Regiment he wish'd to defraud them to a <u>man</u> and I being ordered...to Investigate...the Claims of the Recruits against the Said Serjeant Major I am sorry to say they were in such a Train, that I did not Imagine that any Man born could have been Capable of such gross abuses – & Impositions as he had endeavoured, to Impose upon them His Conduct to me – was Really what – I never Experienced – in any Situation in Life, – through drunkenness and being so Glaringly detected – wrought upon the mans mind in such a manner as to Render him in a State of Madness – the Last Interview I had with him was about 11 o'clock at night with a party of the poor Recruits who had been Grossly Impos'd upon by him. I had a Great deal to do In preventing him from Committing Voilence upon them as for myself the usage I Receiv'd was – <u>malicious</u> and Particularly more so as I never merited such Treatment – from any man much Less from him whom I always supported
...I humbly Recommend Serjeant Hugh MacBean to be his Successor.[98]

* * *

The weather in June 1795 in south west Scotland was pretty miserable for the Lt Colonel commented in a letter of June 2nd to Sir James that: 'The weather is very much against us, it is so wet we can't make use of our field tho' all are very desirous of exercising themselves,' and Watson commented on June 8th:

'We are constantly out when the weather permits – I trust you will hear good accounts of us soon.'[99] On the same day the Lt Colonel wrote to Sir James: 'If you can learn any thing from Ld Adam, with regard to our movements, I hope you'll immediately communicate – as this state of uncertainty is unpleasant – we have improved considerably since we got together and don't lose a day that it's possible to be out – If we remain here a fortnight I think the old part of us will do us no discredit – tho' there's more sick than I cou'd wish, that is between thirty & 40 – but very few of that number dangerously so.'[100]

The sick report[101] for June 15th submitted by the surgeon's mate Thos Stephen showed that there were 33 sick and unfit for duty and that there were a miscellaneous set of illnesses affecting the regiment. These were:

Cough – spitting blood
Cough – hectic
Cough etc
Cough & Pain at breast
Debility
Boil on toe
   on arm – 2 men
   on legs
   on leg
Gun shot wound – Sgt Beaton. A. Fraser
Amputated leg – John Grant
Piles
Fistula in Ano
Dyspepsia
Herpes on leg
Blister at Breast – 3 men
Flux
Sciatica
Excoriation of thighs
Wound in leg
Fever – in hospital – 2 men
Feverish – 3 men
Rheumatism
Bilious Complaint
Venereal Warts
Erysipelas

Relations with the local Dumfries people seem to have been good for on May 28th David Stacey, Provost of Dumfries and one of the Deputy Lieutenants of the County wrote to Sir James:

> I have much pleasure in informing you, that during the stay of the Regt. in this Town, their Conduct has been such as to merit the Good opinion of every person, and I have not heard the least Complaint against a single Individual of them.[102]

Accordingly therefore, the magistrates of Dumfries had no hesitation in asking for the help of soldiers to assist in arresting a troublesome tinker, John O'Neil, his two sons and their wives. On June 9th a party of First Fencibles under the command of Sergeant Peter Beaton set out to arrest the O'Neill family but in the fray the O' Neils wounded sergeant Beaton and Privates John Grant and Alexander Fraser. On the following day the Lt Colonel wrote to Sir James describing the incident:

> Last night the civil Magistrate applied for a party of a serjt. corporal & 12, to aid in apprehending some Irish tinkers who were in an house about a mile & an half distant in order to comprehend them – On the party's approaching the house & requiring admittance the tinkers fired on them and wounded Serjeant Beaton very severely in the hand & groin – John Grant of Glenmorison a Grenadier in both legs, & one Fraser of the light in the arm – the two last are very much hurt as the tinkers arms were loaded with very ragged sluggs & small bullets – a surgeon immediately attended from town & dressed them, but he has not yet been able to extract the lead – the party soon after the tinkers fired, pushed on to the house fired in at the windows without doing any mischief, forced the door & tho' they had suffered so severely, abstained from bayonetting them when they called for mercy
>
> One man & two women in mens cloaths were brought in prisoners – two men in the darkness, made their escape, but one of them is apprehended and brought in this morning and a party is just going out on information to apprehend the other – our Surgeon is confined – but you may be assured that every attention will be shown to the poor fellows, who are as good men as any in

the Regt. – Fraser's arm rec'd the whole charge, which by the by saved his heart – I'm much afraid Grant will be lame for life as he rec'd his wound in the small of both legs – Beaton I hope will soon be well.[103]

On June 13th the Lt Colonel sent a progress report to Sir James on the state of the wounded men:

I am sorry to inform you that I was present in the Infirmary this morning with Dr Gilchrist when poor John Grant's leg was amputated – the mortification was advancing rapidly – and the leg was so wounded as to be unfit for use – it was cut off below the knee – he bore it with heroism and the Drs think he will recover – Fraser's arm is also in a bad way, but they have not yet pronounced on him – Beaton will do well. They are in a most comfortable room and has the utmost attention care and kindness.[104]

On June 28th Dr Gilchrist sent a further progress report to Sir James:

Alexr. Frasers arm is greatly mended, and now, to all appearance, doing very well – For these two night past John Grant has been suffering a good deal of pain and distress, from the large sores which he has, poor fellow, on both legs, so that yesterday we were again a little uneasy about him. Today he is not so poorly as yesterday – Beaton is doing well enough and the consumptive patient (Chisholm) is going on as before.[105]

On August 10th Dr Gilchrist wrote again to Sir James

I am truly concerned to inform you that, after the expectations we had entertained of poor John Grant's recovery, there now appears to be little room to hope for it. Though he was reduced to the most weak and emaciated state after the amputation of the one leg, and the great discharge which took place from the extensive sore produced in the other, yet, as the parts came to have a healing and favourable appearance, we flattered ourselves that he would recover...but for some weeks past, it appeared that he was making no Progress, notwithstanding the use of every cordial & nourishing thing that his stomach would receive.

Beaton & Fraser are almost well.[106]

Beaton and Fraser survived but John Grant died on August 16th. The people of Dumfries were determined to treat the injured soldiers and their

153

relatives properly, David Stacey writing to Sir James on September 23rd:

> At a meeting of the Gentlemen of the County, a short while ago they agreed to pay Fifteen Guineas for behoof of the poor fellows who were wounded by the O'Neils, and at the same time the magistrates agreed to pay an equal Sum...with a request that you would take the trouble of distributing it according to the Circumstances of the men, or as you should judge proper...enclose you a Bill on the Bank of Scotland for Thirty Guineas, which pray have the goodness to distribute.[107]

and on October 2nd David Stacey wrote to no lesser person than the Rt. Hon. Henry Dundas:

> In the month of June last, Sir James Grant's Regiment of Fencibles...were called out to support the Civil power, in Comprehending three Irish vagabonds, who were a Terror of the neighbourhood – and in the Execution of this duty, a Serjeant and three Soldiers were severely wounded – One of the Soldiers was under the necessity of having his leg taken off, and soon thereafter died in our Infirmary. The Serjeant (Patrick Beaton) and Alexander Fraser one of the Soldiers, are both incapable of doing farther duty, and are therefore very proper objects to be recommended to His Majestys Board of Chelsea – As these poor fellows were wounded when supporting the Civil power of this place, I cannot help being warmly interested in their favour...And I earnestly Solicit your Good offices in procuring the King's letter for Serjeant Beaton, and the out Pension for Alexander Fraser.[108]

Beaton and Fraser never fully recovered from their wounds. Fraser was discharged from hospital in Dumfries only to be readmitted to the Infirmary in Edinburgh. Beaton rejoined the regiment but it was not long before he was sent to London to try to obtain a Chelsea pension. Watson wrote to Sir James on September 21st:

> I inclose a pass to be signed by you to take Serjeant Beaton to London – Beaton wishes to have a little money in advance on purpose to <u>enable</u> him to Reside in <u>London</u>...Your Honour Can advance the length of four <u>Guineas</u> to Beaton, at present as that will not be near his proportion when the dividend is made.[109]

On October 26th Sir James reported the outcome of this visit to David Stacey:

The Surgeon of Chelsea hospital...seeing that he was a fine young man...gave a very superficial look at his wounds told him as he was a serjt. he would have no occasion to use his hand for the firelock & reported him still as fit as ever for his Majestys Service – The consequence was his application for Chelsea was rejected – The poor fellow felt himself hurt at such a reception & without waiting at London...he put his foot in a ship and is now with the Regt at Dundee.

Poor Fraser is still in the Infirmary, but I am told much better, tho' it is believed his arm will never be fit for service.

Nothing further happened until Sir James took up the cudgels again on behalf of the two men by bringing their case to the notice of the Lord Advocate to whom he wrote on February 24th 1796 referring to:

the great propriety of procuring the out pension of Chelsea to Sergt. Peter Beaton & Alex Fraser private Soldier in the first Fencibles Sir James incloses Provost Staceys & Dr Gilchrists Letters which may elucidate their situation to his Lordship –

When Mr Dundas was here he approved & in consequence Sergt. Beaton was sent up to London from his own eagerness in too weak a State for he has never been able to do anything since he returned – Alex Frasers wounds detained him in the Infirmaries of Dumfries & Edin. till now – Lord Advocate knows that John Grant died

Peter Beaton attended at the Board but unfortunately his situation not being properly represented & his appearance as a Young man Dr North at the Chelsea Board said a sergt had no occasion to carry a firelock & he was still as fit for duty in consequence of which the poor man was sent Back to the Regt. since which time he has never been able to do anything for himself & others and now lies in a fever occasioned by distress and disappointment – He had an additional wound in his thigh & has still a Ball which has not been extracted

Frasers wounded arm speaks forcibly for itself as he is entirely disabled – he is a good man

Sergt Peter Beaton is a young man of good Education & so much real merit in his Profession that all the officers looked upon him as worthy of a commission...He is now entirely disabled and dispirited.

As a result of Sir James's persistence some progress was made and Fraser was sent to London to try to obtain a Chelsea pension, carrying with him the following note to army agent, James Fraser:

> As the Bearer Alex Fraser private Soldier in the First Fencibles cannot speak English I direct this letter solely to you as I suppose you have retained the Gallic. Give him what money he may have occasion for & have him taken care of as he is a stranger and does not speak the language – he is a worthy good man;

and to Watson he wrote on March 14th:

> Alex Fraser...is gone up to London to endeavour to obtain the Chelsea...His wounds and the loss of the use of his arms are so very apparent that I think they cannot with any propriety refuse it – I have got my friend Mr Russell of the Infirmary here to write to a Surgeon at London to accompany him to the Board...
>
> Beatons Brother came up for him with a horse & he is gone to Urquhart to recover his health.

Following Fraser's visit to the Chelsea Board Sir James was able to write again to Watson on April 12th to inform him that: 'Alex Fraser has got the outpatient on the 6th Inst. I wish poor Beaton had been with him,' but Beaton soon had another chance to get a Chelsea pension, Sir James writing to James Fraser on May 31st:

> Sergt Beaton...is gone up again to try to get the Pension...from the Severity of the wounds the long illness and some effect it has had upon his whole System is from being one of the ablest Serjts. in any Regt. now rendered absolutely incapable of doing anything for himself or the Service...This fine young man volunteered upon that nights service & has now lost his health & powers for Life – The good of the Country calls for kind attention to him.[110]

There is no record of whether Beaton obtained an out pension but it is recorded in Regimental Orders on September 3rd 1796 that Sergeant Peter Beaton was 'removed to a Company of Invalids'.[111]

I ~~John Grant~~ do make Oath, that I am by Trade a
~~Taylor~~ and to the beſt of my Know-
ledge and Belief, was born in the Pariſh of *Abernethy*
in the County of *Inverness* that I have no Rupture, nor ever
was troubled with Fits, that I am no ways diſabled by Lameneſs or otherwiſe,
but have the perfect Uſe of my Limbs; and that I have voluntarily enliſted my-
ſelf to ſerve his Majeſty KING GEORGE the THIRD. as a private Soldier
in the Regiment of Fencible Men, commanded by Sir *JAMES GRANT* of
GRANT, Baronet, upon Condition that I am not to be marched out of *Scotland*,
except in Caſe of an actual Invaſion of *England*; and upon Condition alſo, that
I am not to be draughted out of the ſaid Regiment into any other Corps; and
that I am no Apprentice, nor belonging to any Militia, or any other Regiment or to His Majeſty's Navy; and that I have received all the enliſting
Money which I agreed for. As Witneſs my Hand, this *first* Day of
April 1793 *years*

John Grant

Witneſs preſent

To wit

*T*HESE are to certify, that the aforeſaid *John Grant*
Taylor aged *27* Years *5* Feet *8½* Inches high,
Brown Complexion, *Brown* Hair, *Grey* Eyes.
Came before me. one of His Majeſty's Juſtices of the Peace for the County
aforeſaid, and acknowledged that he hath voluntarily enliſted himſelf to ſerve
His Majeſty KING GEORGE the THIRD, in the aboveſaid Regiment. He
alſo acknowledged he has heard the Second and Sixth Sections of the Articles
of War read to him, againſt Mutiny and Deſertion, and took the Oath of
Fidelity mentioned in the ſaid Articles of War.

I have examined the above-named Man,
and find him fit for His Majeſty's Service.

Surgeon

At Castle Grant this first day of April 1793

Sworn before me *James Grant, J.P.*

ARTICLES of WAR.

[Sect. II. Art. 3.] Any Officer or Soldier who ſhall begin, excite, cauſe or join, in any Mutiny or
Sedition in the Troop, Company, or Regiment, to which he belongs, or in any other Troop or Company
in our Service, or in any other Party, Poſt, Detachment, or Guard, on any Pretence whatſoever, ſhall
ſuffer Death, or ſuch other Puniſhment as by a Court-Martial ſhall be inflicted.

[Sect. VI. Art. 1.] All Officers and Soldiers, who having received Pay, or having been duly enliſted
in our Service, ſhall be convicted of having deſerted the ſame, ſhall ſuffer Death, or ſuch other Puniſhment
as by a Court-Martial ſhall be inflicted.

[Art. 2.] Any non-commiſſioned Officer or Soldier, who ſhall, without Leave from his Commanding-
Officer, abſent himſelf from his Troop or Company, or from any Detachment on which he ſhall be com-
manded, ſhall, upon being convicted thereof, be puniſhed according to the Nature of his Offence, at the
Diſcretion of a Court-Martial.

Attestation form of John Grant dated 1st April 1793[GD248/464/4/1]

i

Honoured Sir

I have been endeavouring to obtain a Ferloe to Elgin - that I might converse with your Honour - but it would not be granted me — My health is broke and the thoughts of my Wife and destitute Babes are ready to sink me altogether — being a Stranger here I cannot expect any person would trust me so far as to advance my bounty-money for me — But if your Honour would favour me with a Ferloe to Perth I make no doubt of obtaining it, and would not pretend to a Discharge from the service untill it was paid — Dear and Honoured Colonel, be so good as consider my Case — and order me to have liberty to wait on your Honour at Elgin - or if a Ferloe to Perth can be granted me as may seem to your Honour most proper — and pardon this trouble from

Honoured Sir

Your most humble Ser

Forres 21st June 1793

John Fraser

P.S. Be so good as favour your poor servant with an answer

Private John Fraser to Sir James Grant 21st June 1793[GD248/684/1/3]

I wrote you this morning; by Nelly's letter just rec'd my Infant is rather easier; tho' I think his fate is sealed — I feel it a duty to wait tomorrow morning of Monday morning's post, to receive Lord Adam's answer, which ought not to be but favorable — If it comes not, I shall set out, as I feel an impelling power beyond any consideration in this life, to be enabled to pay the last duties to what I fondly thought might have been one of the props of my declining life — I know twill pain you to hear your friends distress, its an anguish that none but a parent can feel — May we be enabled to support & bear, what our Maker pleases to inflict

Lt Colonel Cumming's letter of 8th September, 1793, to his brother in law, Sir James Grant[GD248/684/4/1]

Honble Sir

... It will no doubt occasion considerable surprise that the Invalids have not arrived at Glasgow before the marching Divisions but we were detained by contrary winds untill Saturday Evening when we got aboard & set sail Sunday morning at one o: clock – the wind was pretty favourable untill the afternoon of that day when it became boisterous & contrary – we were nearly opposite Montrose but were obliged to turn back to Stonehaven where we landed about 4 o'clock in the Afternoon – we were in great danger the sea washing over us several times but we at length fortunately effected a landing here – we were by far too much crouded there being about 120 in the hold of a small vessel the Soldiers wives & a great many of the Soldiers themselves say positively they will not set foot aboard the vessel – now

Dr John Grant to Sir James Grant, 7th October, 1793 [GD248/684/5/1]

iv

Honble Sir,   Castle Grant 20th Jan:ry 1794.

I duly received your Honours letter of the 8th instant — I really have not taken upon me to prolong any mans furlough — Many of them were at me asking it & representing their bad State of health & that they were unable to travel, all I told them was to set out as soon as they were at all able, & if their Furloughs were then run, that I would give them a Pass This indeed I have given to severals of them, & if in this I have acted wrong I shall not do it more

James Grant, the factor to Sir James Grant, 20th January, 1794 [GD248/685/3/1]

Adjutant James Watson to James Grant, the factor, 4th April, 1794[GD248/469/9]

John Grant, junior, to factor James Grant, 10th April, 1794[GD248/464/9]

May 2ᵈ 1794

Sir

I was favour'd with your letter
of Apr: 25 of last month, to which I am
sensible I ought to have returned a
more early ans — The circumstance
of my coming of age in Septr next,
makes me desirous off withdrawing at
present frm a military life, that
I may have the more leisure to exam
into the state of my affairs, & see
in what situation they are — I
therefore beg leave to offer the resignation of my Compy, which I hope
will meet with your acceptance.
and am Sir —

Yours &c
A McDonell

Resignation letter of Captain Alexander (Alasdair Ranaldson) Macdonell, dated 2nd May, 1794[GD248/465/9]

viii

Dr James

Your Lt Col is most importunate, to
remain absent — and I have been
oblidged, to write him — I cannot feel
at Liberty, to depart from H. M's
positive orders — for all officers, to be
present — at this season of the year — &
I give it you, as my opinion — that it
would be much wiser, for him, to resign —
and stay, to look after his immense —
additional fortune — & numerous family
than to be at all times, asking leave
of absence — which Both you, & he well
know, has been — & will be the Case —
I remain My Dr — at all times much and very
faithfully — Yours

Colonel —
Sir Jas Grant &c &c &c

Ad. Gordon G.

Lord Adam Gordon to Sir James Grant, 6th April, 1795 [GD248/690/3/1]

ix

We Lachlan McIntosh & Duncan McDougal two the unfortunate poor men soldiers of the first Fencibles condemned by the Sentence of the Court Martial in June last at Musleburgh Camp & afterwards reprieved by Your Majestys Clemency upon agreeing to go to the South Wales Brigade now lie in the miserable Prison at Portsmouth amongst Thieves and Robbers without Bed or Cloathing & almost starved to death ————— We are fully sensible of our delinquency & of the mercy intended to be shewn us by your Majestys most gracious pardon upon the terms of going to the South Wales Brigade — But the remaining in this sad State in such Camp is scarcely better than death — And as two of us suffered for that unhappy Frenzy of a moment, & we can appeal to our Officers for our former behaviour, & for our deep & immediate Contrition, & to Genl Hamilton who delivered the terms of your Majestys gracious & merciful pardon for the manner in which we received it by coming & gratefully — We Humbly implore that our past sufferings may be considered so far sufficient, as to prevail upon Your Majesty, to take us out of this said dungeon, & allow us to serve your Majesty & our Country in any part of the World where your Majesty shall see fit to send us to where our Behaviour we trust in the almighty will testify that your Majestys mercy is not misplaced

Sir James Grant's draft petition to the King purporting to come from the condemned mutineers [GD248/2028]

Private Malcolm Grant to the factor regarding his cow 8th August 1796 [GD248/456/5]

Place — as Courious Peice of Busness hapned about her a Short time Since Lieut Colonel Lord Hume of the 10 Militia has Seen her for Several times Watching down the River Side and always made it his Study to attend as I hear her time as posible But one Evening was using twoo much Freedom She got Clear of him went home and told her Mother Brother and Sister that She was So much Troubled with him She Could not venter to walk the Streets — her Brother one Evening thought & fit to put on their Sisters Clothing went the Usual walk and Up Comes Lord Hume how Began his old Tricks By using twoo much Fredom he took of one of his Batons and Strack Hume in the head Cuting him Severly he has Been here Since and married to one of the Duke of Buccleughs Daughters it has Been told here in many Different ways But the above is the Right way as I'm ad it My duty to Enquire

Sergeant Donald McIntosh to Adjutant James Watson 1st December, 1798 [GD248/467/3]

Chapter Five

A second Mutiny

'They were running about not knowing what they were doing'

On June 11th the First Fencibles mutinied again but the event that triggered the mutiny was in itself trivial. According to Mackintosh[1] the regiment was exercising in a field outside the town and at 4 o'clock* the adjutant informed the men that they could now return to barracks in order to purchase their meal. Whereupon one of the Grenadiers, John Anderson, muttered: "High time at any rate." The adjutant overheard this remark and reported the culprit to the Lt Colonel who had him confined to the guardhouse. Several of his comrades tried to release him but the ringleaders were arrested and the Lt Colonel ordered a Garrison Court Martial. However, whilst the prisoners were being taken from the guard room to the court room some fifty or sixty soldiers with fixed bayonets attacked the escort which consisted of the sergeant major, a corporal and six men. The sergeant major thought resistance was pointless and allowed the prisoners to run off with the mutineers. The officers led by the Lt Colonel and the adjutant followed them and re-arrested the prisoners who submissively agreed to return with them to the guardhouse and order was finally restored.

On June 12th, the day after the mutiny, the Lt Colonel took the precaution of writing in Regimental Orders 'In future all officers are to appear under arms, with their Regimental Pistols'[2] and he sent a brief note to Sir James which was carried by Glenmoriston to Edinburgh:

> Major Grant will inform you with much regret of the bad behaviour of our men – and that the Strathspey people have taken up the trade of the Macdonnells – I have not time to be more particular but that we are all affronted & heart-broken with their ingratitude, as never men were more kindly dealt with.[3]

This letter was annotated by Sir James: 'Altyre 12th June – 95 as to M___y' as if he could hardly bring himself to use the word. Sir James set out

---

Footnote:
*Watson in his evidence at the subsequent Court Martial gives the time as one o'clock.

157

post haste for Dumfries, arriving there in the early hours of June 14th from where he sent the following note to Lord Adam Gordon:

> I have the Honour to acquaint you that I arrived here about one oClock in the morning when everything was perfectly quiet & good order prevailed Universally – I likewise have this day seen the Regt at Parade behaving extremely well, & I understand a number have expressed their sorrow, & shame that such a shamefull affair had happened – Colonel Cumming says that good Order has subsisted from the time they were paraded after the Mutiny.[4]

Whilst Sir James was hurrying through the night from Edinburgh to Dumfries the Lt Colonel was writing him the following letter:

> You will be anxious to hear of us, after seeing the Major & my letter of yesterday – we have ever since been perfectly quiet, & I have reason to believe sorrow and shame has succeeded guilt – I am also of opinion, that as the officers were prepared, on their guard, and armed, that we might have perished yesterday – but it was an hazardous experiment, and we were advised by Colonels de Peyster & Blackwood* to take the method I have adopted, of insisting on a general Court-martial – Example must be made & the guilty must suffer be they who they may – I am sorry to add that your own recruits and the Strathspey people in particular are the most guilty, and many of those who have been [torn] with favors by your family.[5]

This second mutiny was viewed much more harshly by the Commander in Chief than the earlier one at Linlithgow the previous year and the regiment was ordered to march to Edinburgh forthwith. On June 16th Sir James wrote a very humble letter to Lord Adam:

> I have the Honor to acquaint you that the first division March'd this morning for Linton
>
> Tomorrow another division consisting of four companies for Selkirk & Biggar
>
> On Thursday a Division of three companies for Peebles
>
> On Saturday last division of two companies marches for Moffat...
>
> as I acquainted your Lordship, I arrived on Sunday morning,

Footnote:
*Colonel Blackwood was the Garrison Commandant at Dumfries.

and Immediately at Parade ordered the preparation for marching...but on account of the Necessary Enquiry which took me and all the other officers up the Rest of that day till past the post time I could only write the few lines I sent...

The Regiment in General seems much hurt with the Late affair, & the prisoners to repent much of their Folly but no attention is paid to their Petitions as it appears they were guilty...

I have the Honor to Remain with the utmost Respect & Anxiety for His Majesty's service.

My Lord, your Lordships most obedient humble servant[6]

When the enormity of their crime and the probable consequences of it began to dawn on the offenders they, as Sir James had indicated to the Commander in Chief, began to 'repent much of their Folly' and wrote to Sir James on the same day as he had written to Lord Adam:

Our destination seems to us to be awfull, but we as Candidates for mercy, sensible of the Crimes we have been guilty of; implord forgiveness and promises in the strength of divine providence, still to Morass any system that may prove Injurious to Character or Country and if it is in your Honours power to act as a mediator betwixt Lord Adam Gordon & us as we trust it is to acquitt us, we totally Rely upon your Goodness hitherto experienced – Had we been sensible of the danger to accrue, we should have been mute; but Rely and depend upon your mercy, willing to Return to our duty as Tyrants against such practices as we have been, accustomed to, and devotees for Establishment and Crown and Dignity

Sic Subscribitus
Lachlan M'Intosh
Charles M'Intosh
Alexr Fraser
Duncan M'Dougald
James M'Donald
Dumfries 16th June 1795

* * *

On June 22nd Watson who was in command of the detachment bringing the prisoners to Edinburgh Castle wrote to Sir James from the Howgate at 3pm:

I have given the party & prisoners a little refreshment, here & we proceed I Expect to be at Edin. Castle by 7 oClock at furthest – the party has hitherto behaved themselves as well as I could wish – the <u>Prisoners</u> are all <u>Contrition</u> & Sorrow.

and at 8 o'clock he wrote from Edinburgh Castle:

I arrived at this place with the Detacht. and Prisoners – under my Command at 7 o clock – in Perfect Good order – a young Lad Cameron of Capt. Grants Company Excepted who fell sick at Howgate, but I presume that by the Time this reaches he will be arrived at Peebles, as I directed him to do I believe his indisposition arose from a foul Stomach, but I left him in a fair way to get clear of it & I hope he has Returned

The Ceremony of Delivering the <u>Prisoners</u> over & waiting on the Commg offr Colonel Scott, has taken up Some time – however now I am perfectly Clear and I have enclosed the Receipt for their bodys to the Lieut. Colonel at your Lodgings to convince him that everything <u>is done</u> as he wished it & also agreeably to your orders to me on that Subject

I humbly beg leave in a Particular manner to Recommend to your notice the Good Conduct of the Detachment, they in fact did everything I could wish as Good & <u>obedient</u> Soldiers – every individual of them Seem'd impressed with the necessary duty they were Employed upon – The behaviour of the Prisoners was such became their unfortunate situation – entering at the Barrier <u>Gate</u> and <u>walking</u> up to the <u>main</u> <u>Guard</u> <u>threw</u> a <u>damp</u> upon all their Spirits – but more particularly <u>McIntosh</u> indeed the whole of them were staggered at the <u>unwelcome</u> Reception they met with at the Guard House – I went in with the Adjutant of one of the Battalions of the Brigades, by Colonel Scotts desire on purpose to see if they had Claims as to subsistence they all said that they had now and always had every Claim duly paid them when due from the first fencibles, the manner they expressed themselves was pleasant, Respecting the Regt in General, altho' they may have Cunning Enough to Dissemble – I understand they are to be put in Seperate Cells from one another this day at Guard mounting – this will mortify them beyond anything that could possibly happen to them for they Depended much upon Enjoying one anothers Society – I shall take the Liberty of Explaining all Particulars when I have the happiness of seeing you on tomorrow night or wednesday morning without fail

I am sorry to say the Last part of our march was not Pleasant for it Rained incessantly upon us from Howgate to this Place.[7]

* * *

Back home in Strathspey the local people were shattered by the news of this second mutiny, the factor writing to Duncan Grant of Delshangie now factor of Urquhart:

I am exceedingly vexed at the late mutiny in the first fencibles – Their Character is now blasted forever – I have had no certain accounts yet who they are that are imprisoned but I fear some of them will suffer.[8]

Unfortunately, there are no letters giving detailed first hand accounts of this second mutiny. Dr John Grant, the factors son, was ill in bed and will have had nothing to tell his father. Lt John Grant junior, who had written such a long letter to the factor after the mutiny at Linlithgow had transferred to the 97th Regiment. Chaplain James Grant was still on leave in Urquhart. Of the quartet that had written to the factor after the mutiny at Linlithgow only Watson was a leading player in the Dumfries mutiny but for once he was strangely silent. We are dependent, therefore, upon the records taken at the subsequent court martial for a detailed account of the mutiny. The court martial opened on July 6th at Musselburgh, with Colonel Wemyss of the 2nd Fencibles presiding, and lasted four days. The first witness called for the Crown was Watson who gave the following evidence:[9]

On thursday the 11th of June last...about 10 o'Clock in the forenoon he happened to see the 1st Major Grant who said the men must not be kept so long in the field again as the Magistrates of Dumfries had been at considerable pains for collecting meal from the Country...The Regt immediately after this marched to the Exercising ground. he was directed by Col. Cuming to put the Regiment in proper order for a field day. after the battalion was collected the Col. took command and exercised them ...till near 1 o'Clock. The Deponent then took the liberty of informing the Col what Major Grant told him...that they must be in Town which

161

Col. Cuming agreed to, and desired the Deponent to communicate the same to the Battalion which he did...one of the men replied very loud there is no occasion for an excuse we have been long enough here already this was said by one Anderson but none of the Prisoners present – The deponent went on and said your conduct as being under arms is very improper and that he the Deponent would report him to the Lieut. Colonel – he took him accordingly up to the Lieut Col. who immediately ordered him to the guard he was marched immediately to Town. The Battalion continued about 10 minutes longer in the field...was then ordered to march to the Dock and was there dismissed...Deponent went to the George Inn and remained there about 1/4 of an hour and on going to his own room he met Ensign James Grant who was then officer of the Guard who told the deponent a good deal agitated "I am sorry to inform you that the Strathspey men are assembled and are now in a state of mutiny at the Guard House"...The Deponent went immediately to the Guard House...there were about 20 or 30...men present...he spoke to them and asked them what they meant...he was answered by one Forsyth that they meant to release the Prisoner as he considered his crime to be trifling – The Deponent immediately replied – Forsyth you are doing a very improper thing and in the meantime I shall put you into (prison) the Guard House – The Deponent immediately seized him by the breast...and thought he pushed him into the Guard House...he found the men pressing close upon him he turned about to them he heard one of the men...say Dam it have him out...The Deponent said "you shall not have him out with my Life I keep this door"...the deponent then found it necessary to extricate himself from the disagreeable situation he was in and for the first time since he has been in the regiment use his stick – he struck severals of the men with his stick & said "dont blame me – I am determined you shall not have him" – when he found the stick had no Effect he drew his sword and said "the first man that comes nigh this Door I shall run him through the body"...he thought that he had confined Forsyth in the Guard House – but was answered that he got off in the confusion upon looking round he saw Forsyth with 5 or 6 more men standing very unconcerned as if nothing had happened The Deponent went up to him and seized him by the breast and said "Sir I am determined you shall be secured – you being one of the principal Instigators of this affair". The Deponent brought him accordingly to the Guard House...and got assistance from the Prisoner Anderson...by this time the Deponent was joined by the 1st Major and most of the officers then in Town he was desired by the major...to reinforce his Guard with a Subaltern and 30 men which he immediately did...The Major said that as every necessary precaution had been taken he would refer doing any thing untill the Lieut Colonels arrival [The Lieut. Col. was then taking a ride out of town]...about 4 o'Clock...about 2 hours after the disturbance...the Col. sat by him and said " Watson you are a good deal confused what is the matter with you – out with it" – The Deponent replied " Colonel there is a good deal the matter with me I am sorry to inform you a disturbance having happened"...The Col. answered they had no occasion for they received every indulgence and said... "I am determined to have them tried by a Garrison Court Martial*"...The Court sat in the mess room of the Geo. Inn...the court proceeded to Examine witnesses...the Prisoners were remarched to Prison as the Court was fully satisfied of what was laid against them...when they were carrying the Prisoners back to Prison...he heard a great noise on the street...on coming downstairs the witness was accosted by two Towns people who said to him " For Gods sake do not go to the street if you value your life"...immediately on coming out to the street he saw great confusion...and...about 50 or 60 men with fixed bayonets on the street he saw several of the officers amongst the men with their backs to him...Captn. Grant said... "I believe they have already rescued the Prisoners and I believe the Lieut. Colonel is now in chase of them" – the witness said to the men "unfix your bayonets directly it is a shame for you to behave in this manner"...upon looking round he saw the Lieut. Col. coming out of the Lane with

Footnote:
* At the garrison court martial John Anderson was sentenced to 150 lashes for 'unsoldier like behaviour under arms' and James Forsyth to 650 lashes for 'insolence to the adjutant' but both these sentences were ultimately remitted.[10]

the Prisoner Anderson linked in his arms...the men obscuring the Lieut. Col. they gave a Shout...they disengaged the Prisoner from the Col. who said you have taken him from me but you have taken him Cowardly...he did not observe any of them [the prisoners] more active in the mob than the rest. he cannot condescend if Chas MacIntosh and Jas MacDonald had their bayonets fixed...he observed Lachln MacIntosh by being tall running across the Street the men were very furious – the Col. said there is nothing more to be done untill they went to the Parade...he [the Colonel] told them that he and the officers had condescended upon those that had been most active in the mutiny and they were picked out by the Colonel...Jas MacDonald was picked out and confined as being thought the most culpable.

The second witness for the crown was sergeant major MacBean who stated that:

He was coming from the Geo. Inn about 7 o'Clock in the Evening Conveying the Prisoners from the Court Martial to Prison – there was a croud of Soldiers met him some with fixed bayonets and some not – he got a little startled when he saw them they took hold of the Prisoners and forced them away...The Deponent desired the Escort to recover their arms and make no resistance as it was needless – they carried of the Prisoners into a close that was on the right hand by that time Col. Cuming came out and followed them – he cannot say if the party followed the Prisoners – the Witness cannot say that any of the Prisoners were on the Party that forced Forsyth and Anderson from him – he did not observe any of them as he was a little blinded...he saw Col. Cuming coming back with one of the Prisoners...the Prisoner was coming back quietly with the Col...he saw a croud about the Colonel after coming down the Lane and the noise of shouting amongst the Croud – he saw three of the Prisoners amongst that croud Jas MacDonald Alexr. Fraser & Lachn. McIntosh he did not observe them doing any thing more than the rest but Fraser & MacIntosh having their bayonets fixed he did not observe them near the Colonel at that time.

Glenmoriston was the third witness for the crown and he gave the following evidence:

he observed two of the Prisoners there [near Col. Cuming] MacDugal & Fraser – he cannot say that he saw them in the act of charge but their bayonets were very close...The Col. drew a Pistol out of his Pocket and levelled it at the head of one of the soldiers who drew back – he thinks it was to Fraser's head the Col. pointed the pistol it was then they raised up their arms – upon this the officers went in amongst them – the Disturbance immediately dispersed very much and the Drum was beat for the Parade they immediately all went down to the general parade...the Prisoners were picked out – the five men were looked upon at the time as being most active, Chas MacIntosh the little one after the croud was dispersed the Deponent saw him but he had not his bayonet fixed

The fourth witness for the crown was Captain John Grant, junior* who stated that:

Alex Fraser and Duncan MacDougal was there [at the entrance to the lane when the Colonel returned] – he does not recolect that any of the rest was there the Deponent heard the croud in a general voice say "stick them stick them" in galic he cannot say any of the prisoners said "stick them"...Col Cumming drew a Pistol and presented it to Alexr Frasers head...on Col. Cumings presenting the Pistol they drew back soon after some unfixing their bayonets and others not...He saw the Col. return as he thinks with Forsyth – he does not recolect if both the Prisoners were with him – the one he saw was coming quietly with the Colonel.

The court then adjourned for the day, reconvening at 10 o'clock on the morning of July 7th. The fifth witness for the crown was Captain John Rose of Holme who gave evidence that:

About 7 o'Clock in the Evening he was in the heart of the croud – he saw a great croud of Soldiers with fixed bayonets. The witness demonstrated with them and told them what a foolish thing they were doing...he spoke to them in Galick some of them answered

Footnotes:
   *There were two Captains named John Grant, John Grant of Rippachie who was the senior of the two and John Grant of Rosefield or Auchterblair who was known as Captain John Grant junior. In his account of the Dumfries mutiny Prebble[11] confuses Captain John Grant of Rosefield with Lt John Grant junior of Delcroy who was now serving with the 97th Regiment.

and said the men were confined for a frivolous cause – the Deponent said they were not judges of that – he saw Lachlan MacIntosh amongst the croud he observed him particularly because he is from the neighbouring Parish.

Other officers and non commissioned officers gave evidence for the Crown. Lt Thomas MacDonald 'observed Lachlan MacIntosh amongst the croud he did not see any of the other Prisoners there – The Deponent did not observe Lachlan MacIntosh doing any violence more than the rest...he did not see any of the other Prisoners if they were there'. Lt Allan Grant 'saw Lachlan MacIntosh amongst the croud, he observed him as being tall...he saw neither C. MacIntosh or MacDonald he would know them as as they belonged to the Company the Deponent belongs to'. Lt Charles Grant 'saw Chas MacIntosh in the croud he observed him as being particularly insolent to the Colonel – he seized his forelock as if he was to strike the Colonel...he does not recolect to see any of the other Prisoners'. Sergeant Peter Grant 'saw Alex Fraser and Lachlan MacIntosh at the disturbance...Lachlan MacIntosh...had his bayonet fixed – he did not see any of the rest of the Prisoners there he saw Alex Fraser have his bayonet fixed all the men had their bayonets fixed...he would have known the other three Prisoners if he had seen them there'. Lt Theodore Morison 'saw Chas MacIntosh in the croud he observed him by being in a great passion he heard him damming if any of the Officers would strick him once they would not strick him twice' Corporal Michael Meredith's evidence cannot have been of much use to the Crown for all he had to say was that he 'thought really in his heart that the men meant no harm to the Col or the Deponent if other ways they might easily have done it'. Sergeant Robert Grant 'saw Lachlan MacIntosh amongst them he saw Jas MacDonald in the rear...Lachn MacIntosh was there with fixed bayonet he saw James MacDonald fix his bayonet...he saw Alex Fraser he had his bayonet fixed along with the rest...he saw Col Cuming take a Pistol and keep it at the head of Fraser, and the rest of the men were drawing back after that'. Captain Simon Fraser 'saw Jas MacDonald there...they were running about not knowing what they were doing some had their bayonets fixed and some not...he is certain he saw none of the Prisoners in the Circle round the Colonel'. Achindown 'saw the Colonel draw a Pistol and putting it to one mans head...on which the witness said for Gods sake dont fire it Col. the Col gave him a sign as it were he did not mean it as he thinks He thought after this they were more pointed he took out his sword and kept down their bayonets. The Deponent spoke with them in Erse being the language he thought they understood best. he does not think any of the Prisoners had their bayonets pointed to the Col....The Deponent asked what was their meaning they replied that they thought they were ill used by Col. Cuming the Commanding Officer and the Adjutant'. Lieut. George Reynolds 'was in such a flurry that he did not know any of the men...he saw Lachlan MacIntosh he took notice of him as he belonged to the Company he Commands. he desired him to go to the Parade he returned his bayonet and said he would go to the Parade he saw Chas MacIntosh at the time the Col was surrounded at the back of the croud he marked him as being so low. he cannot say that any of the other prisoners were there. he heard the men say they were very sorry for what they had done after the Colonel drew the Pistol. this was after the mutiny was over before they went to the Parade'.

Sergeant John Hutchieson is recorded as testifying that: 'He did not observe them point their bayonets against any officer he heard the officers desire them unfix their bayonets which they immediately did.' Sergeant Hutchieson was evidently doing his very best for the prisoners as his evidence clearly enraged Colonel Wemyss, the President of the Court, for on the same day he wrote to Sir James:

> As President of the General Court martial sitting here upon the trial of five prisoners of the Regiment under your command, I am directed by the Court to inform you, that from the great prevarication in the evidence of Serjeant John Hutchison* of the 1st F. Regt. the Court are unanimously of opinion, that he is a very unfit person to be a non Commissd. officer in any Corps.[12]

Sergeant John Grant from Balnaclash, the recruit enlisted by Miss Grant of Grant, told the court that he 'demonstrated with them and desired them do nothing against their officers Duncan MacDugal answered and said the witness was worse himself than any of the officers'.

On that note the second day's evidence ended and the court adjourned. On July 8th Lt Colonel Cumming-Gordon was called to the witness box. From his evidence it would seem that he was in a rather defensive frame of mind and he may have been worried that the mutiny reflected badly on his leadership. His evidence as recorded by the court was as follows:

Footnotes:

*As a result of Colonel Wemyss letter, sergeant John Hutchieson was reduced to the ranks and then discharged from the regiment.[13]

This witness concurs with Adjutant Watsons testimony untill the setting of the Court Martial (the witness wanted to be allowed to give an account from some time prior to the Mutiny to account for his being armed with Pistols that day this was objected to on the part of the Prisoners which was sustained by the Court)...The Deponent thought that the urgency of the case justified his holding a Court Martial at an unusual hour which would be about five o'Clock in the afternoon. the officers were ordered to Court and the rest of the officers to arm themselves with Pistols that Evening...he should also mention that it had been previously hinted to him that they would not allow these men to be punished and that they would shoot the Adjutant...on coming out at the Inn door several voices were crying that the Prisoners were rescued seeing a number of men running up a Close...he followed them up that Close and...came up to the Prisoners he remonstrated with them on the folly of their conduct they said they were forced from the Guard and that they were sensible of their conduct and would follow the witness wherever he wished them to go. he desired each of them to take hold of the skirts of his coat and that he would conduct them to the Guard House...they went out in another close a little above the George Inn there was a rush of men ran in on the witness immediately as he came to the street and took the Prisoners from him...those behind pushed on those that were beforehand charging the witnesses in every direction with fixed bayonets he endeavoured to keep off the bayonets of those in front and feeling himself protected behind whom he afterwards understood to be 1st Major and Capt Jno Grant Junr. words in Erse passed amongst them which he understood afterwards to be divel damn you stick them stick them...he observed Lachn MacIntosh Dn. MacDugal pushing particularly these two men were swearing and were Particularly violent by this time they surrounded him very narrowly he turned to the right he observed Fraser half the length of the bayonet near him L. McIntosh and McDugal was on the Left then on which seeing himself in so serious a situation he drew a Pistol & pointed it at Frasers head who immediately took fright and staggered back finding the good effect it had on him he carried it round the circle which had instantaneously the effect of their carrying their arms...severals of the Officers by this time joined and a few of the Serjeants ordering the men to go to their private parades which most of them did. a few remained among whom was Chas MacIntosh the witness immediately knowing him to be disorderly form the commencement of the regiment he spoke to him and said "what you lilliputian are you doing here" he struck him at the same time with the articles of war which he had in his hand under the ear MacIntosh replied and damned the Deponent for a bugar "why do you strick me" the witness thought him so insignificant went down to Parade and met Lachln MacIntosh he told him that he had remarked his conduct to which he replied he was indifferent whither he did or not...he then ordered out the Colours and endeavoured to get the men to Parade as soon as possible the Deponent formed them into a Circle he read the Articles of War against Mutiny and made his comments upon them he mentioned the enormity of their conduct...he went through the Ranks with the first Major and Adjutant and pitched upon the 2 MacIntoshes MacDugal and Fraser and two others which he added to the list he sent them to the Guard House under strong Escort...there was a message sent to him from the Guard House. he spoke to two of the men and being satisfied they were not as culpabable as the rest he set them at liberty but being informed of Jas MacDonald being very active...he ordered him to confinement.

The Lt Colonel's evidence concluded the case for the Crown. Witnesses for the prisoners were then called. Capt. Robert Cumming and Adjutant James Watson gave evidence on behalf of Lachlan McIntosh. They both said he was orderly and obedient. Private Alexander McIntosh gave evidence on behalf of Duncan McDougal that he was standing at the rear of the crowd. Adjutant Watson and Capt Lt Allan Grant both testified that McDougal 'always behaved like a soldier'. Capt. Simon Fraser called on behalf of Alexander Fraser testified that he 'he always behaved in every respect like a soldier'. Watson was also called by Fraser but was clearly unwilling to give evidence on his behalf confining himself to saying that he could 'say nothing as to Frasers general character'. Private Alexander Shaw was called by Corporal James MacDonald and gave evidence that MacDonald advised him to go to the Parade. Capt. John Grant, senior said that MacDonald was 'a soldier like well behaved lad'. Watson it was recorded 'gives the strongest testimony that words can give of his character good and excellent behaviour as a Soldier'. Finally on behalf of little Charles MacIntosh, Private Alex Fraser testified that 'he did not hear Chas MacIntosh give any bad language to the Colonel'. It would be nice to think that this Private Alex Fraser was one of the accused who was selfless enough to think of another in the same dreadful situation as himself, but this is unlikely as there were as many as nine Private Alexander Frasers in the regiment! Both Capt Lt Allan Grant and Lt Richardson said that MacIntosh 'always behaved very well and like a soldier'. Private James Fraser testified that 'he saw Chas MacIntosh on the Street that he was going down the street saying he was not in the mob...and that the first thing he met with was to be struck by the Lieut. Colonel'. Charles MacIntosh also called Watson who told the court that he had nothing to say in MacIntosh's defence.

The Court then adjourned but did not publicly give its verdict until July 16th. The verdict was that:

> The Court upon full consideration of the Evidence of the whole matters before them were of opinion, that the above named Laughlan McIntosh, Duncan MacDougall, Alexr Fraser, James MacDonald & Charles McIntosh are one and all of them Guilty of the charge...and it was the further opinion of the Court, that the said Lauchlan McIntosh, Duncan McDougall, Alexr Fraser, and Charles McIntosh, be, and they are thereby Adjudged to suffer Death, It was also the further opinion of the Court that the said James MacDonald, be, and is hereby Ajudged to receive Five hundred Lashes in the Usual Manner; but in respect of his exemplary good conduct previous to the Mutiny charged, and the excellent Character he bears as a Soldier, they recommend him to mercy.

Watson's evidence must have been very compelling for the court to recommend Corporal MacDonald to mercy.

On the same day it was stated in General Orders issued by Lord Adam Gordon that:

> Major General James Hamilton is hereby directed to see the said sentce carried into Executtion in so far as regards the Prisoner Alexr. Fraser upon Friday next the 17th July Currt. upon the Links or Sands of Gullen, when & where the said Alexr. Fraser is to be shot to Death.

The above three prisoners Adjudged to suffer Death, viz Lauchlan McIntosh, Duncan MacDougall & Charles McIntosh, are to draw Lotts, to suffer may fall, to be shot to Death at the same time & place with the prisoner Alexr. Fraser...the punishments so justly awarded to the other three prisoners are hereby Suspended untill His Majesty's Pleasure be known.[14]

On July 10th, after the trial was over but before the verdict was known, Sir James begged Lord Adam to show mercy to the prisoners, writing:

Allow me earnestly to petition for those unfortunate young men, of the First Fencibles, and humbly to implore that his Majestys mercy may be extended towards them – Ignorant of what the sentence of the respectable Court martial may be, I shudder at the thoughts, that according to the laws of the army, it may be very severe against some of them -

The suddenness and unexpectedness of the affair – the immediate good order and regularity which almost instantaneously took place by the Spirit, Coolness and activity of the Lt. Colonel, on the one hand and the sense of duty, which pervaded the whole Regiment on the other – The Submission and deep contrition which the Prisoners evidenced – The regularity with which the duty of bringing them to the Castle by their fellow Soldiers of the Regiment was performed – the sense of the consequences of such a crime with which they are now deeply impressed – and the serious warning which the Regiment has since got by the publication, of His Royal Highness order, of the late punishments in England, will I hope have weight with your Lordship, and excuse my giving you the trouble – I need not point out the laudable Characteristic which the Regiment afforded the day before in the affair of the Tinkers, from which three brave fellows be now miserably wounded and in very great danger, in the excellent institution the Infirmary at Dumfries Neither need I say, that in no one quarter, where they have been, has an individual a complaint against them – These unfortunate young men are otherwise of good character, were I am convinced impelled by no malevolence, or the least intention to do hurt, and are the Children of good and loyal subjects – may I supplicate that their youth, and inexperience may plead in their favour – The manner in which his Majestys mercy /

if such shall be his pleasure / may be exerted, I will not pretend to suggest – But I trust in God, it would not be misplaced – These poor unfortunate young men, in the bloom of life, may yet serve their king and Country with merit either in the army or navy – and in the full confidence that sufficient warning of the Consequences of such Crimes has now been impressed, I once more humbly supplicate His majestys mercy in their favour, & subscribe myself with dutifull attachment to His Majesty, & my Country, & sincere respect for your Lordship.[15]

Sir James wrote again to Lord Adam on July 12th after he had been privately told the verdict of the court and the sentences imposed:

When you did me the honour this day to mention to me the sentence agst the unhappy prisoners I was so Thunderstruck with the extent of it, that I could not ask your Lordship whether we might still have room for requesting a delay for a Humble Petition to His Majesty for Mitigation.

I am with much anxiety & the most perfect esteem respectfully etc etc.[16]

Sir James was certainly all of a twitter for he mistakenly dated this letter June 12th but he was not too distraught to attend to business matters for on the following day, July 13th he wrote to the factor at Grantown:

Immediately, or as soon after you receive this as you can, you will set out for this place & bring my List of Debts & every paper as to money matters & business that we may arrange our matters during the Vacation – Mr Alex Grant promised me to write to you as to any other papers that may be necessary, but come you must and the sooner the better – I saw your son perfectly well Yesterday in Camp and see him every day.

and on the back of this letter there is scrawled, in an unfamiliar hand, the following note:

Four of our unhappy Prisoners are condemned to suffer capitally viz Alex Fraser Duncan MacDougal Lachlan Mackintosh & Chas Mackintosh & Sir James & I ordered to see the Sentence put in execution next Friday morning halfway twixt the two Camps Sad Business!

Ld Adam has approved of the sentence, & it was intimated last night – He does not send it to the King.

James Macdonald is sentenced to receive 500 lashes but recommended to mercy.[17]

On July 17th at 6 o'clock in the morning the prisoners were transported from Musselburgh to Gullane in two mourning coaches accompanied by the Reverend Robertson MacGregor, minister of the Gaelic chapel in Edinburgh and the regimental chaplain, the Reverend James Grant. The coffins were carried in a cart immediately behind the two mourning coaches. Alexander Fraser's sentence stood but as he had indicated in General Orders the previous day a degree of clemency was shown by the Commander in Chief who remitted the flogging of Corporal James MacDonald and ordered that only one other should be shot. Lachlan McIntosh, Duncan McDougal and Charles McIntosh drew lots. The lot fell on Charles McIntosh.[18]

There have been differing accounts as to how the two condemned men behaved. According to Mackintosh[19] the *Edinburgh Advertiser* reported that Fraser carried his mutinous disposition to the grave and endeavoured to create a fresh mutiny. Charles McIntosh on the other hand behaved with great resignation and submitted to his fate with great calmness. Prebble[20] states that the *Advertiser* reported that Fraser was calm and McIntosh turbulent at the end but the regimental chaplain wrote to the factor on July 22nd:

Poor Charles MacKintosh's fate was very hard indeed ! but he met death like a hero.

He truly died nobly.

As the chaplain was with the two men at the end there can be little doubt that his version of events is the correct one.

Last minute reprieve of the death sentence, or the drawing of lots when only some were to be reprieved, was common army practice. Lt John Peebles cites two such instances in the American War of Independence. The first being the case of a young soldier who got drunk and lost his way in the night and was sentenced to death for desertion but was pardoned 'at the foot of the gallows'. The poor man 'who behaved very well and peninently at the approaching scenes of death, fainted with joy when his pardon was pronounced'.[21] The other case involved two Grenadiers who were sentenced to death for desertion 'but as one was to be pardon'd they drew lots, & he who drew the fatal billet was executed in sight of ye Army at Noon'.[22]

Recent events had certainly taken their toll of Sir James and his family for in his letter of July 22nd the chaplain concludes:

> I left the Grant family as well as could be expected yesterday. Sir James has suffered extremely, by the late unhappy catastrophe. I pray that a general peace and good understanding maybe soon reestablished never to be broken again. this is much wanted & tho I do not wish to anticipate evil – am afraid all will never again concord or assimilate perfectly unless a certain high officer resigns – which nothing but a principle officer would induce him to do – I can assure you tis fear alone not love that procures obedience at present in the lower orders...
>
> I intend if 'tis Gods will that all is well at home to return to the Regt. again in Sept. meantime Mr McCulloch the Suthd. Chaplain does the duty for his own Regt. & mine.[23]

There can be little doubt that the chaplain thought that the Lt Colonel, because of the harsh discipline which he imposed upon the regiment, was in a very large measure responsible for the mutiny.

Rippachie also wrote to the factor on July 22nd indicating the distress that the recent events had caused:

> Sir Jas. Lady grant & family are well but our late dismal business gave them much trouble & uneasiness – I hope we shall never have occasion to witness such a scene.[24]

The factor, who was now aged 62, was not at all pleased at being summoned so peremptorily to Edinburgh and wrote to Duncan Grant:

> Sir James Grant has lead his commands upon me to go up to Edin. & that I must if at all possible set out by end of next week...it is exceedingly inconvenient for me to go but the bound must obey – yet I expected I was to have no more Journeys to Edin.
>
> By first Tuesdays post we will have by letter & in the Publick papers the particulars of the execution of the most unhappy condemned Mutineers of the Ist Fencibles – It is said only two of them were to suffer Death I sincerely pray that the whole may have got off with their life & be transported, be it where it will.[25]

The weekly regimental returns dated July 22nd simply stated: 'Dead – 2'.

However the monthly return of August 1st reported 3 dead in July.[26] We do not know who this third person was but it does help to remind us that death from natural causes was not all that uncommon.

* * *

Sir James continued his exertions on behalf of the reprieved men and the families of the executed men. On July 19th he wrote to 'Mr MacGregor' a vintner at Fort George who was probably related to Charles McIntosh's wife:

one was condemned absolutely & the other three ordered to cast Lots for life when the unfortunate one fell to the fate of the poor man who bore his sentence in a most becoming manner – It is not imagined they had any premeditated intention but just a sudden passionate impetuosity – sometimes what young highlanders may be guilty of – but of no long continuance at same time you may judge that mutiny & fixed Bayonets cannot be permitted although we may regret severely in our hearts the necessity of punishment – I write this for your satisfaction and wish to inform you that the poor lads widow is gone back to serve a very worthy Gentlewoman a Mrs Grant who will take care and look after her conduct.

The following day Sir James wrote to Henry Dundas:

Justice is amply gratified in the death of two of the unhappy young men who suffered on Friday last agreeably to the sentence of the Court martial – Let me now earnestly request, & strongly recommend mercy in its fullest extent & a total remission of whipping as to the remaining prisoners & believe that when I do so it is with the fullest conviction that it is highly for the benefit of his Majestys service.[27]

This appeal by Sir James was successful for there appeared in Regimental Orders of July 31st the following intimation:

His Royal Highness the Duke of York having signified to General Lord Adam Gordon that His Majesty had been graciously pleased to approve of the sentence His Majesty had been pleased to grant his most gracious pardon to Duncan McDougall & Lachlan McIntosh...upon condition of their serving in the N.S.W. Corps; as also that His Majesty had been pleased to grant his free pardon

to James MacDonald – he forthwith orders to rejoin his Corps &
Company.[28]

Lachlan McIntosh and Duncan Mc Dougal wrote to Sir James on August
5th from Musselburgh:

> We cannot Rightly Thank Your Honour for what you do for your
> unworthy servants but as far as it lays in our power we will serve
> you in any place we will be put to but we would far Rather Serve
> under your Honour than in any other place but if it cannot be
> Done we heartily thank your Honour for your trouble...We do
> not know how to thank your Honour for all the trouble you was
> put at for us – What ever Place we will be put to its not Ourselves
> that we are sorry for but for our poor parents that we lament that
> their hearts will be broken for us
>
> [signed] Lachlan m'Intosh & Duncan m'Dugald.[29]

In the last week of August the two prisoners were transferred to
Portsmouth gaol to await a ship to take them to Australia where they were to
be enlisted in the New South Wales Corps in Botany Bay,[30] but they had
high hopes of being allowed to transfer to Sir James's Regiment of the Line,
the 97th which was stationed at the nearby Hillsea Barracks. On September
10th they wrote to Sir James:

> As we were informed by Capt. Fraser that your Honour Would
> Do all that Lay in your pour to get us into the 97th Regt. and not
> let us proced any further
>
> Nou as we are in portsmouth only 3 mils frome the aforesaid
> Regt We therefore pray that your honour Will Be So kind as to let
> us knou if theire be any such thing as We Will be Got into it or
> not So as we may not live any longer in hops of Delivrey
>
> Duncan McDugald
> Lauchlin McIntosh
> Main Guard at Portsmouth.[31]

However, their hopes of enlisting in the 97th were soon dashed. Lt John
Grant junior, wrote to Sir James from Hillsea Barracks on September 19th:

> I...went to Portsmouth & represented to Lauchlan McIntosh and
> Duncan McDougall that you had the goodness to apply for to
> have them into the 97th but without success – that you had
> however succeeded in obtaining leave for them to enlist in any of
> the Regiments now embodying in the West Indies where a

number of their own country men were to be officers, and would treat them more kindly than they could expect to be in the South Wales Brigade – they immediately jumped at the proposal & enlisted with Capt. James Grant Kinchirdy for Col. Keppels Regt. who I had purposely brought along wt me, and he has by this post wrote to Col. Keppel requesting to know if this be agreeable to him that they may be attested, of which I presume there can be no doubt, and that they poor fellows shall soon be set at liberty.[32]

But neither was this plan successful for Sir James wrote to Lt John Grant junior on October 5th:

> Dear John,
>
> you may tell poor Duncan McDougall & Lachlan McIntosh that having received so positive a refusal from the Duke of York it is impossible to apply again – Perhaps they may be as fully as well in the South Wales Brigade where Soldiers are held in Estimation If you find out when they are to sail for South Wales & inform me as to who Commands then I shall endeavour to have them recommended to his attention.

Sir James wrote again to Lt John Grant junior on January 25th:

> Dear John,
>
> Has poor Lachlan McIntosh & Duncan McDougall the unfortunate Fencibles been allowed to enlist I am told they have or are they still are in Portsmouth Goal.

On hearing that the two men were still in Portsmouth gaol, Sir James became angry and wrote to Henry Dundas on January 29th:

> I have the honour to enclose a petition from Lachlan McIntosh & Duncan McDougall the two unfortunate Soldiers of the First Fencibles who received His Majestys pardon in June last at Musselburgh Camp upon the terms of going to Serve in the South Wales Brigade as they are fine young men & I am convinced will make good Soldiers I once more am induced to request that their humble request may be laid before his Majesty the more so that their present situation really does not seem to come within the Intention of his Majestys Royal Clemency.

and on the same day he wrote to James Fraser of Ainslie and Fraser:

> The two unhappy men Lachlan McIntosh & Duncan McDougall...wrote to me a most miserable Letter from the Prison

177

at Portsmouth I return their Petition drawn out which you will do me the favour to send to the Commissary Paymaster of the 97th that he may get them to sign it and send it up to you when you will inclose it in the Letter to Mr Dundas & have it delivered to him with the certainty of its being attended to...Could you get any respectable Colonel to present their petition it might save you the necessity of inclosing it in a letter from me which I would prefer as being more certain of being attended to than a Letter, which in these hurried times is often mislaid and thought of no more.

Enclosed with this letter was a petition ostensibly written by Lachlan McIntosh and Duncan McDougall but here Sir James was dissembling somewhat for he had written the petition himself. Loose in his letter book there is an undated letter with many deletions and insertions and written in Sir James's own hand. This is the letter:

To the King's most excellent Majesty

May it please Your Majesty

We Lachlan McIntosh & Duncan McDougal the two unfortunate poor men Soldiers of the first Fencibles by Sentence of the Court Martial in June last at Musselburgh Camp & afterwards reprieved by Your Majestys Clemency upon agreeing to go to the South Wales Brigade now lie in the miserable Prison at Portsmouth amongst thieves and Robbers without Bed or Cloathing & almost starved to death – we are fully sensible of our delinquency & of the mercy intended to be shown us by your Majestys most gracious pardon upon the terms of going to the South Wales Brigade – But the remaining in this sad state is scarcely better than death – And as two of us suffered for that unhappy Frenzy of a moment, & we can appeal to our Officers for our former behaviour, & for our deep & immediate Contrition, & to Genl. Hamilton who delivered the terms of your Majestys gracious & merciful pardon for the becoming & gratefull manner in which we received it – We Humbly implore that our past sufferings may be considered so far sufficient, as to prevail upon Your Majesty, to take us out of this sad dungeon, & allow us to serve your Majesty, & our Country in any part of the world where your Majesty will see fit to send us, where our Behaviour we trust in the almighty will testify that Your Majestys mercy is not misplaced.[33]

There was a speedy response to Sir James's direct appeal to Henry Dundas for on February 5th 1796, Lt. John Grant junior was able to write to Sir James from Hillsea Barracks:

I inclose for your information a Letter I have this instant recd. from the Jail Keeper at Portsmouth informing me that the Duke of York has agreed to allow the poor unfortunate men from the Fencibles serve in the 78th Regt. instead of being transported to the Botany Bay Brigade which is really a fortunate change to them – The Jail Keeper is truly an uncommon good man in his Line – you will observe by his letter that he wishes to purchase McDougall's discharge from the 78th Regt perhaps it is yet too soon to mention any thing of that kind but if wish'd for by you may I suppose be effected afterwards without your being seen in it.

and the enclosed letter read:

To Captn* Grant Hilsea
Portsmouth Gaol Feby 5th 1796

according to my promise I inform you of the Result of your and my Petitions Respecting Duncan McDougall and Lauchlin McIntosh They are both pardoned and are to join the 78th Regt as Soldiers.

[signed] G. Lascombe Keeper His Majestys Goal Portsth.

I should be Happy If It is Possible to Buy McDougalls free Discharge you will be I hope Good enough to acquaint me if it is Possible.[34]

To which Sir James replied on February 9th

Dear John,

I have this moment your Letter as to Lachlan McIntosh & Duncan McDougall having got into the 78th Regt – it goes to the Cape of Good Hope & the East Indies which is surely the best thing that could happen to the poor lads & I trust their future conduct will be such as to merit the Clemency shown them you may certainly give Mr G Luscombe what you mention in consideration of his kindness to these unfortunate poor lads & you give them two guineas a piece from me towards Cloathing

Footnote:
*John Grant junior of Delcroy had been promoted Captain in December 1795.

them in case they do not get Bounty from the 78th – I do not see any propriety in an attempt to procure Duncan McDougalls Discharge – What can be the reason for such a proposal.[35]

So in the end both men were lucky. They were initially sentenced to death and then reprieved only to be sentenced to be transported to Botany Bay. Eventually through the efforts of Sir James they were allowed to enlist in the 78th and serve in the East Indies. Prebble[36] was unaware of this correspondence and concludes that the two men sailed with Kinchurdy's Company for the West Indies – a station where fever was rife and a much less favourable posting. Prebble also states that there is no record of the ultimate disposal of James MacDonald, but indeed there is, for Robert Grant of Boat of Cromdale wrote to the factor on May 20th 1799 shortly after the regiment was disbanded:

> As I have informed you concerning James MacDonald's impertinence by visiting Lady Grant to grant him permission to fish on Spey your proclomation was strictly intimated yesterday by William Grant, he had the assurance to be fishing all this morning at Cambruich which I can prove by clear evidence along with me at the same time – I suppose he means to pay no attention to your orders he thinks to proceed as he don at Dumfries and Linlithgow[37]

Chapter Six

Dundee and Ayr

'in little Kilts neatly dress'd'

During, and for some time after the trial of the mutineers the regiment was encamped at Musselburgh and routine camp life continued. General Orders for July 4th stated: 'Commanding Offrs. of Regimts will be so good as order the Tents to be turned up & straw air'd in fine weather the necessaries* to be filled up, and new ones dug every eight days'. In Camp Orders for August 10th it was stated: 'The old straw from the Mess Tents is to be collected in heaps in the rear & after the Officers have supply'd themselves with what is necessary for their Horses will be carried off by the Contractor whose property the straw is'.[1] General Orders for July 28th stated that: 'The Right Honble. General Lord Adam Gordon having taken into consideration the present high price & scarcity of Flour will dispense with the Troops now encamped at Musselburgh wearing Hair powder until further orders'.[2] Although this was intended to be only a temporary measure, hair powdering was officially abolished in 1795.[3]

The Lt Colonel was also busy making regulations. On July 8th he ordered that:

> As the passes of the Regt. are in General so badly wrote, that the Commanding [Officer] is often ashamed to put his Name to them – In future every Man who wishes to be indulged with a pass, is to apply to the Serjt. Major for a printed one properly filled up for which the man is to pay two pence, he is then to go to the Captain or Commanding Officer of his Company, And get him to indorse the pass on the back by puting down his full name & his Rank in the Regt. upon this being done as specified above the Commanding Officer will sign.

and on August 10th he gave orders that:

> In future no Non Commissioned Officer or Soldier is to presume

---

[Footnote:
  * Latrines.

to Marry without leave obtained in writing from the Commanding Officer...As this order is intended entirely for the welfare & credit of the men, they may be assured that any deviation from it will be severely punished as disobedience of orders.[4]

The unsatisfactory terms of enlistment, namely that the Fencibles were not to serve outside Scotland, led the War Office to encourage Fencible soldiers to transfer to Regiments of the Line. There was an inducement of a bounty of five guineas per man but the War Office was only prepared to pay this money for better quality men. A circular from the Adjutant General's Office dated 28th August 1795 which was sent to officers commanding Fencible regiments stated:

you do forthwith make it known, to the Fencible Corps, under your Command, that such of the Private men therein, as shall prefer serving in the Line, may declare to you their wishes to that effect...on which occasion they will receive a Bounty of Five Guineas

You will be entitled to Charge the Sum of Ten Guineas for every man enlisted in the Corps under your Command in the room of those who may have been received into the Regular Regiments upon the above mentioned conditions...but none are to be accepted of under the size of Five Feet Seven Inches for the Cavalry, and Five Feet Five Inches for the Infantry, nor exceeding the age of Thirty Years.[5]

Eight men from the First Fencible regiment took up this offer. They were all aged between eighteen and twenty three years[6] but it very soon became clear that this arrangement was not going to work for this directive was quickly followed by another on September 15th countermanding it:

the indulgence lately granted to the Soldiers of the Fencible Corps to enlist into Regiments of the Line has been liable to abuses...from the date hereof, no Soldier shall be received from the Fencible Corps into Regiments of the Line, except on consent first obtained form the Officer Commanding the Fencible Corps.[7]

At the beginning of September the War Office sought to ensure that the men were better clothed issuing the following regulations:[8]

Established Proportions of Necessaries for Infantry

3 shirts
2 Pair shoes
1 Pair of Long Gaiters
1 Forage Cap
1 stock
1 Black stock
2 Brushes

The regiment received a boost to its morale when the *Caledonian Mercury* printed a letter from a Musselburgh citizen which read:

It is but justice to say, that no troops ever behaved better, or had more of the approbation and good will of the whole inhabitants of the populous towns near which they lay, than the three regiments of Highlanders who occupied that camp for four months last summer and harvest. They were regular, well disciplined soldiers, and sober, quiet, and inoffensive neighbours.[9]

A letter written by Watson to Sir James on September 19th rather conflicted with the opinion of the *Caledonian Mercury*'s correspondent:

I am sorry to be under the necessity of Reporting the Conduct of our Drum Major which has been truly Reprehensible – he with another Drummer of the Regt. were out of camp all night and fell in with some of the inhabitants – and he the Drum Major drew his sword and put several of the Towns people in terror of their lives...he is so Completely worthless – that all admonition that can be given him is Entirely Lost upon him.[10]

Another non commissioned officer Corporal Hugh Ellis who it will be remembered 'got two Fingers frost bit' in April 1793 shortly after being recruited [see Chapter 1] was declared unfit for further service by Dr John Grant on October 1st who certified that:

Copl. Hugh Ellis of the First Fencible Regiment has for Four months past been troubled with Scrophula or King's Evil, to such a degree as greatly to injure his health, & render him unfit for Service – that he has had recourse to sea bathing, the drinking of sea water & the other remedies commonly employed in such cases, without the least good effect – that his health & strength are gradually on the decline – and that it is my opinion, that nothing but his native air can reestablish him in his former state of health.[11]

John MacNeil a piper, petitioned one of Sir James's daughters on October 15th, sending her the following memorial:

That your memorialist being at the time of his inlisting agreed for one shilling p. diem, which he enjoyed untill January 94...was then under the necessity of either accepting of eight pence p. diem or undergo Corporal punishment agreeable to the sentence of a Court martial he incurred by being a little elevated with a Friend by which he ommitted a point of Duty

That your memorialist having in his option the result of the Court accepted the former, rather than reproach himself with the latter – that your Memorialist experience many difficultys by his present small allowance which is unattended with any emolument or even perquisite whatever at present -

Therefore he intreats your Ladyship to consider his case and flatters himself your usual benevolence will interceed and procure him the Four pence more p. diem as formerly – that he may have Pay similar to others in his station in Camp.[12]

The Rev. James Grant who had once again gone back home to Urquhart following the execution of two of the mutineers had been given a further extension of his leave. His duties were now undertaken by the Rev. Patrick McIntyre, chaplain to the 1st Battalion of the Breadalbane Fencibles who wrote to Sir James on October 24th:

I hope you will not think it unreasonable that I should make a small charge for doing Chaplain's Camp duty to your Regt. – I need not tell you, that, if I had not been in Camp Mr Grant would have been obliged, either, to attend himself, or employ a depute who would cost him much more money than I mean to charge. Five Guineas for preaching etc. etc. five shillings for the Precentor, will fully satisfy me.[13]

* * *

The Fencibles were posted to Dundee at the end of October and set up Headquarters at Dudhope Barracks on November 1st. The accommodation at the Barracks was none too good. William Chalmers, the acting Barrack

Master wrote to Colonel Delancey: 'The rooms are uncommonly cold and uncomfortable, every seam of the flooring as well as the deficient partition walls made by unseasoned wood so open and occasioning such a draft of wind that they were liker barns than anything else.'[14]

Not long after they reached Dundee a War Office directive dated 25th November 1795 arrived stating:

> His Majesty having thought fit to direct, that from the 25th December next inclusive, the Establishment of the several Battalions of Fencible Infantry in Great Britain Jersey & Guernsey whose Effectiveness do not amount to 700 Rank & File shall be reduced, so as to consist of 500 Rank and File and no more...
>
> I am accordingly to signify to you the King's Pleasure, that you do immediately take the necessary steps for complying with His Majestys Orders...taking especial Care to dimiss those Men, who are least fit for Service.[15]

In February 1794 the First Fencibles had been augmented by two extra companies and each company had been increased to a hundred men – although they had been unable to recruit all these extra men. As a result of this latest directive they found themselves reduced to eight companies of 57 private soldiers in each company.[16] According to Fortescue[17] this was standard army practise. Fencible and militia regiments were frequently augmented and then reduced in the hope of forcing the discharged men, who were by now fully trained soldiers, to enter Regiments of the Line but two could play at that game. The Fencible regiments followed the Directive to the letter making sure they disposed of their worst soldiers.

Watson now did some rather convoluted mathematics which he sent to Sir James on December 3rd:[18]

> our numbers at present is as follows
>
> | | |
> |---|---|
> | Our present strength R & file | 562 |
> | Deduct Corpls | 30 |
> | | 532 |
> | Deduct the establishment after 25th December | 470 |
> | | 62 |
> | Add three recruits not joined | 3 |
> | Total to be discharged | 65 |

In a list of those to be discharged dated December 6th, comments were made in a 'Remarks' column as to the reason for discharge. These included 'Rheumatism', 'Old & undersize', 'A boy', 'Sickly & dirty', 'Old undersize Papist', 'Very awkward & diseased', 'undersize dirty', 'Undersize stubborn', 'Drinks hard' and 'Old & useless'. Alexander Cruickshank who was described as being 'worn out' wrote to Sir James:

> I hop you will exuse me as nesisity makes me trouble you as I am one old man going to be discharged which is greatly in my favour for after all I could do it was hard for me to maintain my family going Removings so oft from place to place...Capt grant Lurg...promised me that Lady Grant would do her Endeavour to get me Recommended for the pention as I have bin so long in the service I Listed november in the year 1777 with Capt. Lowis Lieth of docharn for the 71 Regt. and continued their till having got his Commission in the 77 Regt. in March 1778 which I was taken into that the 77 and Remained there all the time of the america ware I had my discharge in apriel 83...I am sure that it will be hard till get a hous about this tim of year at hom but I trust Every thing to your Honours goodness.[19]

One sergeant, McQueen by name, was determined to stay with the regiment. Glenmoriston wrote to Sir James on his behalf:

> Serjt MacQueen I have taken upon myself to keep him till I have your further orders he is a good able man his only fault is he cannot write and he himself is miserable about it, and says he will note take it except you deliver him the discharge out of your own hand which he does not think you would do.[20]

Sergeant McQueen's name did not appear among the list of the 67 men finally discharged even though he was described as being 'very unfit' in the provisional list. Sergeant McQueen was not alone in wanting to stay with the regiment as Watson explained to Sir James on December 12th:

> I can venture to assert that the poor fellows we were obliged to part, with – has really left us with <u>Reluctance</u> however triffling it may appear to them in conversation when it Came to the pinch that they were to go, they were in <u>General</u> very sorry for it.[21]

In the same letter Watson went on to regret that so many Strathspey men on leave had failed to return to the regiment on time, inferring that the factor was again extending their leave passes:

> I am really sorry to reflect on my country men being so dilatory

in returning from the Country, there are only a few of the Strathspey men made there <u>appearance</u> when all the <u>Urquhart</u> and Strath Rannoch men and some from over the ferry at Kessock have come within a day of there time – I should be sorry to attach any blame, to such a worthy Character but I suspect the factor.[22]

Some of the officers were also worried how the reduction would affect them personally. In reply to a query from Achindown Sir James sought to reassure him writing to him on December 19th:

You are exactly in the same state you have been in since the Reduction of the Augmentation took place above a twelve month ago – you are Capn. of a Company & Supernummary Major having as such command of the Regt in the absence of the other Field Officers.[23]

This reference to the 'reduction of the augmentation took place above a twelve month ago' is confusing, as the directive is clearly dated 25th November 1795. Sir James is presumably referring to the augmentation which took place 'above a twelve month ago' and not the reduction.

The factor had been allowed home by Sir James in October[24] and was frequently involved in sorting out some of the men's home affairs. Sergeant Robert Grant wrote to him on November 6th to thank him for looking after his mother. In the same letter the Sergeant described conditions in Dundee:

There is 5 Companies of us in the Barracks and 5 Companies in the Town and Every article that we need is very Dear in this Town the meal is 16 pence per peck* puntates 10 per peck and the meat 3¹/₂ the lib and 4 the best meat.[25]

The price of meat escalated further over the winter and on May 13th 1796 it was noted in Regimental Orders:

His Majesty has been graciously pleased to order that in conseqce. of the high price of Butcher meat that an allowance of 2d per week being made to every Non Commissioned Officer and Privates of Infantry to commence from 25th of April 1796 & continued... until such time as average Price of meat is at 4¹/₂d per lib.[26]

On February 1st Glenmoriston, once again in command of the regiment, issued the following order:

The Commanding Officer is informed that the Soldiers in

Footnote:
*a peck was half a stone or just over 3 kilos.

Barracks not only throw out dirt & filth from their Windows – but even the Men piss from their Windows & not withstanding of a necessary house they go out & ease themselves all round the Barracks...the Commanding Officer orders such practises to be discontinued.

but the practise was not discontinued and he had to repeat the order on March 13th:

The Commanding Officer is sorry to understand that so little attention has been paid to his positive orders of the 1st February respecting the Barracks as to Cleanliness both in front and rear he assures the Soldiers in Barracks once for all that if he has occasion to remind them of this Order again that he will augment the Barracks Guard double, & cause Centinels to be placed all round the Inversions of the Barracks to prevent such Nausiance in future.[27]

* * *

At the same time as the First Fencibles were being reduced to an Establishment of 500 Rank and File the 97th Regiment was disbanded. A War Office Directive of November 23rd stated:

His Majesty has been pleased to order, that all the Rank & File Fit for Duty in the 97th Regiment of Foot, who may choose to enter into the Marines, shall be permitted to do so; and that the remainder shall be transferred to the 42nd Regiment, together with as many of the Sergeants & Drummers as may be required, by the commanding officer of that Corps

The unappropriated Non Commissioned Officers & Privates, fit for Garrison Duty only, are to march to Chatham; there to be disposed of as may be judged expedient; and such as are entirely unfit for any Service, are to be discharged immediately with the usual subsistence to carry them Home...

The men who shall enter into the marines will receive a Bounty of five guineas...

The Draughts for the 42nd Regiment are to be allowed a Bounty of one guinea & a half each...

His Majesty has been further pleased to order, that the 97th Regiment, being above the number of Regiments of which the

British Infantry is to consist, shall be discontinued on the Establishment from the 25th December next inclusive.[28]

These cannot have been happy days for Sir James. The Fencible regiment which he had raised with such alacrity and at considerable personal expense had mutinied twice, was in disgrace and reduced in numbers whilst his Regiment of the Line was reduced altogether, the men being transferred to other regiments.

There was now a steady stream of applications from the men to obtain leave or even a discharge from the regiment altogether on compassionate grounds. Watson wrote to the factor from Dundee on November 28th regarding the plight – the nature of which is not revealed – of one of those on leave in Strathspey, and many other matters that were harassing him at the time:

> I am directed by Major Grant to acknowledge – The Receipt of your letter respecting Allan Grant whom you report as being unable to Join : he desires me to say that notwithstanding the positive orders given out previous to their departure from this place that poor Allans case is certainly an exception, from it and he desires that you will have the goodness to <u>Renew</u> his furlough for one month say from 6th Decr. to 5th Jany 96 – but on no account, to be prolong'd further witht. an absolute necessity and reasons assigned to head quarters – for that purpose – you cannot possibly Conceive the anxiety that prevails here for the 2d division's Departure the moment the others arrive – they will not be convinced of the Impractibility of the Roads – but from what you say I think it will be Impossible for those already at home to be here in time however all that means to do there comrades Justice will be sett out before this can Reach you – be sure that we have strain'd every point – on purpose to accomodate them all by allowing more really than we can well answer for to go home – I wish they may all be cautious and not Run Such Risks as the last sett did...

> the men are much better of than the officers – they have had a fresh allowance for Bread again...

> will you have the goodness to call upon Mr Huston the post master and desire him to pay some attention to the act of Parliament Respecting the Soldiers Letters for I find that there is

a Great deal of unnecessary Trouble here on account of his charging the soldiers Letters the full postage we recover every farthing of it here after a great deal of trouble from his office he should only make one penny upon it.[29]

By a War Office circular, non commissioned officers and soldiers were permitted to send a letter for 1d, if signed outside by the Commanding Officer. This was a great concession as the ordinary charges for letters were very high indeed. The regular rate for England to Scotland was 1s 8d for a single sheet and 3 shillings for one ounce.[30]

The adjutant was not the only one who was worried about the number of men outstaying their leave for on December 1st Achindown, who was himself at home on leave, wrote to the factor:

> I understand there are severals of our men in Strathspey whos furloughs are near out that you will be so good as Intimate at the <u>Kirk doors</u> of Cromdale Abernethy & Duthil that every man belonging to the first Fencible just now in Strathspey will assemble at Aviemore by nine o'Clock on Tuesday where I have ordered a serjeant & all the men in this Country to be on Munday Night, the Serjeant will have a pass for the Whole & take the Command.[31]

* * *

Pat Copland wrote to the factor on December 31st:

> Inclosed I send you a Discharge for James Smith at Bridge of Curr which you'll have the goodness to fill up, mentioning the ailment for which he was discharged – I think it is something about one of his arms, but you'll see himself, and can be satisfied as to this.

and the enclosed printed form read as follows:

> G R
> His Majesty's Regiment
> Commanded by ——
> These are to certify, that the Bearer hereof ——
> has served in the above said Regiment for the space of —— as a ——
> and is discharged from the said Regiment; he having received his Pay, Arrears of Pay, Cloathing of all sorts, and all other Just Demands, from the time of his Enlisting in the Said Regiment, to the day of his Discharge, as appears by his Receipt on the Back of his Discharge. He is Discharged

And to prevent any ill Use that may be made of his Discharge, by
its falling into the Hands of any other Person whatsoever, here
follows the description of the said
aged —— Years, —— Feet —— Inches high,
Complexion ——, Hair ——, Eyes ——, born in the Parish of ——
in the County of ——, —— by Trade
Given under my Hand, and Regimental Seal, at ——
this Day of —— 179–
and on the reverse of the form was printed
I – do acknowledge to have received all my Pay, Arrears of Pay,
Cloathing of all sorts, and all other just Demands, from the Day
of my enlisting into the said Regiment to this Day of my
Discharge.
To all whom it may concern,
Civil and Military.[31a]

* * *

On December 12th Ensign Thomas Steele wrote to Pat Copland, a personal
friend, a letter which perhaps reflected an air of despondency and lethargy
which now seemed to pervade many in the regiment:
Your kind Letter of the 17th ulto. I duly received, which ought to
have been answered er this time, but I hope for your pardon as my
excuse is so very good, which is I have nothing to do, in which
lethargic state I am certainly the dullest correspondent in the
world...
There is not the smallest news here we are daily Discharging a
few men, in order to reduce the Regt. to the number allowed upon
the Establishment, the next will be a finishing shake to the Poor
Fencibles, as suppose we may look upon this as a Prelude to the
awful Tragedy of cutting up and Discharging the whole.[32]
Watson wrote to Sir James in a more cheerful frame of mind on January
23rd 1796 following the appointment of a new Drum Major:
The Drum Major answers our Most Sanguine Expectation as yet
He has made a wonderfull alteration amongst the boys, already &
I trust he will Continue to the End of the Chapter...
The weather has been for some weeks Back Uncommonly mild

which makes the Situation of the men in Barracks very Comfortable the Detachment in Town are on the best Terms with the inhabitants.[33]

This latter statement does not accord with an order given by Glenmoriston on January 26th which stated: 'The Commanding Officer is sorry to understand that the duty in Town has been of late so much neglected, & particularly on the night of the 25th Inst. while some of the Soldiers very unprudently were out of their Quarters & had the assurance to Maltrate some of the Inhabitants.'[34]

There was much civil unrest in Dundee at this time as illustrated by a letter from Glenmoriston to Sir James written on January 29th:

The Lower set of people at Dundee have been very clamorous for some days past and keept the Majistrates in some terrour threatening to do mischief on acount of the scarsity of male they assembled yesterday from three to five hundred of them in a field closs to the town the majistrates and them had several messages back and fore, we were applied to have one hundred men ready if called for by the majistrates, they were accordingly prepared under the command of the Capn. of the Grenadiers who was antious to distinguish himself in the publick service which being known to the Mob I believe occasioned there dismissing queitely, they are an unreasonable set and many great rascals among them wishing to make a pretence of any thing for a riot and to do mischief, this morning some of them stoped some Carts of meal coming into town to market began to devide it among their friends, a party of our men was immediately ordered out and one of the majistrates along who caught them in the Heart of this bussiness along with the meal, they will I think be made an example of by the Majistrates, who spoke highly of your Regt. and their behaviour...one poor unfortunate young man died the day I arrived at Dundee in consequence of takeing too much Mercury and geting cold with it he thought the more he took the sooner he would be well.[35]

Mercury was used in the treatment of syphilis and sibbens and it may well have been tried empirically in other complaints. The veteran Rifleman Harris, when he went down with Walcheren Fever [malaria] was prescribed mercury both externally and internally. 'I was now salivated most desperately,' he records, 'after which I got a little better.'[36] Patients prescribed mercury took it both by mouth and had it rubbed in to their skin 'until the saliva flowed from their mouths in a steady stream'.[37]

* * *

A London Lottery paid out some huge prizes to the few lucky winners. Major Duff it is recorded won a prize of £10,000.[38] Sir James eager to chance his arm instructed Ainslie and Fraser to buy him two tickets on January 22nd and on the 28th he wrote to them: 'You may register the Tickets & keep them in your Custody only dont misplace them amongst your Regimental papers.'[39]

The spiritual welfare of the men of the regiment was now looked after by the Deputy Chaplain at Dundee, the Reverend Alexander Macgregor who wrote to Sir James on February 9th:

I have met with uncommon Civility & attention from the Officers of your Regiment since I joined them. Divine worship is performed every Sabbath – day at the Barracks & the men regularly attend...

I have translated into Gaelic the english Sermon entitled "The Christian Soldier"...I am convinced it would be very useful in the hands of Highland Soldiers & that they would read it with great avidity as they are exceedingly fond of every publication that appears in their own language.[40]

Also on February 9th Sir James received an unwelcome letter from Mr Gloag reminding him that his account for clothing the First Fencibles was still outstanding. £1072 – 19s was still due for 1794, £1585 – 16s for 1795 and a further £1292 – 13s for clothing provided for the 97th Regiment. Mr Gloags total bill including 'other small items' came to £3790 – 1s although the aforementioned sums would suggest that the total was even larger. As Mr Gloag had 'very considerable demands to answer in the course of this month' he not unreasonably asked if he could have £1500 or £2000 on account, concluding diffidently 'requesting you will have the goodness to excuse the trouble of this'.[41] Unfortunately for Mr Gloag this letter evoked no response from Sir James and he wrote again on March 26th requesting a much smaller sum: 'As I have got no money as yet from the agents...I am forced altho' exceedingly much against my inclination to trouble you for...two accompts for £400 or £500 Each, for the Clothing for the first Fencibles & the other for the 97th Regt.'[42]

On February 21st 1796 the factor wrote to Sir James: 'Lachlan MacQueen had a Bill of his [a merchant named Duncan Robertson] for about £2 as I am told and was going to put him in Jail for it upon this the poor man came to me...& begd. me to enlist him for the first fencibles to save him prison and which I did.' Two days later Sir James wrote to the factor 'regarding Malcolm Grant in Kenlost giving his son Alex to the Fencibles on condition of being allowed to build a house & improve a small spot there....conditions upon which a very good soldier, was got to the Fencibles'.[43] Indeed two recruits were obtained in the course of two days but one was recruited in flagrant breach of Section IX of the the Articles of War.*

On March 7th Watson wrote to Sir James: 'I am truly happy to announce to you – that this moment a proposition was made by the Commanding officer that we Should all Subscribe a days subsistence for the behalf of the distress'd <u>poor</u> of this place which was learned without a <u>dissenting voice</u> & Sanctioned with <u>three</u> cheers by the whole <u>Parade</u>.'[44]

Towards the end of March it looked as if the regiment was going to enlist its first black soldier, Sir James writing to Watson: 'Samuel Tucker the Black is arrived and a very fine man – A Large Boil he contracted at Sea above his Eye has placed him under Mr Bells hands for Lancing it – I wish to send him along with Lt Wm Grant to you but he may not be ready – The truth is he has no desire to join the Fencibles but I hope he will be got the better of.'[45] As there is no further mention of Samuel Tucker in the regimental records it is very probable that he declined to serve.

On April 27th Watson wrote excitedly to Sir James:

> Yesterday we had a grand field day with powder when the officers & men paid the strictest attention and everything went off with Great Eclat – and Gave universal satisfaction to a Genteel assembleage of spectators who all Retired highly pleased with the Good appearance of the Regiment and their performance was Really masterly – we are preparing for another field day against Colonel Cummings arrival & could we know when we are to honoured with our Colonels presence We Shall Be properly prepared.[46]

Footnote:
  *see Chapter one.

Glenmoriston was so pleased with the regiment's conduct that on May 1st he ordered:

> From the General good behaviour of the men quartered at Dundee Barracks & Town the Commanding Officer is prevailed upon to release the Men at present in Confinem't without being brought to a Court Martial.[47]

Both Sir James and the factor received a constant stream of letters concerning the problems of both officers and men. On April 6th Duncan Grant of Delshangie, who was not only Sir James's factor of Urquhart but also a Lieutenant in the regiment, wrote to factor James Grant on April 6th:

> I do not by any means wish to be troublesome to Sir James, but I cannot help to think it hard if the Colonel cannot keep a servant & a man in his own business at home the most part of the year, without it being any cause of grumble among the other Subalterns who are now so numerous in proportion to the men, if my appearing on publick occasions, say reviews & musters would serve for attendance, it might not be against me to remain in the Regiment, but when this does not do; I am really of opinion that it would be my own interest as well as that of my Constituents, to give up the Regiment altogether, did Sir James settle or fix on me a Salary as Factor of Urquhart adequate to my trouble and expence. I gave you a hint of this when I was last in Strathspey & you seem'd to be sensible of the propriety of having a man on the spot to look after the woods, Rivers & mosses etc etc.[48]

On the following day, April 7th, Angus Robertson, a Sergeant in the First fencibles, wrote to the factor:

> My father being here of late gave notice to me that my Brother James has a Cow he intends to dispose of to forward the Rent – As my venerable mother has a desire for the Cow I hope you will give James Credit to the amount of her, being £3-7 and your draught upon the paymaster of the Regt. shall be answered – I must return you my unfeigned thanks for the many favours you have Conferred upon my Parents since my leaving home, and as I esteem it my Duty to aid as far as I Can, Confides you'l order James to deliver the Cow to my mother.[49]

Alex MacArthur a private soldier wrote to Sir James on May 1st 1796:

> My Father Angus MacArthur Farmer in Easter Tulloch Departed

this life about a fortnight ago which indeed leaves my brother Angus & myself in great Distress...the adjutant hade the goodness to apply to Colonel Cumming for one of us to go to the Country and Angus Poor man set out immediately but woes me to relate he hade not the Happiness of finding him alive...may I therefore Request your honour to have the goodness to Discharge one of us from the Regiment that we may have it in our Power to Retain the small spot we have under your Honours Patronage...

We have Every Reason to be well satisfied with our present situation in the Regt. being thoroughly convinced there never was a Body of men collected that has been better used and every liklyhood of continuing under the Present Officers.[50]

Alex McArthur wrote an almost identical letter to the factor on May 17th asking him to intercede with Sir James on behalf of himself and his brother Angus but the factor must have immediately passed this appeal on to the adjutant for on May 9th Watson wrote to the factor:

I was duly favor'd with yours Respecting the Goodmen the MacArthurs – I wrote the young one immediately on Receipt of your Letter, to remain at home till I sent him farther notice – but Really as to his Brother going I am much affraid it will be impracticable at present as we are under orders for air [sic!] but at all Events I shall do my endeavour to Solicit the comming officer in favor of the one you have already at home – but you must not reckon me ill natured if I sett my face against either being discharged – It will not do – we dare not enlist a single man and consequently by the same Rule we dare not discharge any...

Mr John [the factor's son] was thinking to take a hasty Trip to Strathspey but Really I disuaded him from just going for Two or three days & considering his late indulgence – and the Regt going upon a long march & to a Strange place, we could not possibly do without him.[51]

The factor wrote to Sir James on May 22nd:

I will send tomorrow for Angus McArthur – I have been telling him it would be his Brothers & his Interest to dispose of everything by Roup at this time except the Crop in the Ground – That if one of them did not get home by the middle of Augt

196

next to Roup the Crop in the ground that I would do it for them to the best Acct that I possibly could – The land their father had I can set just now to the next neighbour at the same rent – I likewise told Angus that he and his Brother might depend upon getting as good a Farm from you when they came out of the Fencibles.[52]

William King, a Soldier in the Sgt Major's Company wrote to Sir James on May 16th:

I have nothing to Depend upon to keep up my Family Except I make an Honest shift of giving those Bread by my wife keeping a shop as I always did at the Bridge – end of Curr.

...if your Honor would think Rather proper to give in my discharge as I cannot serve your Honor and keep up a small family

....and if your Honor thinks proper to order your Factor to give me this Moor Ground I will Bound myself to Close the whole with a Dyke and Build a House with stone and lime again next year.[53]

On May 26th the factor received the following letter from Sergeant Donald Grant:

I was honoured with your friendly letter of 22nd May I am not unsensible of your friendship from long experience in the Present time. I would be sorie to give you any trouble or introduce any inconvenience on you – Meantime I am urged to acquaint you that I cannot get my Mother made Sensible in Setting that money Suppose I wrote her Six or Seven time it seems she does not understand, that it is entirely for her own benefit I want it settled as I knew not if she had keeped it a year or two more about her hand there would not be any thing of it worth looking after...if she will not be advised by yourself I cannot help it.[54]

It would seem that the old Lady was persuaded by the factor to do as her son suggested for eighteen months later Donald Grant wrote to the factor from Edinburgh Castle where the regiment was then stationed: 'I have sent home the discharge for that Interest; which Interest are to be paid to my Mother.'[55]

The men appeared to be in reasonably good health at this time. The sick report for the week ending May 15th signed by surgeon John Grant showed that there were 34 men sick as listed below:[56]

197

Dislocated fingers
Ulcer on leg 4
Convalescent from fever 5
Ulcer on foot 2
Gonnorrhaer 2
Rheumatism
Wounded finger
Wounded wrist
Boil on knee
Flux 3
Cough. Pain of Breast 4
Ague
Ulcers on thigh
Boil on hand
Boil on thumb
Collect of water in Scrotum
Stomach Complaint
Cough etc., 2
Boil on leg

On June 7th the Lt Colonel now briefly back in command of the regiment wrote to Sir James:

> Two of our men has been unluckily ruptured within this little while...owing to falls – as I don't imagine our Dr knows much about such cases, do you approve of sending them to the Edin. Infirmary...for it is absolutely necessary they should get proper trusses and by proper care & skill they may yet be recovered – There is Ferguson also who from the Evil has a most Shocking abscess in his thigh, which is now discharging immense quantities – by being sent to the Infirmary for some time under the hands of skilful men he may yet be made good as he is a good looking soldier...our sick runs from 26 to 30 MacGeorge of the Grenadiers dangerously ill by the fever – I have offered the Dr to call in assistance if he was not perfectly sure he understood his case.[57]

It might appear from this letter that the Lt Colonel did not have a very high opinion of the regimental surgeon! Nevertheless, John McGeorge did receive proper medical attention for Watson was able to write to Sir James on June 21st that: 'John McGeorge is now entirely out of Danger and is doing well.'[58]

Rippachie described the rather aimless state in which the regiment now found itself when he wrote to the factor on July 3rd:

> All of us of the 1st Fencibles. We eat sleep & are merry & have little else to do – indeed we have a little drill preparatory to the review & Sir Jas will wonder when he hears I am out with Regt. every day – we expect our review this week when I have no doubt but we shall make a most excellent appearance
>
> The men have all got their new Cloathing but will only receive their half mounting when we go to Ayr.[59]

The Lt Colonel was also in a jocular mood, possibly because he was shortly to go on leave again, and wrote to Sir James: 'The major Logie & I spent 3 pleasant days at Panmuir & came in on Monday – Logie near killed himself not with wine, but eating up large bowlfulls of thick cream.'[60]

The conduct of the regiment whilst in Dundee met with the approval of both the military and civil authorities. On July 13th Achindown wrote to Sir James:

> The first Fencible Regt. has been reviewed by Major Genl. Drummond and it is with much pleasure I am able to say, that no vetran troops in his Majestys Service could do more than equal the First Fencibles today, The Genl. was delited with them & made use of some very handsome expressions in their favr. he ordered me to return his most hearty thanks to the officers & men & to say he never saw a better review or a finer body of men.[61]

and Alexander Thomas, the Provost of Dundee, wrote to Sir James the following day:

> I am exceedingly sorry to understand that the first Fencible Regiment leaves this place tomorrow.
>
> Allow me Sir, to express how highly sensible the Magistrates are, of the orderly & proper behaviour in every respect, both Officers & Men during the time they have been here; and to Assure you that leaving us will be much regretted by the Inhabitants at large as well as by the Magistrates.[62]

* * *

On July 19th the regiment started its march from Dundee to Ayr and Achindown reported to Sir James from Dundee:

The first Division of the first Fencible Regiment march'd from here today, for Cupper, I march with 2d & last division to morrow...I never saw a Regiment leave a place with more regrate on the part of the Inhabitants of every rank...I saw with Mr Watson a letter from Lady Grant & one from Miss grant soliciting leave for two men which I have Granted, but I request Sir James will hold a Deaff ear to all Petitions from the Regiment on that head...if a few are smuggled the others think themselves injured by being refused.[63]

The regiment was on the march most days and its route and Headquarters each night is set out below:

Cupar in Fife	19th July
Kinross	20th July
"	21st July
South Ferry	22nd July
Falkirk	23rd July
"	24thJuly
Kilsyth	25th July
Glasgow	26th July
Kilmarnock	27th July
Ayr Barracks	28th July

The routine on most days was for the Assembly to be sounded at 3.30am and for the regiment to march off at 4 am.

Watson wrote from Ayr to Sir James on July 31st:

The last division Commanded by Major Grant arrived here yesterday in Good health & high spirits – This is a most excellent Barracks as far as is finish'd – their is no place for any of the officers but myself & I have just one of the mens rooms – which will Answer.[64]

No sooner had they reached Ayr than there were great complaints because 3³/₄d had been docked from the men's pay. It was not entirely clear why this had been done so Glenmoriston set up a Court of Enquiry which found that it was because a baker in Dundee had overcharged for bread. Glenmoriston ordered the paymaster to refund the sum deducted. Encouraged by this success the men asked that meat, which then cost 4¹/₂d per lb, should be further subsidised but in a reply to Glenmoriston, the Deputy Adjutant General stated that 'I do not think you can make any extra charge on the public on that account'

Moving from one posting to another was sometimes a very expensive business for the married men as illustrated by the case of private Malcolm Grant who wrote to the factor from Ayr on August 8th:

I hope you will order the Cow that my uncle has taken without any orders from me to Return her to Mrs Grant Craggan I have Received five pounds six for her from Lieut Grant Craggan befor I left Dundee which I was in need of as I was obliged to hire horse and Cart in Dundee to Carry my wife and my two Small Children to this place if the money is paid you it may remain in your hands as ill pay my uncle son here which will answer both parties as Lieut Grant is out of the Cow and his money - I have not money to pay him as I have spent it on account of my small family once more I beg youl order the Cow to Craggan as I am in the greatest distress that Lieut. Grant should be in disapointment to want the Cow & his money as I intend to make all the shift I Can to pay my uncle son here or at hom any of them they please - I should not wish on any pretence but the Cow Should be sent to Craggan as Lieut. has been a good friend to me on several occations.[65]

As a consequence of complaints that the men were vandalising the Barracks, Glenmoriston stated in Orders:

In consequence of the Order of the 10th Inst. having in some degree been but little attended to, and this day another Complaint having been made by the Overseer of works that the Fasheens behind the Back wall has suffered very much by being carried away for firewood – The Commanding Officer has found it necessary to plant another Sentry.

There is a reference in Regimental Orders to 'Sheet & Towel money – The pay serjeants of Companies are immediately to collect the said Money and pay it for their respective companies',[66] so it would seem that conditions inside the barracks, at any rate at Ayr, were not as bad as Scobie* described.

* * *

On August 21st the Lt Colonel, accompanied by his wife, rejoined his regiment at Ayr and wrote to Sir James two days later:

Nelly held it out very well till we reached Glasgow, where she was

---

Footnote:
*See Chapter 4.

attacked with the Complaint that bore on her so severely last year...she has confined herself to the house, taken rhubarb in small quantities, and is better today...we have got very good lodgings & have an excellent reasonable mess...

I have allowed 10 per company of the married ones to work...when the harvest comes on, I am clear for allowing three fourths of the whole, will serve them & the country too.[67]

But the Lt Colonel was shocked to learn that some of the Non Commissioned Officers had been working at the harvest and published in Regimental Orders:

The Commanding Officer is very much surprised at a most unmilitary abuse which has of late crept in to the Regt., the blame of which can only attach to Officers Commanding Companies – He means Non Commissioned Officers being permited to work – It is a thing that never was thought or heard of in any regular well disciplined Regimt. & the whole Corps must be sensible is totally subversive of good order & regularity – a non commissioned officer in fact is always on duty, & if he is absent at work, his attention to his Squad immediately ceases – The Lieutent. Colonel is doubly surprised that there shou'd even be Serjeants in the Regimt. who had such mean ideas of their own repectable situation, as to make such an application, which shows their unworthiness & the ignorance of their character which those people had who recommended them – in future as the Commanding Officer wishes to give every reasonable indulgence to the Regiment in work if any non commis'd officer having a Family of chidren, thinks he can better his situation by partaking of such a favour he is to apply to the Commanding Offr. to be returned to the ranks.[68]

The senior officers went on leave, rejoined the regiment and went on leave again with bewildering speed. In response to an order for all officers to rejoin the regiment, Sir James wrote to Lord Adam on October 11th:

In consequence of Your Lordships General Orders – I arrived here yesterday – Major Grant of Glenmoriston is here – Lt Colonel Cumming & the Second Major are expected – From my situation your Lordship will know that it is not perfectly convenient for me to remain here & will therefore I am convinced give me permission to return to my family & other business.[69]

The Lt Colonel did not stay long with the regiment for on October 21st he was writing to Sir James from home:

You probably heard of the escape Burdsyards & I made in attempting to foord Spey & my Consequent rheumatic pains & tooth-ach, which has obliged me to write to the C. O. to return me unable to join & sick in the country – indeed for some time most of the family have been suffering severely from the tooth-ach, which makes me think its something in the air.[70]

Whether or not it was 'something in the air' Lt. Colonel Cumming's toothache got worse and on November 5th he was writing to his brother in law: 'This severe weather bears hard on my rheumaticks, particularly my left jaw bone, which is threatened with suppuration.'[71] He remained at home for some months in continuing ill health, writing to Sir James on February 7th 1797: 'I shall not be able to join for some time, as the least exertion brings on a swelling, that is very troublesome & alarming & God knows if ever I shall be as sound as I was.'[72]

* * *

It now became apparent to the authorities that many of the army chaplains were not performing their duties satisfactorily so the Duke of York established the Army Chaplain's Department this year. He appointed John Gamble Chaplain General. A circular was sent to all chaplains offering them the choice of attending their duties in person with pay of 10 shillings per day or of retiring on a pension of 4 shillings per day. Most chose the pension. Michael Glover[73] recounts the case of one particular chaplain who had been on leave for 52 years when his post was abolished in 1796. On October 14th, William Windham now Secretary of State at War wrote from the War Office to Sir James:

It appearing, that scarcely any of the Chaplains of Fencible Corps, have performed their own Duty, or employed Deputies, and proper measures being now under consideration for providing the Troops with the means of regularly attending Divine Service, I have received His Majesty's orders to signify through you to the Chaplain of your Regiment, that he must immediately join his Corps, and in future attend his Duty in person.[74]

But it was not until February 18th 1797 that the chaplain who was now the Rev. Mr McGregor, in place of the ailing Rev. James Grant of Urquhart who was to die in Elgin some eighteen months later,[75] 'returned to the duty with Strathspey fencibles at 2s 6d per day'.[76]

On November 4th Rippachie wrote to Sir James from Ayr: 'All enjoying good health except myself having been confined to bed for a fortnight by a Rose fever.'[77] On hearing this news James Mercer, a merchant in Aberdeen, wrote unsympathetically to his friend: 'I am heartily sorry to find that you are at present indisposed – what you take to be the Rose, may perhaps be the Gout...if you, let me tell you, drank less freely of the Red wine, you would enjoy more exemption from pain, than you do, in the decline of your days.'[78]

Whilst Rippachie lay in his sick bed his fellow Captains took the opportunity of getting a final ruling as to the seniority of the Captains and wrote to Sir James on December 4th:

> Being desirous to have our Ranks adjusted in your Regt without any further delay We wrote a joint letter to the Secretary at War...answer by the Deputy Secretary at War as follows
>
> 'Sir I am directed to acquaint you in answer to your letter...that according to the books of this Office You [Captain Cumming] Captn. Fraser and Captn Rose are the three eldest Captns in the 1st F. Regt. of Infantry
>
> [signed] M. Lewis
> Nov. 23rd 1796'
> Ayr 4th Dec. 1796
> [signed]
> Robert Cumming
> Simon Fraser
> John Rose
>
> P.S. the absurdity of our doing duty in your Regt. and being commanded by an officer of inferior Rank in it will no doubt appear to you to be highly improper and what we cannot subject to.[79]

But the satisfaction that these three Captains had in asserting their seniority over Rippachie was short lived for on January 22nd 1797 Glenmoriston wrote to Sir James with a very different ruling obtained from the Commander in Chief:

> Lord Adam Gordon has just transmitted to me his decision with repect to the memorials of Captns. Grant, Cumming, Rose & Fraser respecting their rank in the Regt. he desires me write you his decision which is that Capt. Grant holds his rank as Senior

Captn. in your Fencible Regt. for his former services in the Army – I have informed all parties of his answer.[80]

So in the end Rippachie had his way!

Sir James wrote to Rippachie on November 28th: 'It is long since my factor applied to me for the first Vacant Ensignancy for his Second Son William & as he is in every Respect of a proper age and the Son of a man whose time is altogether devoted to my business I could not decline his request when an opportunity should occurr by a Vacancy in the Regiment.'[81]

William eventually joined the regiment as an Ensign on May 24th 1797 at the age of 20.

Sir James now wished to purchase Ensignancies in Regiments of the Line for two of his sergeants who were 'as handsome men as are in the army & extremely good duty men', and wrote to Lord George Lennox* on December 2nd:

> Allow me if you can with Convenience to request an Ensignancy in your Regt. for a young man I have a great desire to provide for he has been with me a volunteer in the Fencibles from its commencement acting as a Serjt. to make himself fully master of his profession – He is related to myself and to other respectable Gentleman of my name but has not money to purchase a Commission His name is John Grant he is a very handsome genteel man.

But a note he later wrote to Lt [now Captain] John Grant junior reveals that he had no success:

> I wrote to Lord George Lennox my school fellow and old acquaintance as to a commission for John Grant Belnaclash – who is every way worthy for it – But never received an answer.[82]

Achindown wrote rather gloomily from Ayr to Sir James on December 5th after the regiment had been on manoeuvres:

> I arrived here saturday with one of the Divisions of the Regiment from Kilmarnock, we fell in with the other Division under Glenmoriston's command on the road & marched all in together, We had a very disagreeable days march of it, having rained all the time, we are all snug again in our old good Quarters, officers &

Footnote:
   *Lord George Lennox (1738-1805) Eighth child of the second Duke of Richmond. Promoted Lt. Colonel 33rd Foot 1758 at the age of 20. Brigadier 1763. Major General 1772. Full General 1793. m. 1758 Louisa d. of the 4th Marquis of Lothian. Father of the 4th Duke of Richmond.

men all well except Rippachie who is really very ill with his leg....I am sory to hear Altyre still continues ill with Rheumatic pains.[83]

By the middle of December, some of the non commissioned officers and men were again misbehaving causing Glenmoriston to write in Regimental Orders:

On account of the late intemperance and unsoldier like behaviour of some of the Non Commiss'd Officers & privates of the Regiment in Town at Improper hours, the Commanding Officer has th't proper to order the present Guard to be augmented...

The non Commissioned Officer [of the Guard] is...to patrol the Streets immediately after Tattoo beating, & pick up all Soldiers found out of Barracks, or quarters, and confine them during the night...he...is to specify the time they were taken up, & the state they were found in, whether <u>Sober</u>, <u>intoxicated</u>, or <u>Riotous</u>...The Non Commissioned Officer of the Town Guard is to be answerable that he does not directly or indirectly interfere with any of the inhabitants of the place, upon his <u>peril</u>.[84]

* * *

On December 15th, 17 French ships of the line with 19 frigates, 7 transports and 18,000 men sailed from Brest and arrived at the mouth of Bantry Bay off the south west coast of Ireland on December 20th. General Dalrymple who could only muster 1200 men stationed his small force at Brandon to cover Cork and waited for the French to attack. Fortunately they never did because strong easterly gales prevented them from landing and scattered their fleet which was forced to return to Brest.[85] It was not until January 2nd that Major Grant of Glenmoriston heard of this attempted landing. The size of the French force, according to the best estimates at the time, was believed to be 25,000 men.[86] There was then great activity. Sir James received instructions from the Deputy Adjutant General 'to desire you will order the Regiment under your Command to hold themselves in Readiness to march on the Shortest notice'.[87]

On the same day Glenmoriston wrote to Sir James:

Some of the meddling officers of this Regt are desireous that we should offer our services for Ireland and having mentioned it to a few of the men without my knowledge or aprobation, I thought it proper as comdg. officer to call the officers together to day and forbid them saying any more on that subject to the men that unless you and all the officers were unanimous in that measure it would only be disturbing the quiet of the Regt. which we formerly experienced and answer no good purpose.[88]

Two days later Glenmoriston was able to assure Sir James that 'the Irish mail of this day has brought the agreeable intelligence that the French Ships sailed from Bantray Bay on the 25th Inst. without Landing a man & that it is thought that the storms has damaged them so much, that they must Leave the Coast'.[89] Glenmoriston wrote again on January 13th: 'The Gordon Regt I understand by a Letter to Watson this day from Glasgow, have refused going to Ireland all but one Company & I question whether they would go to England again except the French were actually landed there, I do think our men would have gone if we were all clear for it among ourselves, but it would be too much of me to take upon myself to try it without you or Coln. Cumming were present.'[90] This sensible approach by Glenmoriston was to set in train an unpleasant series of events which became known as the 'Infamous anonymous letter' which was sent to Lord Adam Gordon and read as follows:

To Lord Adam Gordon
My Lord
    On the invasion of Ireland, one of the subalterns of the 1st or Strathspey fencibles, confident he was doing his duty asked the men of the Company to who he belonged, if they would go to Ireland, upon their answering in the affirmitive it was made known to major Grant Commanding Officer, when the Subaltern Officer was publickly reprimanded for his conduct, and after Calling a meeting of the Captains the whole was publickly enjoined upon no account whatever to spake to the men of going to Ireland. The following is a list of the officers who I understand refused to go.

Both Majors, all the Captains and most of the Lieutenants are then individually named and the writer concludes: 'By these means a good body of men is lost to their Country...author wishes to be unknown.'[91]

The original letter was sent by Lord Adam to Sir James who in turn forwarded it to Glenmoriston who replied:

    Inclosed I return the anonamous letter; after parade I called a meeting of all the officers, when I shewed it to them, they all read it, and swore against the villanous performance & its author, agreed it was a forged hand but could not condescend on any person but seem'd to think it was (strange to tell) among ourselves.[92]

After seeing the letter, the officers wrote a short letter to Glenmoriston which they all signed and which was then immediately transmitted to Sir James by Glenmoriston and read: 'In consequence of an anonymous Letter wrote to the Commander in Chief, we the Officers of the first Fencible Regiment, think it our duty to assure you that the Contents are Totally false & malicious in the utmost degree.'[93]

But this was by no means the end of the matter as the subject kept resurfacing causing Achindown, who was by then in temporary command of the regiment, to write to Sir James as late as the end of October 1798: 'It has & is still reported in Edinr & Glasgow & every where that the first Fencibles refused to go to Ireland, this report is by no means agreeable to the officers or men of your Regiment & which I took upon myself very flately to Contradict by saying they never was asked.'[94]

The Lt Colonel was unable to rejoin the regiment at the time of the threatened invasion because of unfortunate injuries he had sustained following a fall. Sir James wrote to Glenmoriston with the details:

> I have only time by this post to acquaint you that in consequence of a severe fall down a stair about a fortnight ago Col. Cumming Gordon is totally disabled from attending his Duty he cannot move without crutches & can neither turn himself in bed or bend his Body but is rendered as helpless as a Child & added to which his Testicles are so swelled that he is in continuous Agony which the medical people say time and rest can only remove – He is in the utmost misery at not being able to be with you at this critical juncture...I rejoice my Dear Sir that you are with the Regt.[95]

The threatened French invasion alarmed the government who ordered Sir James 'to recruit to the full Establishment with the utmost possible despatch'. Sir James then wrote to Watson: 'As our Regiment is now so remarkable for fine men I have ordered none to be taken but such as are worthy of it & in the fullest degree fit for his Majestys Service...The men to be recruited must be fine young men in the Vigour of life from Eighteen to Thirty.' At the same time Glenmoriston informed Sir James: 'We find 100 stand of arms to the best of our opinion not in case for actual service,' and he requested: 'That a like number of serviceable arms might be delivered in their stead.' Sir James passed this request on to the London agent, James Fraser who took the matter up with the Department of Ordnance who in turn, replied: 'I am directed to request you will acquaint Sir James Grant that as his Regiment was suplied with arms so recently as the year 1794 The Board of Ordnance desires to receive a particular return of those arms which Sir James considers defective before they determine upon his application to have such arms exchanged.' To which James Fraser commented dryly: 'It is a pity such difficulties occur They are not calculated to retard an Enemy Landing.'[96]

The bad behaviour of his men continued to concern Glenmoriston who wrote in Regimental Orders on January 30th 1797:

The Commanding Officer is very sorry to observe that the men of this Regt. have of late taken to the vice of drinking more than ever he knew of before, he is now determined to put a stop to it.

and again the following day he wrote that he:

finds with regrate that so little attention has been paid to his Order of yesterday...he orders from this time forward that every Soldier Lodg'd in Barracks will instantly repair to them at Retreat beating – & their to remain till revallie.[97]

As the war progressed more arms became available to the Fencible regiments and in March Watson was able to inform Sir James: 'We have by Last nights post Received an order from the Commdr. in Chief Intimating that Two field pieces is to be Imediately attach'd to the Battalion, which we are all happy at.'[98] Manning these two guns were a detachment seconded from the Royal Artillery, consisting of one lieutenant, one sergeant and six gunners. The First Fencibles supplied one lieutenant, one sergeant, two corporals and 24 private men. When the great day came to fire the guns, the following appeared in Regimental Orders:

The Detachment pitched upon this day from the different Companies on purpose to be instructed in the Great Gun Exercise, are to parade tomorrow morning at 10 o'clock in little Kilts neatly dress'd & afterwards at such hours as the Officer of the Royal Artillery shall think proper.[99]

* * *

The court martial book[100] lists 23 men who were court martialled in 1797. On March 15th private Jack McEwan was sentenced to 300 lashes, of which 25 were remitted, for absenting himself without leave. On April 7th privates James Grant and James Kerr were each sentenced to receive 300 lashes, none of which were remitted, for absenting themselves without leave, getting drunk & rioting. Private William McKay was sentenced to 300 lashes for striking a sergeant, but 100 of these were remitted. In this atmosphere of harsh discipline, some offences were treated with considerable leniency, as was the case with private James Morrison who was sentenced to 100 lashes, all of which were remitted for 'absenting himself from Guard without leave and going into Major John Grant's tent with a woman of bad fame for a breach of General Orders in bringing spiritous liqours to camp'. Private Morrison's accomplice private James Moore was acquitted of 'neglect of duty and disobedience of orders in allowing James Morrison of said Company and a woman to enter Second Major Grant's Tent while he stood Centrie'. On August 31st private James McEwan was sentenced to 250 lashes for the rather nebulous offence of 'irregular behaviour and neglect of duty and making a practice of it' but all 250 lashes were remitted. On November 28th private Donald Cameron was sentenced to 200 lashes none of which were remitted 'for being absent from Barracks at Tattoo Beating on the evening of the 25th Instant and not returning untill the morning of the 26th'.

* * *

In early March, Rippachie was involved with some pressing business relating to his position as Regimental Paymaster and he complained to Sir James:

> This business has been attended with an inconvenience to me as it has detained me since the 26th Ulto when I proposed taking a jaunt north, but since having caught a severe Cold, and the time allowed me being so short, I am much afraid I shall not be able to overtake it at this time which I consider very hard upon me, as I stand much in need of a little jaunting for the Recovery of my health.[101]

On March 12th Watson informed Sir James of the state of some of the men:

> George Grig asthmatic he is in all likelyhood, a dieing man and till such time as some change takes place it would be cruel to discharge him...
>
> James Grant and Donald Forbes will of course be kept on agreeable to your desire, John Cameron...is a very old Soldier and has serv'd many years in the 66 & 61 Regiments...Alexander Fraser...with the same complaint – he is also an old Soldr...Ronald MacDonald...is a young man and I trust he will get over his Complaint which is also a Rupture he comes from Inverness a

Clean <u>decent well behaved man</u> – and he is <u>heart</u> Broke to think
that he would be discharged from the Regiment. I therefore beg
leave to request that you will Suffer him to Remain as he is for a
little Time Longer…James Ritchie…the Doctor thinks him in such
a State as to warrant us to discharge him.[102]

Grigg died ten days later.[103] On May 16th Watson sent a list to Sir James
of those who had been discharged on health grounds recommending some
for a pension and others not:

We have now Got Clear of all our supernumerary men and we are
perfectly complete at this moment, and I trust we shall continue
for some time in that state…The following are a list of those
discharged and the Reasons why
Corpl. Thomas Stuart in the Country
Privates   Alex Fraser –   Recommended
             John Cameron –Ruptures
   Discharged and not Recommended
James Ritchie – Rupture
Duncan Murray – Sore Leg
*Peter Farquharson Malingerer – Bad Character
*Farquharson has defied every measure us'd, he was punished But
to no purpose – he has done no duty for 12 months[104]

The two men 'recommended' were sent to London in order to try to
obtain a Chelsea pension.

* * *

At the end of May the regiment received orders to encamp on the Links at
Ayr[105] together with the Gordon Fencibles and a Regiment of Royal
Artillery. The three regiments were formed into a brigade under the
command of Major General Drummond.

In Brigade Orders it stated that 'The Brigade will parade at eleven in the
morning and at half past seven in the evening'. This routine was followed
daily during the brigade's stay in camp. Brigade Orders also stated 'No
smoking to be allowed in tents'. Major General Drummond had 'no
objections to a certain number of men going to see the Races, But as the
course is above a mile from the Camp it will be necessary that they should
have leave from their Commanding Officers who will permit as many men
per Troop or Compy. as they think proper'.

On July 3rd Brigade Orders stated that 'Major General Drummond has ordered that the Palliases* are to be delivered back to the Commissary tomorrow from the tents in consequence of an order from the Commissary General in England, as the camp is expected to be in readiness to move on the shortest notice.[106] On August 17th it was stated in orders 'Major General Drummond desires that the Walls of the Tents may be put up this evening and the blankets put out to Air and this practise will be observed in future for a few Hours every good day'.[107] There is no record whether the palliases were ever reissued, but if they were the men would have been very comfortable with palliases and blankets.

* * *

The Lt Colonel, his health restored, rejoined the regiment at the end of May. He had settled his affairs at home which involved the purchase of some land from the Duke of Gordon to add to his new estate at the cost of £8,000. Most of this he funded from his recent inheritance but he was still looking for a loan of £2,000 and he turned to his brother in law for help with the request that 'it wou'd be very obliging if you could accomodate me with £500' but Sir James who had financial worries enough of his own replied: 'I have really no money to advance for you.'[108]

It was not only the Lt Colonel who had financial matters at the forefront of his mind. On May 27th, in consequence of a mutiny in the fleet, the pay of a private soldier was increased from 6d to one shilling per day but there were various deductions for 'messing' and 'necessaries' which left the soldier with only one shilling and sixpence per week and even this was subject to 'the accustomed deductions for washing and articles for cleaning his clothes and appointments'.[109]

An order from the Adjutant General's Office issued at the same time as the pay rise made provision for the war time escalation of food prices and stated: 'That if meat of the quality proper to be provided for should exceed the price of sixpence per pound or bread of the household quality the price of one penny half penny per pound such extra price shall be allowed by the publick upon a quantity not exceeding three quarters of a pound of meat and one

Footnote:
    *Pallias. A bed made of sacking and filled with straw.

pound of bread per day for each man.' In July it was stated in Brigade Orders at Ayr camp: 'The Contract for supplying the camp with meat being now compleated, the Regiment will receive on Thursday 6th Instant Two pounds of meat per man, and on monday following one pound and one half per man and continue the same proportion twice a week Mondays and Thursdays.'[110] From this it would appear that the men were none too badly fed although weights of meat were inclusive of the bone.[111]

The Lt Colonel wrote to Sir James on May 27th shortly after resuming command of the regiment lambasting one of the private soldiers with his wicked wit and also describing the social life at Ayr:

> I have had a letter of Mr Copland's to the adjutant about one Forsyth ...being very ill of a consumption – the man is in as perfect health as I am, & thank God, I was never better – the fellow who carried the lie to the country deserves to be punished...It has been a cooked up business between the two – I need hardly recal to your remembrance that Forsyth is a bad man, a principal mutineer at Dumfries...
>
> The weather has mended much since I wrote you last & we are very comfortable – The town is a Scene of constant gaiety We have Capital races every Friday, elegant Dances on Mondays, besides intermediate fete's etc; etc.[112]

On June 6th the Lt Colonel wrote a long letter to Sir James which contained a further description of life in the camp:

> Fortunately yesterday was the only good day we have had, and the line turned out to fire the feu de joie was a striking sight – the concourse of spectators was immense & the scene beautiful – our line of parade is like a bowling green – The Dragoons in new cloathing were on the right of the line, then our Regt. the Artillery with their Guns and the Gordons on the left – the whole looked wonderfully well – Soon after the General came on the ground, a signal was given on which seven guns were fired, then our Regt. a volley & then the Gordons, which was repeated twice more, after which Watson being placed in the centre of the whole line gave the signal when God save the King was repeated with three cheers, the whole spectators joining.

Adding inconsequently:

> Venereals is the disorder most prevalent, being three or four times

more than ever before in the Regt. – 30 sick 13 venereals.[113]

Away from the parade ground, the men did not behave so 'wonderfully well' and on August 27th the Lt Colonel wrote in Regimental Orders:

> The Commanding Officer is exceedingly sorry to understand that some of the Men of the Regiment have of late persevered in a scene of drunkeness and irregularity that if an immediate stop is not put to such practices they will bring infamy and disgrace to the Regiment and Ignominy on themselves.

and again two days later:

> A Court of enquiry to be held tomorrow morning at 10 oclock to enquire into a dispute between some Soldiers of the Princess of Wales Light Dragoons, and some of the 1st Fencible Infantry.[114]

There is no mention of the findings of the Court of Enquiry. It is therefore likely that this was a trivial incident.

The officers did not allow these incidents to interfere with the carefree attitude which pervaded their social life as described by Rippachie who wrote to the factor: 'No news here we are all very gay – Balls etc etc almost every night.'[115] The only cloud on the horizon was the weather. Watson wrote to Sir James on August 7th: 'We have a great deal of Rain and Blowing weather here for some Ten days past this day is more favourable and I trust the weather is a little settled,' but on September 6th the Lt Colonel wrote: 'Last night we had an hurricane – many of our tents tore & were blown down.'[116] The Lt Colonel wrote again to Sir James on September 14th:

> Our review is just over...The general & a numerous crowd of spectators, amongst whom was Ld Eglington & several officers, were much pleased with our appearance tho' in their old cloathes, the men were clean, & arms acoutremements & powdered hair in the highest order – They marched past in quick & slow time, with the utmost correctness & their close firing cou'd not be excelled by any Regt. in the service – The manouevres were done with quickness & precision, & upon the whole they did themselves & their officers much credit.[117]

Hair powdering had been officially abolished in 1795 but in some regiments, the First Fencibles being one of them, this practice seems to have continued for a while.

The Lt Colonel soon changed his tune about the clothing complaining to Sir James on September 26th:

I have now to mention Mr Gloag's conduct, your cloathier – on inspecting and comparing the cloathing by General Drummond the 2d day after the review they were notoriously & evidently deficient in colour & quality, to the pattern suit – and had not the General been very good natured...he would not nor should have passed them – the waistcoats too are shamefully bad & not fit to be seen with the Gordons – and the shoes were of such quality that the Grenadier Company with justice refused thirty pairs.[118]

The First Fencibles were stationed at Ayr for 18 months and according to the *Glasgow Courier* they were 'distinguished by the most perfect regularity and propriety of conduct'.[119] In early September they were put under orders to be ready to march but to where they did not know. 'We are in hourly expectation of our route but have not an idea where,' wrote the Lt Colonel on September 21st, adding: 'I am dreading the little Fife towns or some such.'[120] On September 26th they received orders to march in three divisions to Edinburgh Castle 'at which we all rejoice,' wrote Rippachie to Sir James.[121] The camp at Ayr broke up on October 2nd 1797[122] but, according to Mackintosh,[123] the regiments good conduct for over two years was once again marred by a riot on their last evening. No details of this riot have been found but The Lt Colonel wrote in Regimental Orders:

The Lieutenant Colonel has Lord Adam Gordon's orders to express to the Regt. his Lordships very great disapprobation of the shamefull riot that too many of them were engaged in the night previous to their leaving camp a conduct which sullied their former good character for these two years past – To his Lordships levity and the intercession of the Lieut Colonel those offenders are indebted for not being brought to severe and Just punishment and it can only be their Commanding Officer being inabled to report to his Lordship at a future period, their regret for the past and their present and future good behaviour that they can expect to be reinstated in his Lordships good opinion.[124]

Chapter Seven

Edinburgh Castle, Irvine and Disbandment

'when men are not employed in doing right, they are generally doing wrong'

On September 27th Major General Drummond gave the Lt Colonel his orders to march to Edinburgh but could not allow the regiment to leave without 'expressing his approbation...of their conduct and behaviour during the Campaign'. The Lt Colonel gave his own directions for the march and ordered that:

> On the march which is about to take place exact and implicit attention to be paid to following particulars. The line of march is to be four deep in all cases except when the middle of the Road is deep and wet and the sides dry in which case two deep will be permitted. The Officers to remain attached to their companies though the Commanding Officer has no objection Officers Riding provided one a Company is always on foot, but those who ride, are to dismount and march in and out of all towns, with their respective Companies the Non Commissioned Officers and men are to march and their Knapsacks on and no man is permited to remain behind or be absent from his Company, on the footing of his being a married man.[1]

The soldiers' feet may have been helped on the march to Edinburgh by a recent discovery, information about which was privately circulated:[2]

> A method has been discovered by Mr JAMES WILSON, which, upon the application of a certain material, for the preparation of which he has received His Majesty's Patent, and which has, upon Experiment, been found to answer the intended Purpose, by effectually, and in the most simple Manner possible, preventing or removing the Soreness which Soldiers often experience in their Feet during or after a March.
>
> METHOD OF PREPARATION
>
> The Gut, termed by Butchers the Bung Gut, of an Ox, Cow, or sheep, is to be cleansed by scraping gently, with a blunt Knife or edged Stick, and Water, and is then to be inflated until it is dry;

when the Wind is to be expelled, and the Skin will occupy a small Space, laid by for use. When required, a Piece sufficient to cover the whole or any Part of the Foot that is injured is to be applied, softened in water; and as it has already appeared, by Report of the Regiments where it was tried, never once failed of Effect...One Intestine will make five or six Coverings, and in the Country may be Purchased for a Penny or thereabouts...The Reason for its superior Efficacy for the Purpose in Question, to Bladder or various Substances that have been tried, is that from Peculiar Delicacy of Texture it seems to supply a new skin to any part affected, and accomodating by its Flexibility to the exact Shape of the Foot, excludes atmospheric Air, Sand or any other irritating Matter.

The women and children that made up the regimental camp followers had somehow to get from Ayr to Edinburgh. The sight of these appalled the Lt Colonel who wrote: 'We have a terrible sight of women no less than 196 women & children of private men – an increase of 49 women since we came to Ayr.'[3] The official figures were even higher being 187 women and 104 male children and 110 female children.[4]

On October 5th the first Division of the First Fencibles marched into Edinburgh Castle[5] and their arrival was watched by the Commander in Chief. On October 8th the Lt Colonel wrote to Sir James: 'We are all now safely arrived – Lord Adam saw us incog. as we marched in & was much pleased with us – indeed we are infinitely before the Regt. we relieved,'[6] but the state of the men's clothes was so bad that the Lt Colonel had to inform Sir James:

> Lord Adam Gordon called on me here yesterday & asked me to what it was owing, that our Regt. was so long in our old cloaths & in such inclement weather – I told him it was from the cloathiers not supplying us with materials in proper time to make them up – He desired me to express to you his disapprobations of such delays, that it was to you he looked & that he hoped you wou'd guard against it in future etc.[7]

Lord Adam's visit spurred the Lt Colonel to pay a call on Mr Gloag following which he reported back to Sir James:

> I have had an interview with Mr Gloag who is so fair & is a man of so many words that it is impossible to part with him in hostility – Bygones cannot be mended but we have agreed that more attention

shall be paid in future to our <u>requisitions</u>, & that as he has now <u>timely</u> notice, everything shall be provided in <u>time</u>. He says, that if you will agree to go to the same expence as Lord Breadalbane, the cloathing of your Regt. shall be <u>equally</u> good – that he was allowed for them from 1/3 to 1/6[d] per coat more than for us.

On October 9th, soon after arriving at the Castle, the Lt Colonel issued strict orders that:

> In future an officer of a company is Regularly to see that the Barrack Rooms are properly Sweept out, Beds turned up and windows opened by 9 oclock – The Captains and Commanding Officers of Companies, to be answerable that this order is strictly complied with – and also to make preparations that Butcher meat may be bought and their companies entered on regular messes by Friday next – on monday the 16th their will be a General Review of Arms and accoutrements, at which time it is expected the whole will be in the highest order and proper repair – The Commanding Officer is sorry to observe a very great remissness and unattention to duty, on the part of Non Commissioned Officers commanding Guards in allowing men on duty to pass the Barrier and go to the town, as also in permitting the Centries to be in their Boxes in fair weather contrary to every military rule any Centry found in his Box in future, except during rain, shall be subject to an extra guard and a Non Commissioned Officer allowing any man on duty, or any Soldier without a pass to be out of the Garrison, shall be tried and punished for disobedience of orders.[8]

Again on October 14th he ordered that:

> No Pots, water, ashes tea leaves, or anything else to be emptied over any of the windows on any pretence.

and on October 9th:

> It is Lord Adam Gordon's order, that all officers, absenting themselves from their Corps without Leave, shall, on their return to Quarters, be put under arrest by their Commanding Officers, and reported to the General Officer Commanding.

But he was also capable of being indulgent:

> The Commanding Officer agrees to permit six married men per Company to sleep in town quarters very contiguous to the Castle;

and pragmatic:

The Surgeon to give in to the Commanding Officer tomorrow at Guard mounting a return of the men of the different Companies who from Confinement and the use of Mercury are unable to do duty in kilt – in order that they may be provided with an uniform trowzie to do the Castle duty.[9]

Following the imposition of this strict discipline, the Lt Colonel felt able to write to Sir James on November 2nd:

We have had but one man corporally punished since I joined in May & that was <u>wicked</u> <u>black</u> <u>Forres</u> <u>Morrison</u> twice in camp, <u>once</u> <u>for</u> <u>theft</u> – I flatter myself & feel both credit and comfort in it, that I have now got them into being as orderly a well disciplined happy Regt as any in the service, and firmly believe no man in it, can say I treated him with improper or unmerited harshness...you know when men are not employed in doing right, they are generally doing wrong, but by keeping them in a state of activity & employment we keep them happy.[10]

He also gave Sir James some news of a new recruit:

The fine young savage MacLean arrived today, when he was brought for me to see, he came up to the fire side & wanted to sit down – He is in a state of nudity only got 2 Gs – to whom are we to apply for bounty to rig him out?

The Lt Colonel, who was now Commandant of Edinburgh Castle, may have 'flattered himself' that he had turned the regiment into a well disciplined and happy one but he continued to draw attention to misconduct in Garrison and Regimental Orders of which the following are excerpts:

Edinburgh Castle 7th November 1797

Garrison Orders

The Commandant has seen with much concern the late shameful neglect of duty in the Non Commissioned Officers, both Invalids and Fencibles in permitting sentries to relieve one another, for which two Non Commissioned Officers were this morning reduced – he is determined to put a stop to such unmilitary practices in future and any Non Commissioned Officer again Offending may depend upon being Corporally punished.

Edinburgh Castle 9th November
Garrison Orders

In future no women except those of the officers and Store Keepers families residing in the Garrison, are permitted to come into the Castle or go about in it after Tattoo beating as the Commandant is extremely surprised to have been informed, that women belonging to the Invalids were last night going about bawling out the Counter Sign.

Parole Galloway
Counter Sign Jupiter

Edinburgh Castle. 14th November
Regimental Orders

In future if any woman is found emptying out dirty water or other nastiness over the windows of the Barracks, Stairs or passages, She shall be turned out of the Barracks.

Edinburgh Castle. 30th November
Regimental Orders

The Commanding Officer is extremely sorry to observe that the frequent readings of the Articles of War more and frequent Injunctions of the Lieut. Colonel and Adjutant have not had the effect of preventing the mens quiting their arms when they are posted centries, this is an offence so highly unmilitary, that the Commanding Officer is determined to try by a Court martial, the first man caught in such a situation.

Edinburgh Castle. 27th December
Garrison Orders

The Commanding Officer is sorry to be under the necessity of repeating the orders of 25th October respecting Beggars. He therefore orders that in future the serjeant of the Barrier Guard will give orders to their Sentinels not to allow any Beggars or people under that description to enter the Garrison.

Edinburgh Castle. 14th January 1798
Garrison Orders

The Commanding Officer from the best motives, has deviated in some degree from the Standing Orders of the Garrison, in granting standing passes to some young men of the Regiment, on purpose to attend the school, But he is extremely sorry to observe, that great abuses, has and is still makeing of those indulgencies, he is well aware that this does not apply to all of the above description, still this is not the properest place perhaps to discriminate, how are worthy or not worthy of such indulgencies.[11]

It was not only the Lt Colonel who was a strict disciplinarian for Glenmoriston, in the absence of the Lt Colonel ordered that:

On account of the duty that the Regiment is employed upon in this Garrison, The Commanding Officer finds it absolutely necessary to have the Battalion out every morning in future at six o'Clock mondays and saturdays excepted till further orders.[12]

Whilst stationed at Edinburgh Castle one of the duties of the regiment was to provide guards for French and Dutch prisoners of war. Soon after they arrived at the Castle there were complaints about how they were performing these duties. Malcolm Wright, the Commissary of Prisoners complained to the Lt. Colonel at the beginning of November:

I take the liberty of addressing you at present on the subject of the escape of three Dutch Prisoners yesterday from Fountain Bridge Prison

The Frequency of these accidents of late impresses me with apprehension that either the number of sentinels are too few, are injudiciously posted or extremely remiss in their Duty; and I am the more confirmed in this that there never was an instance of an escape from the prison in question when the number of prisoners was comparatively great and unquestionably equally disposed to avail themselves of the inattention of Sentinels – what render the late escapes more unaccountable is their being effected in fair day Light and always from the Airing Ground – The escape of yesterday happened that instant the Turnkey had gone in to his lodge to Dinner – and who upon his coming out, in the space of less than half an hour, found the said three prisoners were off, and the three contiguous Sentinels closed up in their Boxes. - It is unnecessary for me to apply to the Commander in Chief on this Subject, because I am fully persuaded that you will do every thing that is proper not only in punishing the Sentinels of yesterday if you are satisfied that Culpability is attached to them / of which I have not much doubt / but in giving such particular instructions as will prevent such things in future.[13]

The local hospital for troops based at the Castle, was of course, the Edinburgh Infirmary. Replying to an enquiry from Lord Adam, M. Lewis at the War Office wrote on October 26th:

In answer to your Lordship's letter of 21st instant I am directed to acquaint you that...the managers of the Infirmary at Edinburgh charge eight pence per day for every soldier admitted therein.[14]

The performance of the regiment at drill was still the evoking the highest praise, for the Lt. Colonel reported to Sir James on November 16th:

This morning by appointment at 12 o'Clock we marched down to the King's parks...we went thro' our marchings, firings & evolutions, in a manner that everybody present said could not be surpassed – Generals Drummond & Lumsdain & Colonels without number, were present & Col. Mackay told me in marching up, that he had never been more gratified.[15]

* * *

There are constant reminders of the hardship of life for the men at this time and how much they depended on the good will of those in better circumstances. On November 10th agent James Fraser wrote:

I have much pleasure in acquainting you that Corporal Thomas Stewart...of your Regt. obtained the out Pension and in Consequence of an application to the Secretary at War I have been authorised to advance him Pay from 5 May last so that Stewart has gone home <u>rich</u> & happy.[16]

The two brothers, Alex and Angus MacArthur, both now returned to the regiment and stationed at Edinburgh Castle, wrote to the factor on November 9th:

As the duty is so hard in Edinburgh Castle it will be impossible for us to go home this season...we leave it [their late father's croft] to your own management to do with it as it were your own business and as you have been a friend in former times we still rely upon you as a friend though at a distance.[17]

On November 22nd, James Smith in Laggan petitioned Sir James on behalf of his son:

That the petitioner has received a letter from his son James Smith who is in the first Fencibles whereby the petitioner is informed that his said son has been sickly for some time back and is at present in the Royal Infirmary at Edin. the said James Smith in his letter to his Father say's that if a Furlough could be procured for him, he hopes the Country air would Contribute much to his recovery as his disorder seems to be of a consumptive nature -

That the petitioners wife is bedfast and very anxious to see her son especially since she heard of his sickness May your honour for the above reasons be graciously pleased to order a Furlough to be given to the said James Smith that he may come to Strathspey for a short time and this the petitioner hopes your honour will do as during said James Smiths illness he can be of no service in the way of duty at the Regiment.[18]

On receipt of this petition Sir James set enquiries on foot and on December 4th Watson replied:

James Smith has been poorly with a cold, which none of us escap'd – Less or more, on account of our sudden change of quarters, from the camp to warm Barracks, The Reason of his going to the Infirmary was merely on this account – that there is no Regimental Hospital with the garrison, so let the complaint be never so triffling the Patient is sent to the Infirmary.[19]

So it would seem that James Smith's plea for leave on the grounds of consumption was spurious.

* * *

One boy sent to Inverness to learn the fife, caused some trouble according to the Inverness solicitor, James Grant in a letter to the factor of November 22nd:

One of the boys you sent to learn the Fife here...had enlisted with the 79th Regiment – when I heard of it, I wrote to the officer who had enlisted him and got the enclosed answer very politely giving him up. It seems however that the little Rascal is determined to give trouble & not only say he will inlist with another Regt. but refuses to go to Mr Blair. I am therefore immediately to make out a petition against him on which I shall get a warrant to put him in prison until he shall come to a proper sense of his misconduct.

and on November 30th he wrote again:

an uncle of his applied to me to let him out of Prison he & another man becoming Security for the boys future good conduct, I consented to him being set at liberty. The boy is exceedingly spirited & Mr Blair tells me remarkably clever & as he seems sensible of his misconduct, I hope there will be no after complaint of him – He was in prison four days.[20]

* * *

There was now unexpected trouble from Achindown who had been allowed leave on August 30th to stand in the local election at Nairn, with the proviso that he returned to the regiment at Ayr as soon as the election was over. This he signally failed to do which prompted Watson to comment that he had 'really mistaken himself'.[21] When he eventually reported at Edinburgh he was arrested for being absent without leave. The Lt Colonel described the ensuing events to Sir James on November 16th:

The old major joined monday and according to orders was put in arrest & reported – He at first went like a madman & set the whole world at defiance – breathing nothing but independence & contempt. He wrote a foolish letter to Ld Adam which I wou'd not agree to send, which wou'd have made matters much worse – Next morning he descended from his high horse, & copied a letter which I gave him...we are sorry to see the poor man so altered...& yet he has the folly & perversity to be keeping a woman here who will lead his family to ruin.[22]

But it seems that all charges against Achindown were dropped for on December 5th, the Lt Colonel who was again going on leave wrote: 'The old major is so deaf and doited, that I shou'd not wish to leave him long, with the charge of this place...in fact he is almost finished.'[23] Both majors had now taken mistresses.

At the turn of the year men were again wanting to get home, James Rattray writing to the factor: 'I hope you will ask the favour of him [the adjutant] that I might get a short time in the Country again in the spring as my assistance would be very necessary to my parents as they are in much need of it Ever Since I left them.'[24] One sergeant, Robert Grant who had already returned to Strathspey, caused the Lt Colonel to send a dire warning to Sir James that 'there is a report here that late Serjt. Robert Grant carried home a venereal, that he gave it to his maid, she to her lover, & that the parish of Cromdale will be in a state of infection if not attended to'.[25] Venereal disease was rife in the regiment at this time. A note dated January 22nd 1798 states that there were 16 men from the regiment in the Infirmary. One had a fractured jaw, one had fever, two had rheumatism and twelve were 'venereal'.[26]

By now the regiment was again fully up to strength, the Lt Colonel writing to the factor on February 14th 1798:

It will be necessary for us both to stop recruiting till we have farther directions from Sir James for just after I wrote you, I enlisted three very fine young recruits, two of them grenadiers; and a 4th one a little before that time – As we have been so lucky, I suspect we are more than compleat, so that any extra men will fall on the Colonel – I know that he wou'd not mind it for one or two good men to wait a vacancy, but we would wish to saddle him with as little that way as possible – I would not advise you taking more under size, as we are now such a large bodied Regt.

Ten guineas is now only given by the Line Regts. & we should never give but <u>five</u> as the overpluss is to cover any outlays or expences & we can get as many men as we want for that bounty...

Don't think in future to give beyond £5-5.[27]

* * *

Meanwhile, Watson had fallen head over heels in love and had confided the fact to his friend Rippachie but a problem had arisen in which Rippachie thought Sir James could help, so he wrote to him in early March:

You have no doubt before now heard of Mr Watson's having made his addresses to a young Lady in Dumfries & to which circumstance I have become a sort of confident. I have good reason to believe the Parties are fully agreed but for the interference of some of the young Ladies friends...there seems to be a sort of stop to the business at present which a letter from you to me giving your opinion of Mr Watson...may be of use to Mr Watson, & it is from my attachment & friendship to him & knowing also the merit of the young lady with whom I have the pleasure of being acquainted that I give you this trouble...Mr Watson and I are engaged to Supp on Sunday in Company with some of the young ladies near connections & by being able ostensibly in your letter to support the character I have already given of him will I think forward the business and in which he seems most anxious for a favourable termination.

Sir James readily agreed to assist and wrote to Rippachie from his Edinburgh home in Queen Street:

You judge perfectly right when you are of opinion that I would be happy to serve Mr Watson – I have the highest Esteem for him both as a man & an officer, & I should consider our loss as irreperable were more flattering prospects to deprive us of him while we exist as a Regt.[28]

Sadly, there is no record of whether or not Watson finally won over his lady friend from Dumfries, but he must have continued to keep in touch with her for a friend, Sergeant Donald MacIntosh, wrote to him from Dalkeith on December 1st 1798:

I have Received your Letter in Dumfries But had not the opportunity of Writing you Sooner – our acquaintance there Returned from their jant somedays Before I Left that Place – a courious Peice of Business hapned about her a short time since Lieut. Colonel Lord Hume* of the 10 Militia has seen her for several times Walking down the River side and always made it his study to attend as Near her time as possible But one Evening was using twoo much Freedom She got Clear of him went home and told her Mother Brother and Sister that She was so much Troubled

Footnote:
*Alexander, 10th Earl of Home (1769-1841) Colonel Berwickshire militia. Married Elizabeth, 2nd daughter of the 3rd Duke of Buccleugh.

with him She could not Venteer to walk the streets – her Brother one Evening thought fit to put on His sisters Clothing went the usual walk and Up Comes Lord Hume now Began his old Tricks By using twoo much Freedom he took one of his patons and strack Hume in the head Cuting him severly – he has been here since and married to one of the duke of Buccleughs Daughters it has Been told here in many Different ways But the above is the Right way as I made it my duty to Enquire at one of the Serjts of this Regt that were their at the time it hapned.[29]

A further reference to Watson's possible marriage is to be found in a letter from a Miss Jean Grant from Forres. Writing to Watson she says:

Betty is sitting by me she desires me say that when she was in London she was informed you was just going to be married to an airshire young Lady and that when she came to Edin she expected to be introduced to Mrs Watson She is surprised she has heard nothing of it since.[30]

There are two bundles of James Watson's private letters amongst the records of the First Fencibles[30a] from which it is clear that women were attracted to him. There are a number from Lady Grant and there is one from Lt Colonel Cumming's mildly flirtatious daughter Margaret, newly wed to Captain Madden of the 15th Regiment:

Immediately after the ceremony we came here to dinner where papa had invited a large company to meet us...

you must endeavour to get into Mrs Isherwoods good graces that you may be of her little card partys...

I need not say how happy I sh'd be to introduce you to Capt. M. I told him you had been in the secret.

The budding Bard of Paisley expressed the views of the local ladies regarding Watson in the following two lines:

The Fairfield Ladies wept full Sore
Th' Adjutant they'd see no more[31]

It was not only women who found Watson attractive. Amongst his letters is one from a young Glasgow man:

I know that the silly effusions of a young person engaged only in study, by no means agree with a man whom is in active business...

a report of all the Fencible regiments going to be disbanded, prompts me to enquire...of the truth of it indeed, alas! I have little doubt. Forgive the effusions of friendship I can scarcely proceed, – what will you do, – go into a marching regt. and bid adieu to Britain...To dwell upon this subject is not agreeable and to seek for another would be absurd. The case may be better than I imagine; from my heart I wish it

Watson had a younger brother John, who was valet to Sir John Dashwood. In his correspondence with his elder brother, John Watson admits to being poor, his salary never exceeding £40 per annum, but is content that he has 'a Clean Shirt and a ditto behind and that is more than Everybody can say'.

Watson did eventually marry and have a family for he wrote to his mother from Guernsey in 1809, where he was serving in an unidentified regiment with the rank of Captain, telling her that 'Mrs Watson and the young ones are doing well - three of them goes to school daily...on the whole they are a thriving family - as ever a poor man was blessed'. As ever a dutiful son he enclosed an order upon the Postmaster at Grantown for £5.[31a]

* * *

New Orders for the defence of Edinburgh Castle were issued by the Lt Colonel on April 25th:

> In consequence of the number of Prisoners of War now in the Garrison the Commandant finds it necessary to make an alteration in the order of the 21st Oct. Last relative to the Alarm Posts, to the following Effect, The Security of the Garrison within is the first object on which account on any Alarm by day or night the Companies including Cooks Servants and every Denomination are to assemble Instantly in the Barrack Square where they are to be served with ammunition – The Grenadier Company are immediately to move off to the Lower French Prison and Line the Pallisadoes fronting the Doors of the Cells, The Light Infantry and Lt Colonels to take possession of the Hawk Hill Gate and Loop Holes above it the 1st Majors and Capt. John Grant Junrs. to repair to the Magazine and Laboratory, Capt William Grants to the Barrier, the Artillery to repair with their arms to the Laboratory, Man and load two Six pounders with Grape Shot to be Ready to proceed wherever their services might Be required, the Rest of the Battalion and Invalids to remain in the Barrack Square to wait orders.[32]

On May 16th the Lt Colonel wrote to Sir James to say that he had 'got a small house, looking to Leith Links with great difficulty'. By now some five months later, private James Rattray's appeal to the factor to get him discharged in order that he might get home to Strathspey to assist his elderly parents, had reached the Lt Colonel who, in the same letter to Sir James gave his terse reply: 'I cannot discharge Rattray a made Soldier for a recruit, when the <u>enemy are at our gates</u>, & I have told him twas dastardly to ask it.'[33]

There now arose a dispute between the subalterns and the quartermaster, Lieut. James Carmichael, the subalterns writing to Sir James:

> We the Subaltern officers...feel ourselves called upon to state to you our hardship...
>
> Lieutenant & Quartermaster Carmichael, has very secretly obtained an order from the Commander in Chief dispensing with his mounting Guard, or doing any duty that may interfere with the Quartermasters department.
>
> ...Mr Carmichael when he obtained his double commission understood he was to do & did till very lately has always done both duties, we trust and rely that you will not allow us, to be saddled with such an hardship...as it is known to the whole Regiment, that the duty has been constantly done by the Qr Mr Serjeant whose abilities in that line makes the Quartermaster a mere sinecure.[34]

Eight of the subalterns signed this letter and their grievance was supported by the Lt Colonel who wrote in orders:

> In Consequence of a representation from the whole Subalterns the Commanding Officer feels himself under the necessity of ordering Lt Carmichael to Resume his Subalterns duty when it comes to his turn in the Roster.[35]

Whilst in the Castle the regiment kept a visitors book but the entries in it are somewhat mundane. Visitors had to state the reason for their visit which was recorded as either 'business' or 'curiosity'. Amongst those calling on business were Patrick Lee, Innkeeper of the Black Bull at the top of Leith Walk whose Inn the regiment often frequented and Mr Russell and Mr Grant, surgeons in Edinburgh, coming no doubt to attend a sick soldier at the behest of Dr John Grant. A number of Royal Navy seamen came out of 'Curiosity'.[36]

The regiment received orders to leave their quarters in Edinburgh Castle on June 8th and 9th and to station three companies at Leith, four at Musselburgh, two at Prestonpans and one at North Berwick.[37] On June 2nd the Lt Colonel issued one of his last orders as Garrison Commandant:

> As the Regiment is soon to march to summer Cantonments the Commanding Officer takes this Opportunity of returning his thanks to the Officers and men in General, for the Handsome, soldier like manner in which they have carried on the duty of the Garrison...The Officers Commanding at Musselburgh and Prestonpans may give passes not exceeding one or two men per day of each of their Divisions to go to Edinburgh but always to return before retreat Beating...As a shamefull abuse has been made of the indulgence of Furloughs, by many men setting aside the fear of punishment for such an unmilitary act and as such offences will in future be most rigidly Guarded against The Commanding Officer now declares that any man in future out staying Furlough or pass, may be assured of being punished for disobedience of Orders and as the number of men following
>
> [Eighteen men then individually named]
>
> have on former occasions outstayed their Furlough from 30 to 190 days...it remains a Standing Order of the Regiment, that none of the above men ever get such an indulgence in future, and that any Officer of a Company backing a Furlough or a pass for any of those men for the Commanding Officers signature, shall be deemed and held himself to be guilty of disobedience of Orders.[38]

At the same time as the regiment left Edinburgh Castle, Lord Adam Gordon retired from his post of Commander in Chief in 'North Britain' and wrote to Sir James:

> His Majesty having been pleased to appoint Lieut General Sir Ralph Abercrombie* to be Commander of His Forces in North

Footnote:

*Sir Ralph Abercromby (1734-1801). Lt Colonel 1773. Major General 1787. Commander in Chief North Britain (Scotland) 1798. Commanded the British Army in Egypt and defeated the French at Alexandria on March 21st 1801 but was himself mortally wounded in the action. Generally regarded as one of Britains best Generals of the Napoleonic wars ranking with Sir John Moore and the Duke of Wellington.

Britain – I am to request of you to signify to the Officers Non Commissioned Officers and Privates of the Regiment under your Command the just sense I have of the Zeal and attention to His Majestys Service and my thanks for their good conduct since I have had them under my Command – Accept yourself my best wishes and believe me at all times.

    Sir your very faithfull

    and Obedt. Servant

    Adam Gordon General

The previous day Lord Adam had sent the following card to the Lt Colonel:

Lord Adam Gordon presents his compts to Lt Colonel Cumming Gordon and the officers of the 1st Fencible Infantry, and requests the Honour of their Company to Dinner on Wednesday next, at the Kings Arms Tavern, a quarter before 5 o'Clock.[39]

* * *

Further bickering now broke out among the officers due to a misunderstanding. This arose because Glenmoriston had left the regiment to take command of the Invernesshire, or First North British Militia with the rank of Lieutenant Colonel on June 19th and Captain Allan Grant was mistakenly gazetted as Major to fill his place. This infuriated Captain Cumming of Logie, still smarting at being outranked as senior Captain by Rippachie, who wrote to Sir James that this was 'a mistake which I have no doubt but you'll be so good as to order to be directly rectified at same time this makes me believe that if you are so good as recommend me as oldest Captn in your Regt for the promotion of Major in Glenmoristons room that it will be complied with as they surely intended two majors for your Regt.'[40] Sir James informed Colonel Brownrigg, the Adjutant General, that Capt Allan Grant being gazetted a Major was an error and added 'this occasions alarm among the senior officers' which it most certainly did, but pointed out that in the reduced state of the regiment there was no necessity to replace Glenmoriston. Sir James also made this clear to no less a person than the Commander in Chief, H.R.H. The Duke of York writing: 'Major Grant of Glenmoriston first Major in the Strathspey Fencible Infantry being promoted as Lieutenant Colonel in the

Argyleshire Regt. of Militia Major John Grant of Achindown becomes our Sole Major.'[41]

* * *

The regiment camped at Musselburgh for two weeks and was then posted to Irvine. The first division assembled at four o'clock on the morning of June 22nd and marched immediately for Livingston where they spent the night. On June 23rd they marched for Hamilton where they rested for a day. Regimental Orders for June 25th stated: 'The General will Beat tomorrow at 2 o'clock in the morning the Assembly at half past Two and the Troop at 3 o'clock when the Division for Irvine and Saltcaots will fall in and march Immediately.' They reached Newmills that night and marched into Irvine the following day.

Two Companies were stationed at Headquarters three at Stranraer, one at Ballantrae, one at Girvan, one at Saltcoats and two at Greenock.[42]

In a letter to Sir James, Watson now highlighted a problem which surfaced during the march from Edinburgh to Irvine:

It has I believe been the universal practice of most Regiments to keep some little Triffle for incidents that Generally happens, in a corp – that can neither appear as a Charge against the public or against the Colonel and I can aver that many Instances of this Kind has frequently of Late Come in Our Way such as assisting any poor man with a Large family on a long march which is often done.[43]

The total bounty for a recruit had by now been increased to £7. 7. 0 of which £3. 13. 6 was paid directly to the recruit. A reward of ten shillings and sixpence was paid for enlisting the recruit and the enlisting officer was paid a further £2. 12. 6 by way of reimbursement of expenses.[44]

The Lt Colonel was now approached by Mr Lee, the owner of the Black Bull in Leith Walk, Edinburgh, requesting an Ensigancy in the regiment for his son Patrick.* The Lt Colonel told Sir James that Patrick Lee was was '21 years of age, 5 feet 7 inches high, well educated & from what I can learn in these times will be an acquisition to us', adding, 'his father has been uncommonly kind to all our Regt' when it was stationed at Edinburgh

---

Footnote:
  *Patrick Lee was commissioned as an Ensign in the regiment on 11th October 1798.[50]

Castle. The Lt Colonel concluded his letter: 'Our men upon the whole are keeping very healthy & are behaving with uncommon sobriety – the people here are astonished at their Quietness & good order compared with the other Corps.'[45]

But he spoke too soon regarding the men's health for on August 23rd he was writing to Sir James: 'You will be much distressed to be informed that poor Lt Richardson is no more – He was found dead & almost cold in his bed at Saltcoats this morning – He had been very ill last spring in Edin. but seemed to be quite recovered – & spent two days here lately very well.' A detachment of the Grenadier company was ordered to Saltcoats to 'attend the funeral Procession of the Late Lieut John Richardson' and 'there to fire three Rounds over the grave of the Deceas'd'.[46] On October 7th the Lt Colonel wrote in disgust to Watson: 'So little attention is paid at the Adjutant General's office in examining the returns that they did not know that Richardson was dead till I mentioned it.'[47] On September 6th the Lt Colonel wrote to Sir James: 'Saltcoats is a fatal place for our corps – Charles MacDonald from Cromdale a young Lad of 20 who has a Bror. in the Regt. died of a violent fever a few days ago.'[48] He ended with a plea to Sir James to recruit taller men 'as we are dwindling away amazingly – we have been parting with tall men and getting pygmies', and on August 30th he wrote: 'The Recruit accompanying Ensn. Grant was a very leper with the itch, & it was with much difficulty he was taken into an house here; attention must be paid to sending them clean in future as such a thing has for long been unknown in this Regt.'[49]

Watson shared the Lt Colonel's unfavourable view of their new posting, writing to the factor on August 13th:

> This is amongst the worst quarters amongst them a dull stupid place – Coals is the staple commodity here....we are so exceedingly scattered that one of us does not know what the other is about but I have frequent correspondence with the out Posts.[51]

The men of the regiment were allowed out, as was customary, to help bring in the harvest. The Lt Colonel, in granting permission for this, stated in orders:

> As it is customary for Soldiers to be permitted to work during the time of the harvest, the Lt Colonel is desirous of granting that indulgence to this Regimt. under the following Regulations – The Captains and Commanding Officers of Companies are to be

answerable, that no bad behaved Soldier, no one addicted to drinking, or who is looked upon as dirty, in any sense of the word, is to benefit by this permission...no man on any pretence whatever, who has been any considerable time in the Surgeon's sick list, or who has not done his duty, as a good soldier is to have this benefit...The Lt Colonel...relies the men will not pressure to raise the common Wages of the Country, or to become the extortion of the farmers whom they are bound to protect.[52]

* * *

The Lt Colonel had intended going on leave on August 31st but news of a French landing in Ireland made him 'stop to see what comes of them'.[53] A detachment of 40 men under the command of Capt John Grant junior was ordered on September 9th 'to hold itself ready to Embark for the Island of Arran'. This was the nearest the regiment ever got to seeing action for on September 12th Watson was able to inform Sir James 'we have had good news from Ireland the few <u>French</u> that Landed have Surrendered, and the Rebels found in Arms, with them put to the sword'.[54]

This second French attempt to invade Ireland met with some initial success. A small force of 1200 troops, under the command of the audacious General Humbert, on board three frigates, sailed from the port of La Rochelle on August 4th. The frigates, flying British colours, anchored in Killala Bay. Humbert disembarked his small force without delay and was joined by 2000 Irish rebels. General Lake with a force of some three thousand Irish militia supported by the Fraser Fencibles was defeated by Humbert at Castleton. After days of rapid manoeuvering Humbert was eventually cornered on September 8th at Ballinamuck by Lake who had now assembled a force of 20,000 men . Humbert surrendered but 500 Irish rebels were cut down by the cavalry as they fled. Many others escaped across the bogs.[55]

* * *

The Lt Colonel now fell out with Rippachie but, from the letter he wrote to Watson, the exact nature of their quarrel is not clear:

Rippachies character is pretty well known & his fondness for dispute, but fortunately for me he has meddled with the wrong man, and he'll remain at Saltcoats & continue under my command. Col. Mackay told me he pestered him with letters after the Regt. marched to get up his correspondence & the Col. was obliged to tell him he desires not to be troubled with his correspondence – They all now know him to be vexatious, disobedient & litigious, and I trust and am pretty certain, that this last affair has dished him up, as he deserves – you may read the above to the Majr. & the rest of the officers – as to himself I don't think I shall ever correspond with him again, as I think it was most unhandsome to send copies of my letters about Ld Duncans getting Rose's shilling to Colonel Brownrigg.[56]

The Lt Colonel was involved in another dispute on his way home to Altyre. This time he fell out with an Inn Keeper, named Bryan, at Kings Wells. The problem arose because Bryan kept him waiting for 6 hours for horses to take him to Hamilton which he and Mrs Cumming-Gordon did not reach till 10p.m. Because of this unnecessary delay, as he saw it, the Lt Colonel refused to pay Bryan for the horses. In consequence Bryan tried to confiscate his baggage. In describing the incident to Watson the Lt Colonel continued: 'As to Bryan, I never was worse used in my life, by him & his men – they may do their best or worst – the man attempted to stop me on the high way & I cocked a pistol at him & said if he offered to touch my trunk I wou'd shoot him.'[57]

Other officers were in more jocular mood, Captain Simon Fraser writing on October 13th to Achindown, who was in command at Greenock:

I own we are like to wear out of acquaintance as well as correspondence but you cannot attribute that more to me, than to yourself you die not black paper to me, since we parted at Leith, so that you might have been dead or run away with by a gang of harlots long 'er now without my knowing anything of the matter or affording you any protection, as I cannot be with you at all times...I am told you had a great rejoicing at Irvine on hearing of the glorious victories obtained over our Enemies on the Nile if I am not mistaken the fumes of the wine you drunk to Admiral Nielsons health had not evaporate when you write to me on the 8th Inst Your letter Smell'd strong of port wine, we were merry here on the occasion all two companies have made a voluntary offer of one days pay for the Relief of the widows and orphans of the brave fellows that fell in their Countrys Cause on the first of August.[58]

On October 1st Watson wrote anxiously to Sir James: 'We are in the utmost anxiety about our Destination for the Winter, most of the regiments are receiving their Routes,'[59] but no orders to move came and three weeks later Watson concluded gloomily: 'By all accounts we are to Remain Scattered as we are for the winter, There's no help since it must be so.'[60]

Soon another unpleasant business struck the regiment. Achindown wrote to Sir James with the details:

> I regrate exceedingly to be obliged to write upon a very Disagreeable Subject which the Inclosed will fully explain, The officers of the Regiment have come forward in so determined a manner, as to render any interference on my part fruitless finding that to be the case, I had no other plan to adopt but such as are now before you a copy is sent Lt Reynolds by this days post. The officers is determined to bring him to a General Court Martial unless he saves them the trouble by sending his Resignation to you.

Enclosed was the following 'representation to the Commanding Officer 1st Fencible Regt. Headquarters, Irvine 25th Oct. 1798':

> A surmise having gone abroad in the Town of Irvine that Lieut. Reynolds of this Regiment, has been in the habit of associating not only with the Lowest Company in Town, But more particularly in playing Black <u>Gammon</u> and drinking with his own servant and some of the Soldiers of the Regiment which is a thing unprecedented in the Army; and not only throws a Reflection upon the Regt. But is otherwise derogatory of good order and discipline...we the under Subscribing officers of the Regiment beg to represent...our determination...<u>not to do duty or associate with Lieut. Reynolds</u> & we request that you will take such steps in bringing this matter to a speedy Issue – that we may not be under the disagreeable necessity of bringing it to a General Court martial.[61]

The Lt. Colonel, still on leave of absence at Altyre, had been kept informed of events and wrote hopefully to Sir James on November 16th: 'I hope Reynold's going to Newton Douglas, his affair will blow over & that he'll amend as he's an useful subaltern,'[62] but Reynolds by now had tendered his resignation to Sir James.[63]

Achindown remained in command of the regiment during the winter, Watson writing to Sir James on December 23rd: 'The Lt Colonel and Major have come to a mutual agreement that they remain as they are for the winter. That is Major Grant remains here as the Lt. Col. pleads the necessity of his remaining at the Head of his affairs for this Season at Least.'[64] The Lt Colonel also informed Sir James of this arrangement at the same time expressing his views on the town of Irvine in no uncertain terms. 'You have probably heard that by the Major's agreeing to stay, I am saved for the present going to that shocking hole Irvine.'[65]

It was now more than five years since the regiment had been embodied and yet Mr Gloag was still providing clothing of inferior quality. Watson wrote to Sir James on Christmas day reminding him of this:

> I am sorry to say that the quality of this years Cloathing by no means has kept pace with the Extra allowce. Given to the Cloathier for the express purpose of having a Better quality – and Really the cloathing of the Regiment is very inferior indeed.[66]

* * *

Meanwhile, on October 25th, Lady Grant had fallen and broken her leg, an event which caused Sir James much anguish. The factor wrote to Duncan Grant with the details:

> I am exceedingly sorry to acquaint you that last Thursday afternoon as Sir James and Lady Grant were returning home from their walk to Grantown and near the little burn twixt Old Grantown and the Castle, Lady Grant slipt her foot by which she fell and broke her leg upon which Sir James had to run to the Castle for Dr Stuart
> ...her leg was bound up by the Doctor on the spot...then carried in on a couch....as yet God be thanked she has no fever...Sir James is very dull and uneasy and will be so till assured Her Ladyship is perfectly out of danger.[67]

Sir James described the fracture in more detail:

> The fracture was the large or principal Bone of her right Leg betwixt the Calf and the ankle & nearest the Calf.

Five weeks later, on November 30th, Sir James was still very uneasy and wrote to Dr Stephen at Elgin:

Tho' I would willingly hope that my beloved wife is doing as well as can be expected and am conscious that all the attention that is possible in a Physician is paid yet as she has now lain five weeks Yesterday I labour under great anxiety and beg you'll come up on receipt of this as your Experience may aid the progress of the Cure and suggest the manner of raising her bed which is so necessary for her health as soon as it can be attempted.[68]

On December 30th Sir James wrote to his brother in law:

Lady Grant is now thank God in a fair way of reestablishment We have given up the Hall entirely to her and she goes easily in a Chair with a footboard & hanging Case for her lame Leg & Rollers from her Room and back again & is acquiring Strength.

On January 6th Sir James wrote to Alexander Grant, WS in Edinburgh:

Lady Grant continues to recover – She was Seized with a violent Stitch in her side which kept her in bed two days but she is now quite free of it.

Progress was slow but steady and Sir James in a letter of March 6th to Dr James Grant at the Cape of Good Hope wrote:

Lady Grant is...so much reestablished as to be enabled to go about pretty easily upon Crutches.[69]

Seven months after she had sustained her injury Lady Grant was able to discard her crutches, Sir James informing the Lt Colonel on May 21st:

You will be happy to hear that Lady Grant walked pretty easily without a staff.[70]

It is easy for us in this day and age to take the fracture of a leg bone lightly but two hundred years ago it was a matter of considerable concern. A contemporary surgeon wrote, regarding fractures: 'The surgeon ought to be very cautious in delivering his Prognostic concerning Fractures. He should avoid being too hasty in promising a quick easy and certain cure.' Complications included 'violent pains, inflammations and convulsions and sometimes even gangrene and death itself, or at best the patient must submit to an amputation'.[71]

* * *

In the regiment some of the men were still being unruly and two court martials took place at Irvine, the first on November 5th where:

Private James Mcnair 'got himself in Liqour' at Saltcoats, stole 100 herrings valued at 6/8. Sentenced to receive Three hundred Lashes of which one hundred and 25 were inflicted and was also sentenced to be Drummed out from his company with a discharge suitable to his character on acount of his being a disgrace to any Regiment.

The second took place on November 8th when:

Corporal Meredith tried for 'being in a constant state of Drunkeness and incapable of doing the duty of a non comiss'd officer'.

Found Guilty and sentenced to be 'Reduced from Rank & pay, and to serve as a private in the Ranks'.[72]

An incident occurred at Stranraer in the new year which culminated in the court martial of Lance Corporal Andrew Cumming and three others. They were tried for 'disobedience of orders in being out of Quarters after Tattoo beating & for joining in and heading a combination of the Soldiers to bedlam uproar & maltreat some of the inhabitants of Stranraer'. Sergeant Major James Grant gave evidence that 'a letter written by the Prisoner in the name of himself and the other men there assembled, Containing what he considered a challenge to some of the Inhabitants to come & fight them'. Lance Corporal Cumming was sentenced to receive 300 lashes and Privates James Davidson, Ewen Fraser and Drummer John McQueen were each sentenced to 200 lashes.[73] They had the dubious distinction of being the last men in the First Fencible regiment to be flogged.

* * *

By early 1799 all immediate fear of a French invasion had passed and rumours abounded that the Fencible regiments, who were now no longer needed, would be disbanded. Achindown wrote to Sir James on March 1st 'to communicate a report in circulation and very much believed in the first Circles here. I have it from different good Authorities That is that the first raised Eight Fencible Regiments raised for limited service, are to be asked to extend their service and if they refused they are all to be marched to the places they were first raised & there discharged'.[74] On March 15th a worried Watson wrote to Sir James in confidence: 'I must now acquaint you Altho – a painful Task that our existence as a Corp is precarious and uncertain, and what makes it still more so that we have not your presence at this critical and Trying moment...you surely most join immediately.'[75]

239

Sir Ralph Abercromby now wrote Sir James on March 13th:

> I have it in command from H R. H. the Commander in Chief, to signify to you His Majesty's pleasure that the 1st Regiment of Scotch Fencibles should be Disbanded forthwith, unless three Hundred private men of the said Regt. shall offer to serve in Ireland, or Europe unconditionally And unless you engage to complete it, to its present Establishment within three months at farthest.
>
> You will observe that no additional of Bounty is to be offered to the men for this extension of Service.

Sir James replied, rather belatedly, to Sir Ralph on March 24th:

> I beg...that I may be enabled to lay the matter fully before the whole Regiment when I shall hope the requisite No of 300 Men at the least may come forward at any rate as they expect it from me it is but justice to give them a trial. Should however our Endeavours at the last be unsuccessful which I hope will not be the Case I think it proper to acquaint you that according to my Letter of Service in order to be reduced or disbanded they must be marched back in a Corps to the County of Inverness or Moray where they were principally raised or as near thereto as possible – They were embodied at Forres.[76]

On March 16th the regiment was ordered by Sir Ralph to gather at Irvine. On March 18th Sir James and his son Frank, responding to Watson's plea, set out for Irvine. Sir James also wanted Frank to replace his brother in law as Lieutenant Colonel. Accordingly, he wrote to the Lt Colonel on the same day as he set out for Irvine:

> I do not imagine considering my duty in the country that they have any expectation of my going either to Ireland or abroad with the Regt. But the Lt. Col. will certainly be at any rate expected...in the event of your Resolution to resign I can turn it to Franks acct. & I may make use of it for him without loss of time.

But their letters crossed. The Lt Colonel was happy to tender his resignation writing to Sir James on March 16th:

> Friendship & affection for you alone only brought me into the Regt. & a regard to Consistency alone made me abide the inconveniences of it all along. I can neither be such a fool at my time of life & with my family...as to think of fighting the wild Irish, or defending the dastardly Portuguese.

On March 20th he replied to Sir James:

I recd. your letter of the 18th – my meaning most certainly is, that you should avail yourself of me, in the best manner to bring forward Frank...you will therefore do with me, whatever is most for the interest of your family.[77]

Although he had been away from the regiment for some time the Lt Colonel had not forgotten Watson writing to him on March 18th:

Whether the Regt. will stand or fall, it is impossible to guess, but this much I take it upon me to say, that as I have found you deserving and have a regard for you, you may be assured, that if the Regt is disbanded I will use every interest I have in this world, to get you soon reinstated in some comfortable military situation...If the Regt. stands I shou'd congratulate you on your promotion [to Captain in command of a company vice Fraser] – From my opinion of Balnaclash if we stand, he'll probably succeed you.[78]

Sir James expressed a similar high opinion of Watson to Colonel Brownrigg:

In consequence of the Vacancy occasioned by Capn. Frasers Resignation.

Lieut. James Watson is the Senior Lieut. on the Roll of the Regiment & as such recommended by me to be promoted to the Capn. Lieutancy...Lieut Watson has been long in His Majestys service in various Climates & universally respected & approved of as a good officer – As an Adjutant few or none can surpass him.[79]

On March 30th Sir James addressed the regiment at Irvine:

My Brave and Honourable Friends

The Continuance of our existence as a Regiment depends upon your conduct this day – If you volunteer to extend your Services unconditionally to Ireland we are to be kept up as the First Fencible or Strathspey Regiment If you do not we are very soon to be disbanded...One hundred and fifty of you have already come forward...I trust that the whole will chearfully come forward without further hesitation.

But not for the first time Sir James's call for volunteers fell on deaf ears and he wrote to Sir Ralph:

Having convened the whole Regt this day...I found that the

sanguine hopes of the officers...were delusive for instead of coming forward to the extent of Three Hundred Privates as required by Government they did not equal the Number that had volunteered before Therefore the volunteering of this Regt is at an end. I acquainted the officers with the reasons which prevented your allowing the Regt. to be marched to the County of Inverness or Forres previous to being disbanded but that you was to give all allowances the same as if they had marched to Forres.[80]

On the following day an indignant Watson described the event to Lady Grant

Sir James arrived here on Friday 29th with the Commander in Chiefs Ultimatum that if the present number of 300 would volunteer for Ireland alone the word Europe which seemed formerly to stagger them so much would be dispensed with This explanation Elated the Colonel and all the officers, and we were no doubt sanguine in the idea that we would still exist as a Regiment but woes me upon trial the Reverse was the effect...to our astonishment scarcely a man would move...Col Frances...I trust...may never again witness such perfidy and ingratitude[NAS GD248/516/14]

On March 31st Alexr. MacKay wrote from the Adjutant General's Office to the Officer Commanding, 1st Regiment of Fencibles:

I am directed to acquaint you that Lieut. Colonel Nixon – Deputy Quartermaster General will disband the 1st Regiment of Fencible Infantry under your command at Stirling on Monday the 8th April at 12 o'clock.[81]

On April 2nd the regiment left Irvine for Stirling and was disbanded on April 11th, handing in its arms at Stirling Castle. An allowance of £104 was given for the march from Stirling to Forres, a distance of 208 miles.[82]

On April 10th Sir James wrote to Watson:

My Dear watson

This being the day fix'd for disbanding the First Fencibles I have only to bid you adieu as a Regiment to which I was very much attached & to every Individual of my sincere & hearty good wishes wherever they go – Had they come forward & prevented our dissolution I should have been glad, because I think it would have been for the Credit & Honour of the Corps in general & of

Individuals in particular – As it is they have performed their engagement to their King and Country faithfully & I have no doubt will deserve the same good Character in whatever Regiments they engage.[83]

On April 17th the factor wrote to Duncan Grant of Delshangie:

Upon Wednesday and Thursday last week the whole of the First Fencibles were discharged – at one time 213 of them agreed to extend their services but at the last the number was reduced to about 50....Colonel Cumming did not go near them at all at the time of discharging them. There were I am told about fifty recruiting parties in the place in wait for them – Mr Watson goes to an English Fencible Regiment called the Surrey Rangers as Captain & Adjutant – John Grant Balnaclash goes in likewise as a Lieut – in short the First Fencibles are now completely scattered and dispersed – many of them have gone into militia Regiments.[84]

On April 18th Watson wrote to Lady Grant describing an extraordinary scene that took place as soon as the regiment had been disbanded:[85]

On thursday last 11th instant, we began early in the morning to deliver in our Arms at the Castle – which was done with the greatest regularity then began a pleasant scene (since our fate was now irrecoverable) The moment the men were divested of their Arms they carried their officers shoulder high thro' all the principal streets of the Town, some of the Companies not satisfied with this mark of respect had carriages previously ordered from whom they Took the Horses and drew the officers through the streets in Triumph. The sensation felt by both officers and men cannot be described.

It can be readily understood that Sir James was most unhappy at the turn events had taken and he wrote to the Lord Advocate on April 23rd:

The situation of my family estate heavily encumbered by over exertion for ages in the Service of their King and Country made me sacrifice my seat in Parliament and my political weight in the country to an office [Cashier of Exercise] which was to enable me to overcome the load that oppressed it – whereas now it is only become a dangerous and unprofitable addition to the Cares which require my attention and that at a time when the duties of my Office as Lieutenant [Lord Lieutenant of Inverness-shire] in an extensive County...involves me in expense and withdraws my attention from my private affairs – not to mention the unexpected reduction of both Regts I had raised in the fullest Confidence that they were to be continued to the end of the war.[86]

Sir James was not the only Commanding Officer to be upset at having to disband his Fencible regiment. The Earl of Breadalbane is said to have been 'completely in the dumps at the late orders'.[87]

Pat Copland wrote to the factor from Edinburgh on April 24th:

As far as can be learned here, only 132 men of the first Fencibles have enlisted, which I imagine will not entirely answer the end Government had in view.[88]

Nor indeed was it the end that anybody had in view when the regiment was first raised in those heady spring days of 1793.

Chapter Eight

Epilogue

'It is not imagined they had any premeditated intention but just a sudden passionate impetuosity – sometimes what young highlanders may be guilty of'

This account of the short life of the First Fencible Regiment of Highlanders raises the question – Why did they mutiny? Not once but twice the private soldiers of the regiment held authority in total defiance. They were in full bloodied mutiny at Linlithgow and Dumfries and they defied their officers on at least three other occasions. Firstly, at Forres soon after they were embodied, then the Macdonell company refused to obey their officers on a second occasion at Linlithgow and the regiment is known to have rioted on the evening of their departure from Ayr although there are no details of this riot, only Lord Adam's censure.

Did the soldiers mutiny because of oppressive behaviour by their officers? Sir James was the Colonel of the regiment but he was a soft hearted and kindly man. He gave his Edinburgh recruits half a crown each with the result that on their very first parade they were all as 'drunk as dragoons' which was the 'devil and all' to the Lt Colonel. This was typical of the man. He often gave men leave, frequently against the wishes not only of the Lt Colonel but also the pragmatic adjutant, as witnessed by the case of Private John Fraser. He went to great lengths to do all he could for men down on their luck. His endeavours on behalf of Sergeant Peter Beaton and Private John Fraser were unremitting. He interceded, with due deference to the authorities, on behalf of the two Dumfries mutineers, Lachlan MacIntosh and Duncan McDougall and when the two were left to rot in Portsmouth gaol he was justly angered. Not for nothing was he widely known as 'the Good Sir James'. Yet it was in his presence at Linlithgow that the regiment first mutinied.

The Lt Colonel, unlike Sir James was a strict disciplinarian. His comment to Sir James from Edinburgh Castle 'you know when men are not employed in doing right, they are generally doing wrong, but by keeping them in a state of activity & employment we keep them happy' underlines his philosophy as does his comment after Linlithgow 'if these miscreants arn't frightened into better behaviour, there is an end of all discipline'. There is no doubt that he could be arrogant. His confrontation with the diminutive Charles Mackintosh at Dumfries when he struck him with articles of war and dismissed him with the gibe 'what you lilliputian are you doing here' is just what one would expect from him as was his threat to shoot the innkeeper Bryan. The chaplain certainly thought the Lt Colonel was too harsh with his men when he wrote to the factor after Dumfries: 'I am afraid all will never again concord or assimilate perfectly unless a certain high officer resigns...I can assure you tis fear alone not love that procures obedience at present in the lower orders.'

Lt John Grant junior, was also aware that something was amiss in the regiment when he wrote to Sir James from Glasgow: 'I am confident their [two sergeants] appointment will give universal satisfaction among the men, which is at present in my humble opinion a matter to be attended to.' It is not clear from this whether he thought the Lt Colonel was to blame for the dissatisfaction amongst the men and it should be remembered that the Lt Colonel was highly regarded by at least two of the officers. Rippachie wrote from Paisley: 'I am very happy to learn Altyre is to be so soon with the Regt,' and, according to Watson, his departure from that place met with 'universal regrate'.

Adjutant Watson was generally held in high esteem by the rank and file. Lt John Grant junior, after the riot at Forres, wrote to Sir James: 'Our Adjutant poor man is more lucky than could almost have been expected for when the orders of I may almost say all were held cheap his was not only immediately obeyed but he was also cheered.' It was quite extraordinary that whilst being held prisoner in Linlithgow Palace, he was able to get the mutineers to drill for two hours until they were so tired they wanted him to stop! Yet at Dumfries some local citizens feared for Watson's safety when he went out into the street to try to quell the mutiny saying to him: "For Gods sake do not go to the street if you value your life." Watson may have been temporarily out of favour at that time for it was his reporting of private Anderson to the Lt Colonel that triggered the Dumfries mutiny.

The private men of the regiment must have been aware of the behaviour of some of the other officers. It was probably known that Quartermaster Sutherland was trying to defraud Sir James and Rippachie's ongoing feud with the other Captains regarding seniority may have filtered down to the ranks. The fact that the Lt Colonel had been 'reduced to the disagreeable necessity of putting the two oldest Lieuts in arrest' will certainly have been known to the men. Otherwise, it can be argued that, by and large, the officers behaved remarkably well towards the men who would hardly have treated them with such affectionate respect the day the regiment was disbanded at Stirling Castle had they felt otherwise.

The same cannot be said of the Non Commissioned Officers. Sergeant Major Donald Ross, it will be remembered, not only 'got himself drunk & so beat that he is not fit to be seen; his face disgracefully marked & has not been able to attend a parade this week', but he also behaved in an appalling fashion towards the new recruits just before the mutiny at Dumfries. Two sergeants were court martialled, one for being 'brutally drunk on guard'. Drum Major Weddell was 'such a Drunken man that we are much plagued wt him and often disappointed – we all wish much to be free of him if another would be got'. The list of Non Commissioned Officers behaving badly is almost endless.

What of the Private soldiers and more particularly their views on flogging? This was certainly a punishment that was frequently resorted to in the First Fencible regiment. It is often stated that Highland soldiers found flogging degrading and demeaning. Prebble[1] makes a particular point of this writing that Highland soldiers 'had a horror of the lash, and rarely committed an offence that merited it...a Highlander's spirit broke under the punishment and he rarely returned to his home afterwards'. Scobie[2] makes the same point, stating that: 'Flogging...was seldom resorted to in Highland regiments, as it was entirely unsuited to the Highland character and susceptibilities', and Fraser[3] wrote that flogging was 'abhorrent to the mind of the Highlanders'. But are these statements a true reflection of the Highland soldiers views on the matter? If they are it seems very surprising that there is so little mention of it in any of their letters. The nearest we get to an opinion on flogging is in a letter from Piper John MacNeil to Miss Grant when he states that he got 'a little elevated with a friend' and was given the option of a reduction in pay or a flogging and chose the former as he did not want to 'reproach himself with the latter'. James Stevenson, writing to his parents in Edinburgh, told them that a friend of his had received a hundred lashes for desertion adding in a masterpiece of understatement 'which were very sore'. Stevenson also told his parents that three others had been 'tied up to be whiped for small offences'. He made no adverse comment on these punishments but then he was not a Highlander and nor were nearly half the regiment.

Alexander-Gordon,[4] describing the reaction to a flogging of a soldier of the 93rd Highlanders, states categorically that there was 'not the slightest trace of that feeling of 'degradation' which according to the sentimentalists...

overwhelms not only the man who is flogged but also his comrades'. Glover[5] does not make any mention of Highlanders having a particular aversion to flogging. Indeed, although not referring specifically to Highlanders, he goes so far as to say 'the punishment was not really resented by those who were liable to it'. So what lead to the various mutinies and riots which broke out from time to time? In the case of Linlithgow there was one specific issue, as it seemed to the mutineers, namely that they were about to be forced to go to England despite the specific undertaking by Government that they were not to 'to be marched out of Scotland, except in case of an actual Invasion of England'.

The issue that triggered both the second Linlithgow 'riot' and the Dumfries mutiny was a sense of injustice. The soldiers felt that a comrade had been arrested for a trivial offence and this went against their sense of fair play. It should be remembered that anger at perceived injustice to an individual soldier was also the reason behind the mutiny of the Breadalbanes at Glasgow. Forsyth[6] is certainly of the opinion that a sense of injustice was the cause of the Dumfries mutiny. He states that 'a spirit of discontent had been awakened amongst the men' and that they 'dreaded that there was a design to entrap them into foreign service'. Forsyth believed that Private Anderson's arrest and almost inevitable impending flogging for what was after all only a 'jocular remark' incensed the men. At Linlithgow Watson, who Lt John Grant junior thought had 'a very strange & uncommon knowledge of the minds of the lower order', thought that 'they had wrought themselves up to such a Degree of anger and Revenge without the smallest occasion whatever that they thought it was necessary to give way to their wild Ideas'.

Sir James suggested that a similar reaction was behind the Dumfries mutiny when he wrote: 'It is not imagined they had any premeditated intention but just a sudden passionate impetuosity – sometimes what young highlanders may be guilty of.' At the court martial after the Dumfries mutiny Corporal Meredith made the very pertinent point that he 'thought really in his heart that the men meant no harm to the Col...other ways they might easily have done it'. Might it not be that the Highlanders were more hot headed and quicker to see a grievance than their Lowland and English counterparts? Judge Advocate Larpent certainly thought so. He recalled an incident when a young corporal of The Black Watch, who, having been rebuked for neglect of duty by his Lieutenant, promptly shot the Lieutenant through the heart. 'It seemed to be,' mused Larpent, 'an excess of Scotch pride.'[7]

The factor who knew the Strathspey people intimately made the very telling point that 'they might have stood firm to the terms of their attestation without breaking into the stores & taking possession of the ammunition'.

* * *

What purpose did the regiment and the other Fencible regiments raised so suddenly at the outbreak of war serve? Historians disagree as to how close the country was to revolution in the early days of the Napoleonic wars. Sedition was rife in the cities and large towns but Cookson[8] tends to play this down stating that there was an 'enormous gap between the threat of revolution as imagined by government and ruling groups and the innocuousness of physical force protest in the actual event. Violent disorder, for the most part, remained localized, limited in its aims, and easily subdued'. On the other hand Wells[9] believes that the threat of revolution was very real and 'must be taken very seriously indeed'. Fortescue[10] states 'the home army...was not designed primarily for defence, against foreign enemies, but simply and solely for the purposes of domestic police'. This assessment of their role is confirmed by Lt Colonel Cumming who commented to Sir James after the riot at Forres: 'The people of the Town have been infamous Instruments in seducing the minds of the men, to whom I have explained that it was not for a foreign enemy we were raised, but merely to keep such rascally spirits as every town in Scotland were full of, in order.' In the short life of the regiment there were certainly many occasions when they fulfilled this purpose. At Glasgow the Lt Colonel informed Sir James 'from anonymous letters, & the evil spirit of the lower class of the people, I have been induced with the Provost's approbation to serve out loaded Cartridges to the guard'. At Paisley, Glenmoriston found 'a prodigious crowd of the lower orders assembled they have been threatening mischief for some time but our appearance I think has had a very good effect in this place I do not think they can do any longer here without the military'. At Dundee, Glenmoriston reported to Sir James: 'The Lower set of people at Dundee have been very clamorous for some days past...we were applied to have one hundred men ready if called for by the majistrates'.

If this was the real *raison de etre* for the regiment then it certainly served a useful purpose.

Chapter Notes

[NAS = National Archives of Scotland (formerly the Scottish Record Office)]

Chapter 1

[1]   Mackintosh, H. B. (1934) The Grant, Strathspey or First Highland Fencible Regiment. 1934. p15. Elgin: Yeadon.

[2]   Prebble, J. Mutiny (1975) Mutiny: Highland Regiments in Revolt 1743-1804 pp. 183-197 London: Penguin.

[3]   Churchill, Winston S.(1957) A History of the English Speaking Peoples. Vol iii p.232. London: Cassell

[4]   National Archives of Scotland (NAS) Seafield Muniments GD248/2026

[5]   NAS GD248/683/2/1

[6]   NAS GD248/2026

[7]   Prebble, J. (1975) Mutiny: Highland Regiments in Revolt. pp.302, 306, 307-309. London: Penguin.

[8]   Mackintosh, H. B. (1934) The Grant, Strathspey or First Highland Fencible Regiment. p.22,26,44,47,87. Elgin: Yeadon.

[9]   NAS GD248/691/4/2

[10] Holmes, Richard (2001) Redcoat: The British Soldier in the Age of Horse and Musket. p. 113. London: Harper Collins

[11] Holmes, Richard (2001) Redcoat: The British Soldier in the Age of Horse and Musket. p. 113. London: Harper Collins

[12] NAS GD248/683/2/5

[13] Mcgrigor, James (1861) The Autobigraphy and Services of Sir James Mcgrigor, Bart. Late Director General of the Arny Medical Department p. 10. London: Longman

[14] NAS GD248/2026

[15] Prebble, J. (1975) Mutiny: Highland Regiments in Revolt 1743-2804. p.310. London: Penguin

[16] NAS GD 248/464

[17] Fortescue, J.W. (1905) A History of the British Army. vol. 4 ii, p872. London: Macmillan.

[18] NAS GD248/467/1

[19] NAS GD248/464/3; GD248/2013

[20] Mackintosh. H. B. (1934) The Grant, Strathspey or First Highland Fencible Regiment. pp17-18. Elgin: Yeadon.

[21] NAS GD248/464/8

[22] Mackintosh, H. B. (1934) The Grant, Strathspey, or First Highland Fencible Regiment. pp24-25. Elgin: Yeadon.

[23] NAS GD248/464/1;GD248/464/2

[24] NAS GD248/464/1

[25] NAS GD248/190/3

[26] NAS GD248/683/2/1

[27] Glover, R. (1963) Peninsular Preparation: The Reforms of The British Army. p222. Cambridge University Press.

[27a] NAS GD248/706/2

[28] Glover, Michael. (1977) Wellington's Army in the Peninsular 1808-1814. p.29. Newton Abbot: David and Charles

[29] Glover, Michael (1977) Wellington's Army in the Peninsular 1808-1814.

p.29. Newton Abbot: David and Charles

[30] Haythornthwaite, Philip J. (1994) The Armies of Wellington p. 48. London: Arms and Armour Press.

[31] NAS GD248/464/6

[32] NAS GD248/683/2/4

[33] NAS GD248/464/6; GD248/464/10

[34] NAS GD248/464/10

[35] NAS GD248/695/1/2

[36] NAS GD248/464/6

[37] NAS GD248/464/7;GD248465/5

[38] NAS GD248/465/17

[39] NAS GD248/465/5

[40] NAS GD248/465/5

[41] NAS GD248/465/5

[42] NAS GD248/465/5

[43] NAS GD248/465/6

[44] NAS GD248/464/6

[45] NAS GD248/683/3/2

[46] NAS GD248/464/1

[47] NAS GD248/465

[48] NAS GD248/683/3/2

[49] NAS GD248/464/10

[50] NAS GD248/464/8

[51] NAS GD248/454

[52] Fortescue, J. W. (1905) A History of the British Army, Vol. 3 p.527. London: Macmillan.

[53] NAS GD248/464/8

[54] Haythornthwaite, Philip, J. (1994) The Armies of Wellington. p. 53 London: Arms and Armour Press

[55] NAS GD248/2026

[56] NAS GD248/683/3/4

[57] NAS GD248/683/3/2

[58] NAS GD248/2026

[59] Mackintosh, H. B. (1934)The Grant, Strathspey or First Highland Fencible Regiment p.20. Elgin: Yeadon.

[60] NAS GD248/683/2/1

[61] Haythornthwaite, Philip, J. (1994) The Armies of Wellington. p. 69. London: Arms and Armour Press

[62] NAS GD248/464/9

[63] NAS GD248/683/3/2

[64] Haythornthwaite, Philip J. (1994) The Armies of Wellington p. 63. London: Arms and Armour Press

[65] NAS GD248/468/3

[66] NAS GD248/468/3

[67] Boyd, D.H.A. (1998) Amulets to Isotopes p.36. Edinburgh: John Donald

[68] NAS GD248/683/3/1

[69] Scobie, I. H. M. (1914) An Old Highland Fencible Corps: The History of the Reay Fencible Highland Regiment. p. 48. Edinburgh & London: Blackwell.

[70] NAS GD248/190/3

[71] NAS GD248/454/7

[72] NAS GD248/465

[73] NAS GD248/213/2

[74] NAS GD248/464/5

[75] NAS GD248/464/3

[76] NAS GD248/684/1/3

[77] NAS GD248/468/3

[78] McIntosh, H.B. (1934) The Grant, Strathspey or First Highland Fencible Regiment. p.94 Elgin: Yeadon

[79] NAS GD248/684/1/2

[80] NAS GD248/684/1/3

[81] McIntosh, H. B. (1934) The Grant, Strathspey or First Highland Fencible Regiment. p.33 Elgin: Yeadon.

[82] NAS GD248/2026

[83] Scobie I. H. M. (1914) An Old Highland Fencible Corps: The History of the Reay Fencible Highland Regiment. pp.49-50. Edinburgh & London: Blackwell.

[84] NAS GD248/463/4

[85] Mackintosh, H. B. (1934) The

Grant, Strathspey or First Highland Fencible Regiment. p.22. Elgin: Yeadon.

[86] NAS GD248/464/7

[87] Houlding, J. A. (1981) Fit for Service: The Training of the British Army: 1715-1795 p. 10. Oxford: Clarendon Press.

[88] NAS GD248/468/3

[89] NAS GD248/464/8

[90] Holmes, Richard (2001) Redcoat: The British Soldier in the Age of Horse and Musket. p. 339. London: Harper Collins

[91] Osborne, Brian D. (2001) The last of the Chiefs: Alasdair Ranaldson Macdonell of Glengarry 1773-1828 p.58. Argyll Publishing

[92] NAS GD248/464/3

[93] NAS GD248/463/5

[94] NAS GD248/466/8

[95] NAS GD248/463/5

[96] NAS GD248/684/2/2

[97] Fortescue J. W. (1905) The British Army 1783-1802. p.20. London: Macmillan.

[98] NAS GD248/190/3

[99] NAS GD248/2023

[100] Holmes, Richard (2001) Redcoat: The British Soldier in the Age of Horse and Musket p.324. London: Harper Collins

[101] Glover, Michael (1977) Wellington's Army in the Peninsular: 1808-1814 p. 68. Newton Abbot: David and Charles

[102] Holmes, Richard (2001) Redcoat: The British Soldier in the Age of Horse and Musket p.325. London: Harper Collins

[103] Haythornthwaite, Philip J. (1994) The Armies of Wellington p. 67. London: Arms and Armour Press.

[104] Somerville, Alexander (1967) Autobigraphy of a Working Man pp.195-197. London

[105] Haythornthwaite Philip J. (1994) The Armies of Wellington p. 70. London: Arms and Armour Press.

[106] Hibbert, Christopher (1985) The Recollections of Rifleman Harris. p. 54. London: Century Publishing.

[107] Alexander-Gordon, W. (1898) Recollections of a Highland Subaltern p. 5 London

[108] Glover, Richard (1963) Peninsular Preparation: The Reform of the British Army p.176. Cambridge University Press.

[109] Hibbert, Christopher (1985) The Recollections of Rifleman Harris p. 92. London: Century Publishing.

[110] Glover, R. (1963) Peninsular Preparation: Reform of the British Army. Cambridge University Press.

[111] NAS GD248/464/10

[112] NAS GD248/684/1/3

[113] NAS GD248/2026

[114] NAS GD248/684/3/2

[115] NAS GD248/465/4

[116] NAS GD248/684/3/1

[117] NAS GD248/464/10

[118] Gruber, Ira D. (1998) John Peebles American War: The Diary of a Scottish Grenadier 1776-1782. p. 12. Stroud: Sutton Publishing Ltd

[119] Gruber, Ira D. (1998) John Peebles American War: The Diary of a Scottish Grenadier 1776-1782. p.106. Stroud: Sutton Publishing Ltd

[120] Haythornthwaite, Philip J. (1994) The Armies of Wellington p. 64 London: Arms and Armour Press.

[121] Howard, Martin R. Red Jackets and Red Noses: Alcohol and the British

Napoleonic Soldier J. Roy. Soc.
Med. 2000; 93. 38-41.

[122]   NAS GD248/64/3
[123]   NAS GD248/684/3/3
[124]   NAS GD248/684/3/4
[125]   NAS GD248/684/5/1
[126]   NAS GD248/468/3
[127]   NAS GD248/684/3/4
[128]   NAS GD248/684/4/1

Chapter 2

[1]   NAS GD248/684/4/2;
        GD248/468/3
[2]   NAS GD248/684/4/1
[3]   NAS GD248/684/4/2
[4]   NAS GD248/684/4/3
[5]   NAS GD248/684/4/2
[6]   NAS GD248/684/5/1
[7]   NAS GD248/684/4/2
[8]   Fortescue, J. W.(1905) A History of
        the British Army. Vol.4.i. p.529.
        Macmillan: London.
[9]   NAS GD248/451/1
[10]   NAS GD248/684/4/3
[11]   NAS GD248/684/5/1
[12]   NAS GD248/684/5/2
[13]   NAS GD248/465/4
[14]   NAS GD248/684/5/3
[15]   NAS GD248/684/5/3
[16]   NAS GD248/684/6/1
[17]   NAS GD248/684/6/2
[18]   NAS GD248/684/6/1
[19]   Houlding, J. A. (1981) Fit for
        Service: The Training of the British
        Army: 1715-1795 p. 103. Oxford:
        Clarendon Press
[20]   Glover, Michael (1977) Wellington's
        Army in the Peninsular: 1808-1814
        p. 39. Newton Abbot: David and
        Charles
[21]   NAS GD248/684/6/2
[22]   NAS GD248/1543
[23]   NAS GD248/684/6/2
[24]   NAS GD248/685/3/1/2
[25]   NAS GD248/685/1/3
[26]   NAS GD248/685/1/3
[27]   NAS GD248/685/1/1
[28]   NAS GD248/465
[29]   NAS GD248/685/2/1
[30]   NAS GD248/464/8
[31]   NAS GD248/685/3/1/1
[32]   NAS GD248/2026
[33]   NAS GD248/464/7
[34]   NAS GD248/464/3
[35]   NAS GD248/685/3/1/1
[36]   NAS GD248/685/1/1
[37]   NAS GD248/685/2
[38]   Boyd, D.H.A. (1998)Amulets to
        Isotopes. pp17-19. Edinburgh: John
        Donald.
[39]   Mettler, Cecilia C (1986) History of
        Medicine p. 637. Alabama: Adams
[40]   NAS GD248/2027
[41]   NAS GD248/464/8
[42]   NAS GD248/685/1/2
[43]   NAS GD248/468/3
[44]   NAS GD248/684/6/1
[45]   NAS GD248/685/1/1
[46]   NAS GD248/685/1/1
[47]   NAS GD248/685/1/3
[48]   NAS GD248/685/1/3
[49]   NAS GD248/685/3/1/1
[50]   NAS GD248/685/3/1/2
[51]   NAS GD248/685/1/3
[52]   NAS GD248/685/1/1
[53]   NAS GD248/685/3/1/1
[54]   NAS GD248/685/1/3
[55]   NAS GD685/3/1/2
[56]   NAS GD248/685/1
[57]   NAS GD248/1543
[58]   NAS GD248/685/1/3
[59]   NAS GD248/685/3/1/1
[60]   NAS GD248/685/3/1/1
[61]   Mackintosh, H. B. (1934) The
        Grant, Strathspey or First Highland

Fencible Regiment. p87 Elgin:
Yeadon

[62] NAS GD248/685/3/1/1
[63] NAS GD248/685/3/1/2
[64] NAS GD248/685/3/1/1
[65] NAS GD248/685/3/1/1
[66] NAS GD248/685/4/1
[67] NAS GD248/685/3/1/1
[68] NAS GD248/685/3/1/2
[69] NAS GD248/685/3/1/2
[70] NAS GD248/ 685/4/1
[71] NAS GD248/685/3/1/1
[72] NAS GD248/685/3/1/2
[73] NAS GD248/468/3
[74] NAS GD248/465/11
[75] NAS GD248/1543
[76] NAS GD248/465/8
[77] NAS GD248/685/3/1/2
[78] NAS GD248/685/5/1
[79] NAS GD248/454/6
[80] NAS GD248/454/6
[81] NAS GD248/1552
[82] NAS GD248/454/6
[83] NAS GD248/685/4/3
[84] NAS GD248/686/1/2
[85] NAS GD248/685/4/3
[86] McIntosh, H. B. (1934) The Grant, Strathspey or First Highland Fencible Regiment. p.41. Elgin: Yeadon.

Chapter 3

[1] Prebble, J. (1975) Mutiny: Highland Regiments in Revolt1743-1804. p.277. Penguin.
[2] Mackintosh, H.B. (1934) The Grant, Strathspey or First Highland Fencible Regiment. pp.41-42. Elgin: Yeadon.
[3] NAS GD248/686/1/1
[4] NAS GD248/2027
[5] NAS GD248/2027

[6] NAS GD248/686/1/1
[7] Mackintosh, H. B. (1934) The Grant, Strathspey or First Highland Fencible Regiment. p.44. Elgin: Yeadon.
[8] MacIntosh, H. B. (1934) The Grant, Strathspey or First Highland Fencible Regiment. p.45. Elgin: Yeadon.
[9] NAS GD248/685/4/1
[10] NAS GD248/2027
[11] NAS GD248/685/4/1
[12] NAS GD248/685/4/2
[13] NAS GD248/454/2
[14] NAS GD248/454/2/6
[15] NAS GD248/686/1/1
[16] Fortescue J. W. (1905) A History of the British Army.vol 4.i. p.212-213. London: Macmillan.
[17] NAS GD248/454/6
[18] NAS GD248/454/6
[19] Prebble, J. (1975) Mutiny: Highland Regiments in Revolt 1743-1804. p.299. Penguin.
[20] NAS GD248/464/9
[21] NAS GD248/686/1/2
[22] NAS GD248/454/6
[23] NAS GD248/685/4/4
[24] NAS GD248/464/9
[25] NAS GD248/464/9
[26] McIntosh, H. B. (1934) The Grant, Strathspey or First Highland Fencible Regiment. p.48. Elgin: Yeadon.
[27] NAS GD248/686/1/4
[28] NAS GD248/454/6
[29] NAS GD248/454/6
[30] NAS GD248/465/17
[31] NAS GD248/454/6
[32] NAS GD248/464/9
[33] NAS GD248/464/9
[34] NAS GD248/464/9
[35] NAS GD248/465/1

[36] NAS GD248/686/1/4

[37] NAS GD248/468/3

[38] NAS GD248/686/2/3

[39] NAS GD248/686/2/2

[40] NAS GD248/686/1/5

[41] NAS GD248/686/2/1

[42] NAS GD248/464/9

[43] NAS GD248/2027

[44] Mackintosh, H. B. (1934) The Grant, Strathspey or First Highland Fencible Regiment. p. 52. Elgin: Yeadon.

[45] NAS GD248/465/8

[46] NAS GD248/454/7

[47] NAS GD248/464/9

[48] NAS GD248/465/11

[49] NAS GD248/465/9

[50] Mackintosh, H. B. (1934)The Grant, Strathspey or First Highland Fencible Regiment. p. 51. Elgin: Yeadon

[51] MacDonald, N. H. (1979) The Clan Ranald of Knoydart & Glengarry; A History of the MacDonalds or MacDonells of Glengarry. p.188. Edinburgh: Forrest Hepburn & MacDonald.

[52] NAS GD248/2027

[53] NAS GD248/686/3/2

[54] NAS GD248/686/3/2

Chapter 4

[1] NAS GD248/686/3/4

[2] NAS GD248/687/1/1

[3] NAS GD248/687/1/2

[4] NAS GD248/687/1/3

[5] Mackintosh. H. B. (1934) The Grant, Strathspey or First Highland Fencible Regiment. p.56. Elgin: Yeadon.

[6] NAS GD248/463/7

[7] NAS GD248/64/3

[8] NAS GD248/687/1/4

[9] NAS GD248/687/4/2

[10] NAS GD248/687/3/2

[11] NAS GD248/1543

[12] NAS GD248/465/11

[13] NAS GD248/415/7

[14] NAS GD248/465/1

[15] NAS GD248/468/3

[16] NAS GD248/415/8

[17] NAS GD248/686/3/6

[18] NAS GD248/687/1/2

[19] NAS GD248/465/11

[20] NAS GD248/465/1

[21] Scobie, I. H. M. (1914) An Old Highland Fencible Corps: The History of the Reay Fencible Highland Regiment. p.59. Edinburgh: Blackwood.

[22] Haythornthwaite, Philip J. (1994) The Armies of Wellington. p. 60. London: Arms and Armour Press

[23] Bamfield, Veronica (1974) On the Strength: The Story of the British Army Wife. p.22. London: Charles Knight

[24] Haythornthwaite, Philip J. (1994) The Armies of Wellington. p. 126. London: Arms and Armour Press

[25] Glover, Richard (1963) Peninsular Preparation: The Reform of the British Army. p. 221. Cambridge University Press

[26] Gardyne, C. G. (1901) The Life of a Regiment: The History of the Gordon Highlanders. p.21. Edinburgh: Douglas

[27] Fortescue, J. W. (1905) A History of the British Army. Vol.4. ii. p.907. London: Macmillan.

[28] NAS GD248/688/1/2

[29] NAS GD248/688/1/3

[30] NAS GD248/688/1/2

[31] NAS GD248/688/1/4

[32] NAS GD248/464/3

[33] NAS GD248/688/2/2

[34] NAS GD248/453/3

[35] Prebble, J. (1975) Mutiny: Highland Regiments in Revolt 1743-1804. pp.319-358. London: Penguin

[36] NAS GD248/688/2/2

[37] NAS GD248/688/2/3

[38] NAS GD248/688/3/1

[39] NAS GD248/688/3/1

[40] NAS GD248/688/3/2

[41] NAS GD248/467/1

[42] NAS GD248/688/3/2

[43] NAS GD248/688/3/2

[44] NAS GD248/688/3/2

[45] NAS GD248/455/1

[46] NAS GD248/455/1

[47] NAS GD248/713/8

[48] NAS GD248/713/8

[49] Boyd D. H. A. (1998) Amulets to Isotopes. p.20 Edinburgh: John Donald

[50] NAS GD248/713/8

[51] NAS GD248/713/8

[52] NAS GD248/692/1

[53] NAS GD248/468/4

[54] NAS GD248/713/8

[55] NAS GD248/689/4/3

[56] NAS GD248/689/4/4

[57] NAS GD248/689/4/5

[58] NAS GD248/689/4/6

[59] NAS GD 248/468/4

[60] NAS GD248/688/3/3

[61] NAS GD248/689/4/5

[62] NAS GD248/689/4/5

[63] NAS GD248/689/4/5

[64] NAS GD248/690/1/1

[65] NAS GD248/685/4/1

[66] NAS GD248/690/4/1

[67] NAS GD248/465/9

[68] NAS GD248/690/1/3

[69] Houlding, J. A. (1981) Fit for Service: The Training of the British Army: 1715-1795 p. 3. Oxford: Clarendon Press.

[70] Houlding, J. A. (1981) Fit for Service: The Training of the British Army: 1715-1795 p. 95. Oxford: Clarendon Press.

[71] NAS GD248/689/3/3

[72] NAS GD248/690/1/4

[73] NAS GD248/690/2/2

[74] NAS GD248/690/2/1

[75] NAS GD248/690/3/3

[76] NAS GD248/690/2/1

[77] NAS GD248/690/2/6

[78] Mackintosh H.B. (1934) The Grant, Strathspey or First Highland Fencible Regiment. p. 108. Elgin: Yeadon.

[79] NAS GD248/690/2/6

[80] Prebble, J. (1975) Mutiny: Highland Regiments in Revolt.1743-1804. p. 364. London: Penguin.

[81] NAS GD248/690/3/3

[82] NAS GD248/690/3/1

[83] NAS GD248/690/2/4

[84] NAS GD248/2028

[85] NAS GD248/690/2/1

[86] NAS GD248/690/2/4

[87] NAS GD248/690/2/6

[88] NAS GD248/690/3/1

[89] NAS GD248/690/3/1

[90] NAS GD248/690/3/3

[91] NAS GD248/690/3/3

[92] NAS GD248/690/4/1

[93] NAS GD248/690/4/2

[94] NAS GD248/691/1/2

[95] NAS GD248/690/4/3

[96] NAS GD248/691/1/1

[97] NAS GD248/691/1/1

[98] NAS GD248/690/4/3

[99] NAS GD248/691/1/1

[100] NAS GD248/691/1/1

[101] NAS GD248/463/6
[102] NAS GD248/691/1/3
[103] NAS GD248/691/1/2
[104] NAS GD248/691/1/2
[105] NAS GD248/691/4/3
[106] NAS GD248/691/3/2
[107] NAS GD248/691/4/3
[108] NAS GD248/691/5/1
[109] NAS GD248/691/4/3
[110] NAS GD248/2028
[111] NAS GD248/468/5

Chapter 5

[1]   McIntosh, H. B. (1934) The Grant,
       Strathspey or First Highland
       Fencible Regiment. p.63 Elgin:
       Yeadon.
[2]   NAS GD248/468/4
[3]   NAS GD248/691/1/2
[4]   NAS GD248/691/1/2
[5]   NAS GD248/691/1/2
[6]   NAS GD248/691/1/2
[7]   NAS GD248/691/1/3
[8]   NAS GD248/3417/2
[9]   NAS GD248/689/2/2
[10]   NAS GD248/2023
[11]   Prebble, J. (1975) Mutiny:
       Highland Regiments in Revolt.
       1743-1804. p.373. London:
       Penguin.
[12]   NAS GD248/691/2/1
[13]   Mackintosh, H. B. (1934) The
       Grant, Strathspey or First Highland
       Fencible Regiment. p.96. Elgin:
       Yeadon
[14]   NAS GD248/467/1
[15]   NAS GD248/691/2/2
[16]   NAS GD248//691/2/2
[17]   NAS GD248/451/4
[18]   McIntosh, H. B.(1934) The Grant,
       Strathspey or First Highland Fencible
       Regiment. p.65. Elgin: Yeadon.

[19]   McIntosh, H. B. ibid., p.66.
[20]   Prebble, J. (1975) Mutiny:
       Highland Regiments in Revolt
       1743-1804. p.388.
       London:Penguin.
[21]   Gruber, Ira D. (1998) John Peebles
       American War: The Diary of a
       Scottish Grenadier 1776-1782.
       p.279. Stroud: Sutton Publishing
       Ltd.
[22]   Gruber, Ira D. (1998) John Peebles
       American War: The Diary of a
       Scottish Grenadier 1776-1782.
       p.277. Stroud: Sutton Publishing Ltd.
[23]   NAS GD248/454/8
[24]   NAS GD248/454/8
[25]   NAS GD248/3417/2
[26]   NAS GD248/463/6
[27]   NAS GD248/2028
[28]   NAS GD248/468/4
[29]   NAS GD248/691/3/1
[30]   NAS GD248/463/6
[31]   NAS GD248/691/4/2
[32]   NAS GD248/691/4/2
[33]   NAS GD248/248/2028
[34]   NAS GD248/692/2
[35]   NAS GD248/2028
[36]   Prebble, J. (1975) Mutiny:
       Highland Regiments in Revolt
       1743-1804 p.389 London: Penguin
[37]   NAS GD248/453/13

Chapter 6

[1]   NAS GD248/468/4
[2]   NAS GD248/468/4
[3]   Holmes, Richard (2001) Redcoat:
       The British Soldier in the Age of
       Horse and Musket p. 274. London:
       Harper Collins
[4]   NAS GD248/468/4
[5]   NAS GD248/691/3/3
[6]   NAS GD248/2028

[7]   NAS GD248/691/4/1
[8]   NAS GD248/467/1
[9]   NAS GD248/691/1/3
[10] NAS GD248/691/4/1
[11] NAS GD248/691/5/1
[12] NAS GD248/691/5/3
[13] NAS GD248/691/5/3
[14] Mackintosh, H. B. (1934) The Grant, Strathspey or First Highland Fencible Regiment. p.68. Elgin: Yeadon.
[15] NAS GD248/691/6/3
[16] McIntosh, H. B. (1934) The Grant, Strathspey or First Highland Fencible Regiment. p.57. Elgin: Yeadon.
[17] Fortescue, J.W. (1905) A History of the British Army. Vol. 4 ii. p.889. London: Macmillan.
[18] NAS GD248/692/1
[19] NAS GD248/692/1
[20] NAS GD248/692/1
[21] NAS GD248/692/1
[22] NAS GD248/692/1
[23] NAS GD248/2028
[24] NAS GD248/691/5
[25] NAS GD248/455/2
[26] NAS GD248/468/5
[27] NAS GD248/468/5
[28] NAS GD248/691/6/3
[29] NAS GD248/455/2
[30] I. H. Mackay Scobie (1914) An Old Highland Fencible Corps: The History of the Reay Fencible Highland Regiment. p.199. Edinburgh and London: Blackwood
[31] NAS GD248/452/1
[31a] [NAS GD248/452/1]
[32] NAS GD248/689/3/1
[33] NAS GD248/692/1
[34] NAS GD248/468/5
[35] NAS GD248/692/2/1
[36] Hibbert, Christopher (1985) The Recollections of Rifleman Harris p.122. London

[37] Haggard, W. Howard. Devils, Drugs and Doctors p.349. London: Heinemann
[38] NAS GD248/364/2
[39] NAS GD248/2028
[40] NAS GD248/692/2/2
[41] NAS GD248/692/2/2
[42] NAS GD248/692/3/1
[43] NASGD248/452/2
[44] NAS GD248/692/3/1
[45] NAS GD248/2028
[46] NAS GD248/692/4/2
[47] NAS GD248/468/5
[48] NAS GD248/451/5
[49] NAS GD248/451/5
[50] NAS GD248/453/6
[51] NAS GD248/453/6
[52] NAS GD248/692/4/1
[53] NAS GD248/453/6
[54] NAS GD248/453/6
[55] NAS GD248/456/8
[56] NAS GD248/693/3
[57] NAS GD248/693/1/1
[58] NAS GD248/693/1/1
[59] NAS GD248/465/12
[60] NAS GD248/692/4/1
[61] NAS GD248/693/1/2
[62] NAS GD248/693/1/2
[63] NAS GD248/693/1/2
[64] NAS GD248/693/1/1
[65] NAS GD248/456/5
[66] NAS GD248/468/5
[67] NAS GD248/693/2
[68] NAS GD248/468/5
[69] NAS GD248/2028
[70] NAS GD248/693/4/1
[71] NAS GD248/693/3/1
[72] NAS GD248/694/1
[73] Glover, Michael (1977) Wellington's Army in the Peninsular: 1808-1814 p. 130. Newton Abbot: David and Charles
[74] NAS GD248/693/4/2

[75] NAS GD248/467/3
[76] NAS GD248/694/1
[77] NAS GD248/693/3/1
[78] NAS GD248/693/3/3
[79] NAS GD248/692/1
[80] NAS GD248/693/6/1
[81] NAS GD248/2028
[82] NAS GD248/2028
[83] NAS GD248/465/9
[84] NAS GD248/468/6
[85] I. H. Mackay Scobie (1914) An Old Highland Fencible Corps: The History of the Reay Fencible Highland Regiment. p.110. Edinburgh and London: Blackwood.
[86] NAS GD248/693/6/1
[87] NAS GD248/693/6/1
[88] NAS GD248/693/6/1
[89] NAS GD248/693/6/1
[90] NAS GD248/693/6/1
[91] NAS GD248/694/1
[92] NAS GD248/694/1
[93] NAS GD248/467/1
[94] NAS GD248/697/1/2
[95] NAS GD248/2028
[96] NAS GD248/2028
[97] NAS GD248/468/6
[98] NAS GD248/694/2/1
[99] NAS GD248/468/6
[100] NAS GD248/2023
[101] NASGD248/465/9
[102] NAS GD248/694/2/2
[103] NAS GD248/694/2/2
[104] NAS GD248/694/4/1
[105] NAS GD248/694/4/1
[106] NAS GD248/468/6
[107] NAS GD248/2024
[108] NAS GD248/694/4/1
[109] Fortescue, J. W. (1805) A History of the British Army. Vol. iv. Appendix B. London: Macmillan.
[110] NAS GD248/468/6

[111] Haythornthwaite, Philip J. (1994) The Armies of Wellington p. 62. London: Arms and Armour Press
[112] NAS GD248/694/5/1
[113] NAS GD248/694/5/1
[114] NAS GD248/2024
[115] NAS GD248/453/8
[116] NAS GD248/695/1/1
[117] NAS GD248/695/1/2
[118] NAS GD248/695/1/2
[119] McIntosh, H. B. (1934). The Grant, Strathspey or First Highland Fencible Regiment. p.71. Elgin: Yeadon.
[120] NAS GD248/695/1/2
[121] NAS GD248/695/1/2
[122] NAS GD248/467/1
[123] McIntosh, H. B. (1934) The Grant, Strathspey or First Highland Fencible Regiment. p.72. Elgin: Yeadon.
[124] NAS GD248/2024

Chapter 7

[1]   NAS GD248/2024
[2]   NAS GD248/466/6
[3]   NAS GD248/695/1/2
[4]   NAS GD248/697/3/3
[5]   Mackintosh, H. B. (1934) The Grant Strathspey or First Highland Fencible Regiment. p72. Elgin: Yeadon
[6]   NAS GD248/695/2/1
[7]   NAS GD248/695/2/1
[8]   NAS GD248/2024
[9]   NAS GD248/2024
[10] NAS GD248/695/2/2
[11] NAS GD248/2024
[12] NAS GD 248/468/7
[13] NAS GD248/466/5
[14] NAS GD248/2023
[15] NAS GD248/695/2/2

[16]   NAS GD248/465/9
[17]   NAS GD248/366/2
[18]   NAS GD248/465/8
[19]   NAS GD248/695/3/2
[20]   NAS GD248/456/7
[21]   NAS GD248/695/2/2
[22]   NAS GD248/695/2/2
[23]   NAS GD248/695/3/2
[24]   NAS GD248/453/10
[25]   NAS GD248/695/3/2
[26]   NAS GD248/527/5
[27]   NAS GD248/366/6
[28]   NAS GD248/696/1/2
[29]   NAS GD248/467/3
[30]   NAS GD248/467/2
[30a] NAS GD248/467/2
[31]   NAS GD248/64/3
[31a] NAS GD248/513/17
[32]   NAS GD248/468/7
[33]   NAS GD248/696/2/2
[34]   NAS GD248/696/2/2
[35]   NAS GD248/468/7
[36]   NAS GD248/442/12
[37]   NAS GD248/696/2/3
[38]   NAS GD248/468/7
[39]   NAS GD248/468/7
[40]   NAS GD248/696/3/3
[41]   NAS GD248/1544
[42]   NAS GD248/466/3
[43]   NAS GD248/696/3/4
[44]   McIntosh, H. B. (1934) The Grant,
       Strathspey or First Highland
       Fencible Regiment. p.77. Elgin:
       Yeadon.
[45]   NAS GD248/596/3/4
[46]   NAS GD248/468/7
[47]   NAS GD248/467/3
[48]   NAS GD248/696/4/2
[49]   NAS GD248/596/3/4
[50]   Mackintosh, H. B. (1934) The
       Grant, Strathspey or First Highland
       Fencible Regiment. p.93 Elgin:
       Yeadon.

[51]   NAS GD248/465/12
[52]   NAS GD248/468/7
[53]   NAS GD248/596/3/4
[54]   NAS GD248/696/3/4
[55]   Scobie, I. H. M. (1914) An Old
       Highland Fencible Corps: The
       History of the Reay Highland
       Fencible Regiment. p.205.
       Edinburgh: Blackwood.
[56]   NAS GD248/467/3
[57]   NAS GD248/467/3
[58]   NAS GD248/466/5
[59]   NAS GD248/697/1/1
[60]   NAS GD248/697/1/2
[61]   NAS GD248/697/1/2
[62]   NAS GD248/697/2/1
[63]   NAS GD248/467/6
[64]   NAS GD248/697/3/2
[65]   NAS GD248/697/6/2
[66]   NAS GD248/697/3/2
[67]   NAS GD248/444
[68]   NAS GD248/1544
[69]   NAS GD248/1544
[70]   NAS GD248/1545
[71]   Mettler, Cecilia C (1986) History
       of Medicine p. 871. Alabama:
       Adams
[72]   NAS GD248/467/4
[73]   NAS GD248/466/5
[74]   NAS GD248/698/2/1
[75]   NAS GD248/698/2/2
[76]   NAS GD248/2023
[77]   NAS GD248/698/2/2
[78]   NAS GD248/467/3
[79]   NAS GD248/697/4
[80]   NAS GD248/2023
[81]   NAS GD248/467
[82]   McIntosh, H. B. (1934) The Grant,
       Strathspey or First Highland
       Fencible Regiment. p. 80. Elgin:
       Yeadon.
[83]   NAS GD248/697/4
[84]   NAS GD248/3417/2

[85] NAS GD248/520/9

[86] NAS GD 248/1545

[87] Mackillop, Andrew (2000) More
Fruitful than the soil: Army, Empire
and The Scottish Highlands p.23
East Linton: Tuckwell

[88] NAS GD248/453/6

[10] Fortescue, J.W. (1905) The British
Army 1783-1802. p. 20 London:
Macmillan

Chapter 8

[1] Prebble, J. (1975) Mutiny:
Highland Regiments in Revolt
1743-1804. p.98. London: Penguin

[2] Scobie, I.H.M. (1914) An Old
Highland Fencible Corps: The
History of the Reay Fencible
Highland Regiment. p.59.
Edinburgh & London: Blackwell.

[3] Fraser, W. (1883) Chiefs of Grant.
Vol i. p.456. Edinburgh

[4] Alexander-Gordon, W. (1898)
Recollections of a Highland
Subaltern p.5. London

[5] Glover R. (1963) Peninsular
Preparation: Reforms of the British
Army. p.176. Cambridge University
Press.

[6] Forsyth, W. (1900) In the Shadow
of Cairngorm: Chronicles of the
United Parishes of Abernethy and
Kincardine. p338. Inverness: The
Northern Counties Publishing
Company Ltd

[7] Larpent, Francis Seymour (2000)
The Private Journal of Judge
Advocate Larpent p. 78. Kent:
Spellmount

[8] Cookson, J. E. (1997) The British
Armed Nation 1793-1815. p. 182
Oxford: Clarendon Press.

[9] Wells, Roger (1983) Insurrection:
The British Experience 1795-1803
p. xiv Gloucester: Sutton

Index

Abercromby, Sir James of Birkenbog, 35.
Abercromby, General Sir Ralph, 230, 240.
Aberdeen, 16-17, 19, 29, 31-32, 34, 36, 44, 50-51, 53-56, 65, 67, 141-142, 204.
Amherst, Field Marshall Lord, 48, 90, 119, 135, 138.
America, war with, 15, 37, 50, 173, 186.
Ammunition, 18, 94, 96, 99, 102-103, 106, 110-111, 228, 249.
Anderson, Private John, 157, 162-164, 246.
Anderson, Private Michael, 45.
Army Agents, Ainslie and Fraser, London, 62, 156, 177, 193, 208-209, 222.
Army Chaplain Department, 203.
Attestation 23-24, 26, 30-32, 36, 94, 96, 249.
Aviemore, 72, 77, 147, 190.
Ayr, 65, 69, 108, 181, 199-201, 204-205, 211, 213, 215, 217, 224, 245.

Bantry Bay, French ships anchored in, 206-207.
Barracks, 127-128, 184-185, 188, 192-193, 200-201, 206, 209, 210, 218, 220, 223.
Beaton, Sergeant Peter, 151-156, 245.
Billeting, 34, 50, 74,128.
Black Bull Inn, Edinburgh, 229, 232.
Blackwood, Colonel, 158.
Bounty Money, 15, 24, 26-27, 29, 31, 48-49, 84, 90-91, 116, 129, 141, 182, 188, 225, 232, 240.
Bread, 66, 189, 197, 200, 212-213.
Bread Money, 24, 33, 57, 120.
Breadalbane, Earl of, 30-31, 218, 244.
Brownrigg, Colonel, Adjutant General, 231, 235, 241.

Caledonian Mercury, 183.
Camp followers, 59-60, 66, 120, 128, 201, 217.

Carmichael, Quartermaster James, 108, 120, 123, 127, 129, 141, 148, 229.
Catholicism, 24, 70, 80-81, 117-119.
Chelsea Pensioners, 30, 62, 154-156, 211.
Copland, Pat, 143, 149, 190-191, 213, 244.
Cumming, Lt Colonel Alexander Penrose
Cumming of Altyre, 17-19, 21-23, 27, 33-35, 37-38, 40-44, 47, 49-53, 55-56, 58-60, 62, 66-74, 77, 79-80, 83-84, 87, 110-112, 114, 117, 120, 124-126, 129-130, 132, 134-135, 137, 142, 144-153, 157-158, 165, 167, 169, 171, 174, 181, 194, 196, 198-199, 201-203, 206-208, 212-219, 221-222, 224-225, 227-238, 240-241, 243, 245-246, 249.
Cumming, Lance Corporal Andrew, 239.
Cumming, Ensign Harry, 22, 90-91, 109, 116.
Cumming, Captain Robert of Logie, 21, 28, 39-40, 57, 64, 109, 120, 129, 132-134, 136-138, 169, 199, 204, 231.

Delancey, Colonel Oliver, 128, 185.
Desertion, 25-28, 32, 34, 36, 45, 47, 52, 60, 63, 131, 140, 147, 173, 247.
Dumfries, 65, 96-97, 123, 133, 138-140, 142-143, 146-149, 152-155, 158-159, 161, 165, 171, 180, 213, 226, 245-248.
Dundas, Henry, 1st Viscount Melville, 16-17, 20, 112, 129, 154-155, 175, 177-178, 179.
Dundee, 29, 83, 155, 181, 184-185, 187, 189, 192-193, 195, 199-201, 249.
Drummond, Major General, 199, 211-212, 215-216, 222.
Drunkeness, 27, 32, 34, 41. 45, 50, 59, 66, 69-70, 73-74, 120, 132-133, 135, 150, 173, 209, 214, 239, 245, 247.

Edinburgh, 15, 27- 32, 35, 37-38, 44, 58,

67, 83, 96, 115, 131-132, 138, 154, 157-160, 173-174, 197, 215-217, 219-222, 224, 226, 228-230, 232, 238, 244-245, 247.

Edinburgh Advertiser, 173.

Ellis, Private Hugh, 36, 183.

Ellis, Private George, 29-30.

Erysipelas (Rose Fever) 130, 151, 204.

Fencible Regiments.
    Argyll, 15, 21.
    Breadalbane, 21, 83, 117, 131, 138, 184, 248.
    Fraser, 138, 140-141, 234-235.
    Glengarry, 70, 119.
    Gordon or Northern 15, 17, 21, 59, 87, 89, 94, 96, 98, 100, 109-110, 207, 211, 213, 215.
    Grant, 20-21, 34, 78.
    Reay or Mackay, 76, 77.
    Southern or Hopetoun 15, 21, 83, 115, 134.
    Sutherland, 15, 21, 83.
    West Lowland or Montgomerie, 21, 83, 95.

Forres, 21, 31, 33-34, 36, 39, 41, 42-45, 48-50, 52, 56, 59, 65, 72, 79-80, 109, 129, 134, 142, 144, 146, 219, 227, 240, 242, 245-246, 249.

Forsyth, Private James, 162-165, 213.

Forsyth, Sergeant John, 69, 141.

Fraser, Private Alexander, wounded by Tinkers, 151-156.

Fraser, Private Alexander, Mutineer, 159, 164-166, 168-173.

Fraser, Private John, 48-49, 56, 245.

Fraser, Captain Simon of Foyers, 21, 28, 39-40, 92, 120, 169, 176, 204, 241.

Fraser, Simon, Sheriff of Inverness, 78.

Furlough, 49, 56, 62, 69, 83, 145, 189, 190, 223, 230.

Geddes, James, 29-31, 36, 49.

Gilchrist, Dr, 144, 153, 155.

Glasgow, 32, 45, 52, 54-59, 61, 65, 70, 72, 74, 80, 82-84, 86-87, 90-91, 95, 97, 102, 112, 116-117, 121, 127, 131-132, 200-201, 207-208, 215, 227, 246, 248-249.

Glasgow Courier, 215.

Gloag, John, 38, 67-68, 148, 193, 215, 217, 237.

Gordon, Duke of, 16-17, 28, 212.

Gordon, Lord Adam, 34-35, 37-38, 50, 53, 55, 58, 60, 65, 67, 71, 73, 82-83, 90, 92-94, 112, 114-118, 123, 131-134, 142-143, 145-147, 158-159, 170-172, 175, 181, 202, 204, 207, 215, 217-218, 222, 230-231, 245.

Gordon, Sir William, 83, 125, 134.

Grant, Lt Allan of Mulben, Mulderie or Advie, 22, 120, 139, 166, 169-170, 189, 231.

Grant, Alexander, W.S., Aberdeen, 31.

Grant, Alexander, W.S., Edinburgh, 37, 132, 172.

Grant, Lt Charles, 166.

Grant, Sergeant Donald, 197.

Grant, Ensign Duncan of Delsangie, Factor of Urquhart, 22, 63-65, 161, 174, 195, 237, 243.

Grant, Ensign Duncan, Junior, 22.

Grant, Private Duncan, 63-65.

Grant, Lt Francis, W., Sir James's son, 22, 39, 108-109, 138-140, 240-241.

Grant, Isaac, W.S., 38, 97.

Grant, Sir James, 15-23, 25-35, 37-40, 43, 48-53, 55-80, 82-93, 95-98, 108-112, 114-116, 118-121, 123-127, 129-130, 132-159, 167, 171-172, 174-180, 183-187, 189, 191-215, 217, 219, 222-226, 229-234, 236 -244.

Grant, Dr James, 238.

Grant, James of Heathfield, Factor to Sir

James Grant, 17-19, 25-26, 29, 32, 35-36, 38, 47, 49, 66, 69, 75, 77-78, 84-86, 93, 95, 99, 104, 110, 118, 125-127, 130, 134, 143, 147, 149, 161, 173-174, 180, 182, 186-187, 189, 190, 194-197, 199, 201, 205, 214, 222-223, 225, 229, 233, 237, 243-244, 246, 249.

Grant, Rev. James, 19, 22-23, 26, 28, 35, 42, 63-65, 93, 95, 130, 161, 173-174, 184, 203, 246.

Grant, James W.S., Inverness, 223-224.

Grant, Captain James, of Kinchirdy, 177.

Grant, Ensign James, 22, 162.

Grant, Private James, 48.

Grant, James of Corrimony, 63-64.

Grant, Sergeant Major James, 239.

Grant, Lady Jane, wife of Sir James Grant, 32, 48-49, 51, 106, 133, 174, 180, 186, 200, 227, 237-238, 242-243.

Grant, Dr John, 17, 19, 22, 28, 57, 84-86, 90-91, 93-94, 96-98, 108, 115-118, 120, 143, 144-145, 161, 183, 197, 229.

Grant, Major John of Glenmoriston, 18, 21, 27, 39, 56, 58, 69, 71, 72, 74, 82, 112, 120, 123-124, 130, 132, 135, 139, 143, 148, 157, 161, 164, 186-187, 192, 195, 200-202, 204-209, 221, 231, 237, 249.

Grant, Captain John of Achindown, 18, 21, 28, 39-42, 63, 73, 83, 85, 91, 97, 112, 120, 130, 132-135, 139-140-144, 146-147, 166, 187, 190, 199, 205, 208, 210, 224, 232, 235-237, 239.

Grant, Lt John, Junior 18, 19, 22, 36, 38, 43, 57-58, 73, 76-77, 86, 88, 93, 104-105, 120, 124, 161, 176-177, 179, 205, 246.

Grant, Rev. John of Abernethy, 19.

Grant, Captain-Lieutenant John of Rippachie, 21, 26, 28, 31, 39, 42, 80, 87-88, 94, 97-98, 108, 112, 120, 124, 127, 135-138, 140-142, 144, 165, 169, 174, 199, 204-206, 210, 214-215, 225-226, 231, 234, 246.

Grant, Lt John of Rosefield, 21, 71, 120, 165, 228, 234.

Grant, Ensign John of Kinchirdy, 22.

Grant, Private John, taylor, 25, 32, 49.

Grant, Private John of Balnaclash, 36, 140, 167, 205, 241, 243.

Grant, Lt John of Ballintomb, 42.

Grant, Private John, 56 - 57.

Grant, Private John, son of William, Ground officer, 107.

Grant, Private John, wounded by Tinkers, 151-153, 155.

Grant, Lewis Alexander, Sir James's son, 52, 125.

Grant, Lewis, Factor's son, 85.

Grant, Sir Ludovick, 16-17.

Grant, Private Malcolm, 201.

Grant, Sergeant Mathew, 30.

Grant, Miss, daughter of Sir James, 32, 106, 140, 167, 200, 247.

Grant, Patrick of Glenmoriston, 18.

Grant, Major of Achernick, 17-18.

Grant, Dr Peter, 19, 22, 36, 84, 94, 107, 112, 143, 145.

Grant, Ensign Peter, 22.

Grant, Private Peter of Rothymoon, 75.

Grant, Sergeant Peter, 166.

Grant, Sergeant Robert, 166, 187, 225.

Grant, Sandie, 106, 127.

Grant, Ensign William, Factor's son, 91, 205.

Grant, Lt William of Callendar, 21, 28, 108, 120, 140, 228.

Grant, William, Constable in Grantown, 79, 180.

Grantown, 16, 36, 48-49, 73, 77, 79, 93, 97, 126, 147, 172, 228, 237.

Gullane, 29, 173.

Hamilton, Major General James, 170, 178.

Home, Earl of, 226-227.

Huskisson, William, 20.

Hutcheon, Hugh, 29, 31-32.

Hutchieson, Sergeant John, 167.

Irvine, 216, 232, 235-238, 240-242.

Kilgour, Sergeant Peter, 32, 43.
Killala Bay, French landing at, 234.
King's Evil, 135, 183, 198.

Lascombe, G. 179.
Lee, Ensign Patrick, 232.
Lennox, Lord George, 205.
Leslie, Lt General Alexander, 37-38.
Linlithgow, 81-83, 85-89, 91, 93-96, 98-99,
    101, 105-106, 108-112, 114, 116, 118-
    119, 126, 135, 142, 158, 161, 180, 245-
    246, 248.

MacArthur, Private Alex, 195-196, 222.
MacArthur, Private Angus, 196, 222.
MacBean, Sergeant Major Hugh, 150, 157,
    164.
MacDonald, Corporal James, Mutineer,
    164, 166, 169-170, 173, 176, 180.
Macdonell, Captain Alexander (Alasdair
    Ranaldson) of Glengarry, 21-24, 28, 34,
    39-40, 42, 66, 70-73, 93, 106, 112-113,
    118-119.
Macdonell, Father Alexander, 70.
Macdonell, Lt James, 22-23, 42.
Macdonell, Lt Ronald, 22, 42, 72-73.
MacDougal, Private Duncan, Mutineer,
    159, 165, 167-173, 175-180, 245.
McGregor, Rev. Alexander,173, 193, 203.
Mc Grigor, Sir James, 19, 117.
McIntosh, Private Charles, Mutineer, 29,
    38, 159, 160, 164-167, 169-173, 175,
    246.
McIntosh, Private Lachlan, Mutineer, 159,
    164, 166-173, 175-179, 245.
Mackay, Lt Colonel of Bighouse, 76-77.
McNair, Private James, 238-239.
MacNeil, Piper John, 184, 247.

McQueen, Sergeant, 186.
Meal, 33, 43, 51, 157, 161, 187, 192.
Meat, 49, 187, 200, 212-213, 218.
Mercury, 52, 65, 192-193, 219.
Meredith, Corporal Michael, 166, 239, 248.
Morrison, Private James, 210.
Morrison, Lt Theodore, 166.
Muskets, 35, 50, 59, 103, 106, 111.
Musselburgh, 131, 138, 161, 173, 176-178,
    181, 183, 230, 232.

Nixon, Lt Colonel, 242.

Paisley, 87, 123-125, 127, 129-133, 227,
    246, 249.
Pay, 33, 36-37, 49, 56, 83, 91, 128, 181,
    190-191, 200, 203, 212, 247.
Pitt, William, Prime Minister, 16, 20, 128.
Postage, 189-190.
Punishment, 45-48, 131, 163, 170, 173,
    209-210, 239, 247-249.

Rattray, Private James, 108, 225, 229.
Recruiting, 23-24, 26-32, 78-79, 86, 91,
    119, 126, 134, 138-139, 141, 149-150,
    194, 208, 232.
Reynolds, Lt George, 145-147, 150, 167,
    236.
Richardson, Lt John, 170, 233.
Riding System, 86, 88, 91.
Robertson, Sergeant Angus, 195.
Rose, Captain John of Holme, 28, 40, 92,
    120, 145-147, 165, 204.
Ross, Sergeant Major Donald, 69, 117-118,
    149, 247.

Scott, Colonel, 160.
Sibbens, 64-65, 192.
Stacey, David Provost of Dumfries, 152,
    154-155.
Steele, Ensign Thomas, 191.
Stephen, Dr Thomas, 120, 151, 237.

Sutherland, Private Alexander of the
    Breadalbane Fencibles, 131, 138.
Sutherland, Quartermaster Angus, 18, 22, 28,
    32, 38, 68, 108, 120, 142, 246.
Sutherland, Private Robert, 45.

Tuberculosis, 128, 135.
Tucker, Samuel, 194.
Typhoid, 128.

Urquhart, Lt John, 22, 28, 71.

Venereal Disease, 52, 60, 64, 146, 151, 192,
    213-214, 225.

Wardrobe, Private James, 65-66.
Watson, Adjutant James, 18-19, 22-23, 35,
    37, 42, 44, 49, 59, 73, 83-84, 93-94,
    98-104, 106, 109-110, 112, 124-125,
    127, 133, 137, 139-140, 143-145, 148-
    150, 154, 156-157, 160-161, 163, 167-
    170, 183, 185-186, 189, 190-191, 194,
    196, 198, 200, 206-211, 213-214, 220,
    223-228, 231-237, 239-243, 245-246,
    248.
Weddell, Drum Major, 74, 141, 247.
Wemmys, Colonel William, 161, 167.
Wheeler, Private Edward, 27.
Whooping Cough, or Chin Cough, 72, 79.
Windham, William, 20, 203.

Yonge, Sir George, 20, 75-76.
York, H.R.H. the Duke of, 48, 175, 177,
    179, 203, 231.

Cover & Layout: Stephen M.L. Young
                           Elgin
                           Scotland
                           stephenmlyoung@aol.com

Font: Adobe Garamond (11pt)

Copies of this book can be ordered via the Internet:

                           www.librario.com

or from:

                           Librario Publishing Ltd
                           Brough House
                           Milton Brodie
                           Kinloss
                           Moray IV36 2UA
                           Tel /Fax No 01343 850 617